LIFE, PASSION, AND HEAVY METAL
IN THE FORGOTTEN CONTINENT

HEAVY METAL AFRICA

D1235962

EDWARD BANCHS

WORD ASSOCIATION PUBLISHERS
www.wordassociation.com
1.800.827.7903

ISBN: 978-1-63385-161-0
Library of Congress Control Number: 2016913281

Cover by theBookDesigners
Cover photographs by Edward Banchs
Back and spine photograph by Frank Marshall
Author photograph by Ashley Reynolds
Layout by Jason Price

Published by
Word Association Publishers
205 Fifth Avenue
Tarentum, Pennsylvania 15084

www.wordassociation.com
1.800.827.7903

PRAISE FOR HEAVY METAL AFRICA

"Who knew that Africa had a thriving heavy metal audience? Edward Banchs knew. He's able to convey some of its messy, thunderous glory here."

—Pittsburgh Post-Gazette.

"(Banchs') journey details a continent caught in a tug of war between its troubled past and an ambitious present."

—Metal Hammer

"Heavy Metal Africa is an easy-to-pick-up read with strong detail and impact. Its ability to open minds to a world many do not think about every day is not just powerful, it's important."

—New Noise Magazine

"A brilliant take on not just an overlooked metal culture but a continent that is often forgotten or marginalized."

—Decibel

"...hard to put down."

—Pittsburgh City Paper

"Heavy Metal Africa tells of (Banchs') unusual adventures in a most unusual place."

—Medium.com

"(Banchs) crafts a map of sorts, a deep dive into what the stories of the bands and fans feels like."

—Afropunk

"(A) fascinating and important book that delves into the metal scene in a place most metal fans are not familiar with."

—HeavyMusic HQ

"A superb book. Heavy Metal Africa is a ground breaking and important work."

—Metal-Rules.com

"...when it comes to heavy metal Edward Banchs debunks all the myths around its African scene..."

—GriotMag.com

CONTENTS

INTRODUCTION
A Collision of Passions

London's Heathrow Airport can be a convoluted display of disorder and impatience. I have flown through this airport enough times to be fairly comfortable with its flow and routine. One precise moment, however, broke the mold of the mundane for me. After my flight from the United States, the day was to be simple: Take the train from the airport to my friend's neighborhood, go to a pub while I waited for him to get off work, head back to his place for a shower, a quick nap and then a night out. But on this day, things were different.

"How long will you be in the UK for?" asked the rather large, bald, petulant middle-aged immigration officer, whom I pictured as Mr. Clean (the resemblance to the American cleaning product icon was uncanny) in my head.

"Just two days, then I'm off to Kenya."

"Kenya?" he paused. "Who do you know in Kenya?"

"I'm meeting some people. Well," I hesitated, but, feeling that honesty was perhaps the best policy in this situation, I continued. "I've never met them in person before. We've only chatted on the Internet." My response seemed careless. Mr. Clean stopped what he was doing and glared at me with the look you would give someone who said the wrong thing.

Every passenger flying into Heathrow that day was being questioned, too, I had hoped. "What were you doing in Zimbabwe?" he asked while flipping through the pages in my passport, taking mental notes of my previous trips. Zimbabwe was another country on a tight watch in the United Kingdom, given the political quagmire and sanctions the UK had placed on its former colony, which has fallen to disarray under one of the worst dictators alive. I took that particular trip to Zimbabwe six years prior, but Mr. Clean still asked, "Who did you meet there?" I froze.

I began to panic. Too many thoughts circled around my head as to what was going to happen next. Why couldn't he just let me pass? I took two steps forward in this state of panic, peeking over his desk to see why he could not just stamp me in and let me catch the train so I could meet my friend. My movement caught him by surprise, and he waved someone over. This was not going the way I had planned.

Just as Mr. Clean stared me down, a plain-clothes London city police officer grabbed my arm lightly and escorted me away from the immigration counter without my passport. "Mr. Banchs, please come with us," said the young officer.

"OK. Where am I going?"

"Just come with us," she said, as more officers quickly assembled.

I was being detained.

It never occurred to me that I was the sort of traveler they were looking for. A few days before I landed in the United Kingdom, armed Somali terrorists stormed into a crowded suburban shopping mall in Kenya's capital city, Nairobi, and murdered dozens in a senseless mass shooting. Officials around the world were still piecing together details about what had led to this horrific crime, and who was responsible. And, of course, ubiquitous news reports of terrorists groups communicating with people in the West through Internet chat rooms for recruiting were more than likely echoing through Mr. Clean's head as well as those of the many British officers strategically situated throughout the airport. As it was, Heathrow had a steady stream of traffic to and from Kenya.

Mr. Clean, rightly so, had his concerns.

My "suspicious" travel activity had apparently upset the officers, who questioned me for the better part of an hour. I just told the truth: I was writing a book about heavy metal music in Africa, and I was just going to Kenya for a month to meet and spend time with rock and heavy metal musicians.

"Heavy metal? In Africa?" asked one of the officers.

I was going to be here a while.

I had been asked to follow the police officers to a bench within sight of Mr. Clean, who had left his desk with my passport. Everything was happening quickly. I could still see the immigration counter where I had just been standing, but now sat with two police officers by my side as the younger of the two officers stood directly in front, questioning me – not far from the hordes of people lining up anxious to get into the country to start their vacations and business meetings.

Things got serious rather quickly, and I got real right along with them. Every sort of question was thrown my way in rapid-fire style about who I was visiting in Kenya, how I knew them, why I was visiting the east African nation, and where I was staying. Noting an expired student visa in my passport, one of the officers asked why I had lived in the UK before. I tensed up, and got short with two officers in a desperate attempt to hold my ground. I did not think I had broken any laws and was now being held as a "suspicious" traveler because of the action of a few cowards. So again, I was asked, "Why did you live in the UK?"

"I went to graduate school here," I snapped.

"Where did you study?" asked an officer the second I finished the word "here."

"University of London," I replied.

"What did you study?" asked another.

"African studies," I stated without hesitation.

"Africa? Why Africa?"

That was a question I had been asked before and always found difficult to answer. And still do. Why am I so interested in Africa? I cannot answer this question with the sort of succinct clarity that satisfies those who ask. All that I know for sure is that in my mid-20s, I developed an insatiable appetite for all things Africa and made it a priority to accommodate this interest for the rest of my life. I just found myself drawn to Africa.

My initial attraction to the continent was a mystery to me, as I had known very little about Africa, just assumptions of how Africans lived and what the continent was like. I could say my motivation to learn more came from a newspaper article I read about a conflict occurring in the Democratic Republic of the Congo. The story outlined a horrendous war that had been going on and off for decades and was costing far too many lives. Though I cannot for certain tell you which newspaper I was reading, who wrote the article or what day it was published, it got me thinking more about the world around me. I put down that particular article and decided that I wanted to do more than just work as a short-order line cook in a restaurant for the rest of my life. I viewed Africa as "that" place: the place of misery, famine, war, and unkind and dangerous people. Now I know that simply is not true, but that mentality of assumption kept me trapped in a belief system that I needed to move on from.

I decided to focus my energy on understanding how the world worked and why people lived the way they lived, so I enrolled in Florida Atlantic University to pursue a degree in Political Science and Anthropology. I had hoped to learn a few things about Africa while there. However, the university did not offer courses on African history, nor the continent's politics. Of benefit though was the job I took to get me through college at a bookstore, which provided me the ability to keep up on what books were being released about Africa, and the continent's history. Little by little, my small hobby of studying African history began to evolve into much, much more. A few professors understood my interest on all things Africa and pushed me toward an internship in Washington, D.C., with a lobbying firm that allowed me to work directly with diplomats on matters of development, aid, and foreign policy, which I embarked on during my junior year of college.

Upon my return to Florida Atlantic University to complete my senior year, the idea of pursuing a degree that focused on Africa was well on my mind. I had done a little research already, but was not sure if graduate school was something I would be interested in pursuing. But Africa was consuming my interests, so I decided to apply to graduate schools that offered degrees in African Studies while completing my degree in Political Science and minor in Anthropology. I was accepted into three programs and had to make a decision with the two I focused on: Howard University in Washington, D. C., or the University of London. Living in Washington was a great experience, and I would have easily settled back into that wonderful city again without difficulty. But London was different and a fresh start. Here was a chance to step outside of my comfort zone and gain a different educational experience, and most importantly, a new perspective. This was what I had been waiting for! So I took a great chance and began to prepare myself for a move to the United Kingdom to attend the University of London's School of Oriental and African Studies (SOAS) to focus my attention on post-colonial African politics.

My interest in Africa came later in life, but my love of heavy metal came in grade school and has remained a big part of my identity. The late '80s were a fantastic time to be exposed to this type of music. At the time MTV was playing a lot of music videos featuring over-the-top, out-of-reach, glam superstars. Though the image of neon-colored spandex and hairspray-soaked manes was a bit much for me, the sound pulled me in. I could not get enough of what those guitars sounded like, and what the guitar players were doing with their instruments. Once the '90s came along and I was introduced to thrash metal and hardcore, there was no turning back. Metal became a pleasant addiction. It kept me out of trouble, and introduced me to the best friends I could ever ask for. I spent my money as a teenager on heavy metal albums, took road trips from Altoona, the central Pennsylvania town where I was raised, and even started playing guitar in heavy metal bands. Metal has kept me focused and driven, and I still continue to bond over my love of this music with friends all over the world.

For those outside the genre's periphery, heavy metal is incredibly misunderstood. The uncomfortable "Satanic" imagery that adorns a lot of album covers and T-shirts, as well as the inhuman vocals of many of the genres notables, push people away. Perhaps there was a reason I gravitated to this music and its off-putting, aggressive sound. Heavy metal may have been the perfect soundtrack for someone growing up in a small working-class Pennsylvania town, while being raised by a single mother struggling through the confines of poverty. Maybe this is why the brutality of the genre spoke to me – I found it empowering. It allowed me to find comfort through chaos, and gave me the power to be myself. Heavy metal gave me a voice.

My passions for heavy metal music and Africa collided while I was living in London. Standing at the back of a heavy metal pub in London's historic Soho on a cool, rainy spring night in 2011 with my friend Dave, also a graduate student of SOAS, we both engaged in a deep conversation about our favorite heavy metal bands around the world. Of course Dave asked if I knew anything about heavy metal music in Africa – which, for most metal fans, was overlooked. We were discussing how we had seen metal covered in the metal press from all over the world up to that point – except Africa. Even the popular documentary by Canadian filmmaker Sam Dunn, *Global Metal*, overlooked Africa. It was as if the heavy metal world forgot about Africa. Bands from North America and South America were well established, Australia and Asia had a healthy output of metal bands as well as acts that toured through those continents regularly, and Europe was heavy metal's epicenter. But Africa? Africa was heavy metal's forgotten continent.

Having traveled to Africa a few times before, I told Dave about a weekend I spent in Cape Town, South Africa, in 2007 that began to shape my knowledge on the subject. A friend of mine, Craig – whom I met while browsing metal records in Cape Town – introduced me to an acquaintance of his, Alec Surridge, at a metal bar in the Bellville section of Cape Town. Alec had played in a local band for years, The Warinsane, and was previously a member of the seminal South African band Sacraphyx. Alec knew enough about African metal to tell me about the scenes in Mozambique and Botswana, as well as what he heard about metal in other African countries. My knowledge of African metal, to that point, had been limited to that one encounter.

I relayed the story of my conversation with Alec to Dave, who told me about a photoset he came across of passionate metal fans from Botswana recently published in *Vice* magazine by a South African photographer named Frank Marshall. My curiosity kept growing as this was probably the first time that metal in Africa received any bit of coverage. I returned to the United States for a month in the summer of 2011 to continue working on my master's thesis on the history of Zimbabwe's land reform policies. During my downtime, I began to search for more African heavy metal bands. The initial Internet searches returned very little. The information on African metal was very thin: just a handful of South African bands and a band from Botswana mentioned in the *Vice* magazine piece. But I kept searching.

After I returned to London, I met Dave in the back of the same Soho pub and – several pints in – I laid out my idea for an article, or series of articles, about metal in Africa and was eager to pitch the idea to metal magazines.

The hardest part was finding musicians I could interview. I contacted a blogger in South Africa who goes by the name of Darkfiend and asked him a few questions. He runs the Metal4Africa.com website and, with the amount of knowledge he had on the subject, was happy to share what he knew. And he became my first interview! Two weeks had passed after my first contact with Darkfiend (after sending emails to a number of bands in South Africa), and I had only heard from two more bands. I waited though and after a few more weeks, I had been in touch with a band from Kenya and, surprisingly, one from Madagascar. Soon enough, more bands replied to my interview request (many joked they were on "Africa" time). One contact followed another, and two months after my first contact, I had been in touch with rock and metal musicians in 16 African countries. Everything started to come together.

Also, it quickly became apparent I had more to work with than I anticipated. I felt that I could write extensively about each country and include those as chapters for a book. The book idea had come to mind, but after my first inquiry yielded few results, I decided to just aim for the articles. But now, after a few months, I scrapped the article idea and hashed out the blueprint for this book.

Once I returned to the United States permanently, I gathered my notes and started putting everything together. Fresh off an MA in African Studies and with a lifetime of metal behind me, I began drafting chapters for a book. They were awful. I was frustrated. I was upset because my brain had been pumping out academic essays and I had just worked for months on a thesis, so I was wired into an academic writing style. "Who would read this?" I kept asking myself. It was a terrible feeling. The only thing that felt right was to visit the countries myself to get a better story and a better understanding of what metal scenes were really like on the ground, and not only how metal fans in these countries were living, but also to experience metal in Africa for myself. I knew I had to do it – I had to travel. I felt that I needed to show and tell, and perhaps tell a different story. But how was I going to get the money? I went through academic circles to see about getting grants. Denied. I set up fundraisers through crowd sourcing sites. Nope. I had no money to start with: nothing! This was an incredibly ambitious idea, and I was too determined to give up.

Immediately, I began saving my money, which was difficult. I was in a serious bind when it came to paying my bills and feeding myself. Any job I could get I took; I wanted this. First, I worked as a substitute teacher (and if ever there was a question of my will to finish this book, it was surviving that job) for a year before I could save for the first *Heavy Metal Africa* trip. I returned from that trip and began working at another bookstore before I carelessly used the money I saved for a first and last months' rent on a new apartment in order to buy an airline ticket to Kenya. This put me in a serious bind, but I did not care. Again, I was too determined to get to Africa, and with that airline ticket moved from Florida to Pittsburgh, Pennsylvania, for cheaper rent on the advice of a friend and, again, started to pile on the jobs. I was dead set on finishing this book.

The first *Heavy Metal Africa* trip started with visiting everyone I had contacted in South Africa and Botswana in 2012, two countries I knew had sufficient scenes for me to start with. Once I put myself on the ground, everything became much clearer. Email addresses now became faces and personalities. I had several contacts to go with in those two countries, but once I was there, I was able to introduce myself to more. It seemed that no one took my interest in their bands and scenes seriously at first, but once I made the effort to visit Africa many rock and metal musicians came out of their respective shells because of what they told me I was offering them: an opportunity to be heard across the globe. I could now see how metal in Africa extended deeper than I originally thought.

Considering everything I could have covered, I made the conscious decision only to write about the people I met in the countries I visited. Also, I could not realistically visit all of the countries I wanted to, just the nations that had well-established scenes based on the contacts I had. The only country I had planned to visit and could not was Angola, whose rock and metal scene has blossomed into one of the continent's most promising. As a result of a strict visa policy, I was unable to secure the proper travel documents. The chapter presented in this book on Zimbabwe happened as a result of me being unable to visit Angola.

There were plenty of musicians I could have met, but did not have time to, and plenty of stories that could have filled volumes – especially when it came to the history of rock and roll in Africa – but I kept my focus mostly on the present and active bands. Also, given the how little information existed about the history of rock and metal in the various countries I visited, I had to construct the historical narratives based on the testimonials of those I was interviewing. I relied on consistencies from the more reputable musicians within each scene. My promise to you is that quotes from the musicians presented in the book are as spoken, and any interview that was done through a translator was done so with the honesty from those who were translating for me. It was on their word that what was spoken to me was accurately stated.

Some musicians had already responded to interviews via email responses before we met in person, and agreed to be interviewed again. When we would meet, I asked musicians to choose the places where they felt comfortable and began to record our conversations when it was agreed to. Any topic that was off limits was discussed beforehand, and the names of the musicians in this book are how they asked me to present them. Sometimes I would ask musicians questions about their music and lives through a traditional "question and answer" format, while other times I would just record a conversation that focused more on the stories they wished to share and less on my questioning. While I was excited to learn new things about Africa throughout my travels, I realized that the educational foundation I was traveling with helped in modicum. The book became less about my views, and more about the lives and passions of heavy metal's forgotten continent.

The chapters presented in this book are the snapshots of the places and times I visited in each country, highlighting the best and worst I experienced in Africa over the past five years. In addition to being a personal journey years in the making, Heavy Metal Africa is a unique story, and I am honored to introduce you to the incredible African musicians and fans whose passionate pursuit of heavy metal is recognizable anywhere in the world.

Starting in South Africa in 2012 because of the number of contacts I had established (and because the airline ticket was the cheapest around!), I arrived to a rock and metal scene that was pacing forward rather quickly in one of the continent's largest nations and largest economies. The law of apartheid that divided the nation's citizens for years based on skin color is no more; heavy metal bands are no longer silenced and harassed by the police state that severely enforced a segregation policy that once defined their nation. With apartheid in the rearview mirror, today's South African rockers are benefiting from the ability to move forward in one unifying voice: music. I jumped right into this special country: touring with bands, sleeping on floors, and speaking to an overwhelming amount of musicians from a myriad of backgrounds to understand the challenges they faced moving forward with the underlying burdens of their nation's past.

Botswana – South Africa's northern neighbor – was a place I fell in love with right away. The hot, quiet nation has become the epicenter of the continent's rock and metal scene as a result of the bands Skinflint and Wrust, as well as a few leather-clad rockers known as the "metal cowboys." Botswana's heavy metal scene has since been featured on CNN, The Guardian, *Vice* magazine, and BBC, but so much about this metal community was still unknown at the time I visited the nation. I was excited to see what fueled their passion for metal, and what, if any, obstacles stood in their way. Between long bus rides, spending quiet time with the "first family of rock," loud rehearsals and meeting the faces of African metal, Botswana was special.

Kenya was still in shock from an atrocious mass shooting in September of 2013, the same attack that had me answering questions in Heathrow airport. The rockers in the country found an escape in the music that let so much of that anger turn itself into a positive release. Visiting a wide array of musicians – who chose to meet me everywhere from their homes to pubs and even casinos – I found myself meeting a young generation of rockers who were proud to put Kenya on the map of heavy metal. One of the more challenging experiences of my life, Kenyan musicians confronted issues of ethnicity with me as they struggled to balance tradition with their cosmopolitan surroundings. Also, just about a week and a half into my trip I had been infected with malaria – which was awful! From offering me the chance to meet with rockers who kick-started this movement in front of confused audiences with little means to do so, to bands who are now finding their way to Europe, Kenya exceeded my expectations and challenged my senses.

Madagascar was always a mystery to me. A large nation with a quiet reputation, I was shocked by the amount of poverty that I witnessed upon landing, and delighted to encounter Africa's largest and most vivacious rock and heavy metal community, where rock songs live as anthems, and musicians live with unwavering passion. A nation in crisis, political leaders betraying their own, an ecological wonder in devastation, and people living in a terrible desperation – my perspective was forever altered after leaving this splendid nation in 2014. Madagascar showed me so much with so little. It is unique, remarkable and a memory that is forever wonderful.

From Madagascar I visited Mauritius, Africa's small island paradise. The country is the example of the continent's aspirations of political and economic success. But things are not always how they appear, as I was told of an underlying corruption, geographic fatigue, and abhorrent job prospects that have sent many Mauritians overseas. However, the rock and metal community on the island has begun to embrace their history: a musical tradition that has lent itself to the grooves of heavy metal and an identity that has flourished as a result. Just 100 or so miles southwest is a mountainous formation – about the size of Mauritius – known as Reunion Island, a place that has also embraced its musical traditions. Similar to Mauritius in its size and traditions, this French territory is blessed with remarkable geography and an even more wonderful metal scene that left me speechless. By embracing the once forbidden musical style of maloya, the Reunion scene has uniquely created, "metaloya," a metal sound that bands are ready to showcase to the world.

As a result of poor planning, I was not able to secure the proper travel documents to enter the country of Angola. Instead of wallowing in frustration, I grabbed a flight to Zimbabwe in a spur-of-the-moment decision. The nation has fallen to the status of failed state over the past 20 years as a result of President Robert Mugabe's suppression of human rights and *is* one of the worst countries on the planet to live in. Understanding that Western journalists have been shunned as a result of the government's suppression of free speech, I was still excited to visit the very small rock and metal community. Zimbabwe was the one nation I visited where a rock and metal community lived with trepidation. Devastated by nearly ninety percent unemployment and political sanctions, the very small Zimbabwean metal community spoke to me behind walls, sharing their aspirations, and their fears. Having previously visited this nation in 2007 during one of the worst financial crises in the history of the world – a time when inflation skyrocketed the price of goods by the hour – I was also anxious to see how things had changed in a country where hope is more than a metaphor.

Heavy Metal Africa.

SOUTH AFRICA

1

SOUTH AFRICA
A Past Divided, A Future United

Sixteen hours is a long time to spend on an airplane. But this is where I found myself: on a metallic tube flying over an ocean searching for answers to satisfy my own curiosity, not knowing what was ahead of me, who I would meet or even where I would go. I just wanted to jump into a story that had yet to be written. The continent I had grown fond of still holds a million mysteries, and rock and roll was one of them.

It has been over 20 years since the National Party ended their rule, along with the political system of apartheid. What began as a series of land acts in 1913 evolved into a system of racial segregation in which the minority white population was given the right to own land and businesses, while the remainder of the population was forced to live in separate areas and use separate facilities. As a direct result of apartheid, which was fully implemented as the result of political elections in 1948, South Africa experienced international sanctions and a political isolation that resulted in a musical culture shut off from the rest of the world.

Many spoke of resistance, oppression and fighting against their strong government that exercised no remorse. Heavy metal was so heavily shunned during apartheid that it limited the music to the extreme underground in certain areas as a result of metal fans becoming targets of harassment by local populations. But so much has changed since then, and the musicians performing today were beyond eager to welcome me into their homes, their lives and their stories.

Before meeting the bands of today, I wanted to sit with as many musicians as possible from the previous generation of South African metal bands in order to understand where bands were coming from, lyrically and musically, since heavy metal was as much resistance toward the apartheid government as it was a personal liberation for those performing the music. I also found myself submerged in questions. How did a country of 50 million people find itself completely divided by something that no one alive has any control over – skin color? What is the future of the country and how are things since apartheid ended? Also, what are the challenges for metal bands today in Africa's largest and most recognizable economy? And what needs to change for the genre to expand deeper into the South African landscape? I could not wait to get started!

SHADES OF SHAME

Herman Le Roux was exactly as he described himself: long-haired with a long beard, wearing an Iron Maiden T-shirt. He was happy to greet me at the airport. We had been trading emails for nine months, constantly chatting away about our lives and music, connecting on many levels. After some short pleasantries, we headed to his hometown and South Africa's capital city, Pretoria. I was fairly tired and sat quietly, staring at the overwhelming sight of Johannesburg. The city – with a unique skyline visible from a great distance – and the surrounding areas are saturated with a tangled maze of mega highways that kept coming into view. Every turn and crest on the four-lane-wide road system returned vistas of never-ending neighborhoods, mega shopping plazas and industrial sites. It was difficult to tell where Johannesburg ended and Pretoria began.

Complemented by the purple blossoms of the jacaranda trees outlining the city's sidewalks and roadways, Pretoria's central skyline is an afterthought, as the soft mountains and greenery dominate the views. Driving throughout Pretoria, Herman was pleased to show me the sights while providing encyclopedic facts of his hometown. He commented on the current inconvenience that the government has caused by renaming city streets, not only in Pretoria, but also throughout the country. "This used to be the longest street in the world," Herman said while pointing to a road sign on what was once known as Church Street. "But now I don't even know what it is called, because it is broken up into pieces." Similar frustrations were echoed from most

I came across, as business owners flushed away their cash reprinting ads and business cards. Cities were now littered with the "Know Your Streets" banners, GPS systems were going crazy and citizens who had lived in these places their entire lives were left questioning the motive behind the massive renaming. But in many ways, like Pretoria, South Africa is a changing entity.

Arriving at Herman's home, I was introduced to the rest of his band, Juggernaught, which Herman describes as a "new wave of American stoner rock, but not quite" as they gathered for one of their bi-weekly band rehearsals. Herman's small home also doubled as the base for his mother's business. Herman explained that the band had always rehearsed where his mother owned businesses because of the availability of space. They have rehearsed in a motorcycle dealership, a brothel and now a mortuary. Explaining the space available, it was obvious why they loved their room – and, of course, no one was there to complain about the noise. All others on-site were deceased. Herman asked if I would like to set my bags in the room he had laid out for me. "I would love to," I responded. Walking toward a small, detached room next to the rehearsal space, I asked, "Why is the wall cold?" Herman just smiled. Immediately on the other side of the wall by the bed was the cold room containing corpses! My heavy metal adventure was off to a great start.

Herman and his generation are living in a country that has slowly evolved into a growing economy and a free democratic society. However, today's South Africans are struggling through a near 50 percent unemployment rate, low wages, ever-increasing government corruption and a horrifyingly high crime rate. But what was life like in this country before the transition – that period of time when an authoritative government bowed to the merits of democratic will? "People think that apartheid was a party for white people, but it was really police brutality," explained Herman. I brought up the subject of apartheid to Herman – a descendant of Huguenot settlers to South Africa – to better understand what life was like during that period. There was a shade of unease that was drawn across Herman's face as well as those of his band members, mostly because of the push that so many had made to put that period behind them. Perhaps this was the conversation that many needed to finally have.

"The police force here monitored what was going on in the streets carefully," explained Clifford Crabb, vocalist of the long-running and popular Johannesburg-based power progressive metal band Agro, "If you put your foot out of line, you got fucked up! It was that simple." Life before the end of apartheid for Clifford as a metal fan growing up in Johannesburg, the city at the center of attention during that tumultuous period, was privileged because of his skin color, but burdened by his views. "It was all forced religion and it was forced politics. There was no room to think otherwise. If you attempted to do so, you had it hard. My role as a metalhead was to speak out against apartheid; we [the metal community] did so blatantly. Agro was a mouthpiece for anti-apartheid metalheads. Our lyrics, especially in those times, were very anti-apartheid."

Others relayed similar stories of being shut out by law enforcement and often beaten by law enforcement officers, who were an extension of the authoritarian government. "Back in those days, the police just beat the fuck out of anyone and everyone. Sure apartheid was a big thing then, but anyone who didn't fit into their regime got the shit kicked out of them or worse. The headbangers may as well have been black because the police hated us. They were always fucking everyone up at the metal clubs," recalled Dean Smith of the influential bands Ragnorock and Odyssey. "The government was very oppressive. The police were always raiding the clubs [and] could take you out to a field and beat the crap out of you. And there was nothing you could do," explained Jay R, who owed a heavy metal record store in Johannesburg's Hillbrow neighborhood called Total Chaos during apartheid.

Apartheid, which translates to "separateness," saw its full implementation after the 1948 elections in which the National Party, led by Hendrik Verwoerd,[1] emerged victorious. Non-white groups included black Africans, coloreds (those of mix race), Cape Malays and Asians (those whose ancestry was from the Indian sub-continent). Those who were not white were made to carry identification cards and use separate public facilities, were unable to own land,

---

1   Hendrik Verwoerd was born in the Netherlands and was known as the "architect of apartheid," which he once said was a "policy of good neighborliness." After surviving an assassination attempt by a white farmer in 1960, he was killed in 1966 after being stabbed in the throat by a parliamentary messenger named Dimitri Tsafendas.

prohibited from marriage and sexual relations with whites, barred from voting and were at times forced from land deemed "white" land. The minority white population had, at the height of apartheid, over 80 percent of the land to use, farm, build on and own, while the overwhelming majority of the non-white nation utilized less than 20 percent.

These policies were enforced by a police force that had gained international notoriety for its brutal, at times deadly, enforcement. South Africa's policies of division paralleled those of other African governments, whose politics of racial and ethnic separation were tearing African nations asunder throughout the continent. What made apartheid stand out was the sheer obstinacy and brutality of the police forces and their strict enforcement of the government's ideology.

Apartheid affected every South African's life. It affected how they thought, acted and spoke. Even those in the white population who stood against apartheid were met with heavy resistance, with some having to flee the country for safety reasons. It would not be until 1991 that the government, under the leadership of F.W. de Klerk, began to ease apartheid restrictions, even loosening the ban on political opposition.

The trappings of apartheid allowed the government to separate and divide races because they felt they were not compatible, yet music acted as a force of unity. A trip to the Soweto Township in Johannesburg will find you in the company of photos of legendary American jazz musicians alongside South African political heroes.[2] While the country

---

2   American musician Louis Armstrong even sent a trumpet to South African jazz icon Hugh Masekela as a sign of solidarity.

has a history of protest music and musicians – scrutinized by the government for writing anti-government songs – punk, rock and heavy metal are left out of the discussion by journalists and academics who have researched the history of protest through music in the country.

Western rock musicians were also vocal in their boycotting of South Africa, with the formation of the Artists United Against Apartheid supporting a boycott of the Sun City resort in the country as well as the collaborative performance of the song "Sun City" penned by long time E-Street Band member Steven Van Zandt. Musician Paul Simon himself broke the boycott (landing heavy criticism) by visiting South Africa as part of the inspiration for his *Graceland* album, which featured South African musicians and the musical styling of mbaqanga.[3] Yet, it is unclear how effective the boycott actually was. University of London's Stephen Chan states that the "boycott had little real effect," as labels were still sending music to be played on South African radio, records were still shipped to the country and Western artists were still performing in the country.

Metal musicians and fans were aligning themselves with the West, too, by getting involved in tape trading in the 1980s. At the time, heavy metal and hard rock magazines featured personal ads from metal fans and musicians around the world asking that music from the West be sent to them because of political troubles in their lands, lack of resources or high import duties that made

3   A style of music with Zulu roots performed on Western instruments, mbaqanga served as a great voice for the struggle during the apartheid years. Paul Simon's *Graceland* album and the success of the "White Zulu" Johnny Clegg helped to revive the style of music.

it nearly impossible for them to get new music otherwise. Readers from industrialized nations answered inquiries for new music by sending cassette tapes and even magazines to new and unfamiliar lands as a way to promote their favorite bands and to expose new fans to new artists and trends within the genre. For those sending cassette tapes to South Africa during apartheid, it was not about politics; it was about getting this form of music to an eager audience.

Faced with international sanctions and political isolation because of apartheid, metal was still able to flourish and grow, albeit in very small circles. With the heavy burden of dealing with an extremely conservative consensus and a government that would not tolerate much pushback against a religious doctrine that divided populations based on skin color, metal was relegated to the underground. In some ways it was this isolation that allowed the South African metal scene to develop and form its own identity. The pre-1994 era, marking the official period of rule for the National Party, was an era when musicians composed and performed music influenced by the limited amount of acts they were exposed to, allowing for a better exploration of their creativity.

Throughout the 1960s, '70s, and '80s, many rock bands – including The A-Cads, Rabbitt,[4] Hawk, The Asylum Kids, McCully's Workshop, Housewife's Choice, Freedom's

---

4   A massive success in the country, the peak of their fame is referred to locally as "Rabbit Fever." Featuring members Duncan Faure and Trevor Rabin, Faure would later join the Bay City Rollers and enjoy success with top 40 hits including "Saturday Night." Rabin relocated to England and became a member of the highly influential band Yes.

Children, Black Rose, Radio Rats and The Safari Suits –
set the pace for generations to follow, establishing how
to record, release and promote original music within the
country. The very first heavy metal band in South Africa
is not known for certain, but the evolution of rock to hard
rock spun into the space that bands such as Black Rose,
Suck, Stretch and Urban Assault were able to occupy with
something more expressive. Once the '90s arrived, the
heavy metal culture in South Africa gained the momentum
it needed to become a mouthpiece for a generation looking
to break away from the chains binding them to an ideology
that many did not support. "We had sanctions, so there
were a lot of things we couldn't get in South Africa at that
time, and [because of the sanctions] a real 'do-it-yourself'
culture developed. There was a real brotherhood in the
subculture," remembered Total Chaos' Jay R, insisting that
because of the oppressive – heavily censored state – heavy
metal was able to flourish on its own in South Africa during
the '90s. "It was an exciting time. I can't speak for anyone
else, but I really felt that we were creating something really
special back then. Felt like we were creating something that
would be a bookmark in the South African music history."
Bands like Agro, Voice Of Destruction, and Groinchurn
led the charge and commenced a new dialogue in the South
African musical sphere.

Tall, thin, with a red goatee and straight, restrained, long
black hair, Paul Blom sat with the sight of historic Robben
Island over his shoulder. Set along the Atlantic Coast of
Cape Town, Robben Island is now a tourist site with daily
tours guided by former political prisoners. It was there that

a quiet prisoner, number 46664, sent to prison for treason, sat in a small cell for 18 years dreaming of the day he would be released to lead his nation. The late Nelson Mandela used to stare at the very site where Paul and I sat long before there were shopping malls, movie theaters and pubs lining the heavily visited area. With Mandela's beautiful message of forgiveness and passive reserve, his was a leadership that the world did not expect and will most likely never see again. Through his negotiations with National Party leaders such as de Klerk and P.W. Botha, Mandela fought for not only his African National Congress (ANC) party, but also everyone else's with careful and adroit planning that led to the successful transition that occurred in 1994. Though we sat to discuss his former band Voice Of Destruction's role in the South African music scene and his country's past, Paul glanced over his shoulder and shared that he once met Mandela in July 1998 when the then-President paid an unannounced visit to his place of work – a story he recalled while sharing a photograph of the two shaking hands. Paul, wearing a heavy metal T-shirt and long hair, remembered that Mandela stopped to shake everyone's hand and share small banter. When I asked what Mandela spoke to him about, he joked, "My lip ring!" It was with that topic that we shifted course to something a bit more serious.

"Not until you got older did you realize what was happening; you were really not aware of the atrocities that were happening in the townships a few kilometers away. As kids we were very much oblivious to the unjust activities of the inexcusable regime. We caught glimpses of township raids (on television) but a lot of it was withheld." It was during the apartheid era that Voice Of Destruction had put down its roots, forming as a protest punk band whose lyrics addressed "anti-fascists proclamations." While not an original member (the band formed in 1986), Paul and his brother Francois (vocalist) joined the band in the early 1989 and 1990, respectively, after which the band refocused their energy toward their thrash metal influences.

Voice Of Destruction built a sizable fan base throughout the country over the course of the next few years, "mainly because V.O.D. made the effort to spread their word across the country" at a time when bands in South Africa were not yet making touring part of their routine, explained Paul. They would even release a live video, *Welcome to South Africaaaargh! Live '93*, which further helped the band promote their name within the country. The eventual attention of a European label, Morbid Records (the same company that would later sign Groinchurn), and the subsequent release of Voice Of Destruction's seminal album, *Bloedrivier,*[5] established the band as local legends. The album, which is held in high esteem throughout the metal community in Africa, was recorded in Europe,

---

5   Afrikaans meaning "blood river," the name refers to a historic battle between a highly outnumbered Voortrekker force of roughly 500 versus 10,000-plus Zulu fighters. Led by Andries Pretorius, the trekkers were said to have made a "vow" with God for support. Victorious in their defeat of King Dingane's soldiers, of whom 3,000 lost their lives, a monument was erected and stands today in Pretoria as a repayment to the "vow." V.O.D. chose this title for their album, as Paul explained, because "we are linked to this place [South Africa], and we adapted the title as a protest reaction, not glorifying war between the blacks and whites." The album's cover is a painting by renowned South African activist and artist, Norman Catherine.

becoming the first release outside of Africa by an African metal band.

"We [still] hear from people all over who listened to those cassettes to shreds. It is amazing how word spread before email and the Internet really took off." Contemplative, Paul expressed how content he was at the influence the band had locally: "The punk/hardcore/thrash/death metal blend of V.O.D. made it a more unique band with a sound of its own among many who wanted to emulate Metallica," he stated confidently. Many around South Africa felt that V.O.D. was the one band responsible for establishing the genre locally, as well as the unquestionable pioneers of metal in the country. Though not the first metal band in South Africa, Voice Of Destruction pushed the doors down for the rest. "The stuff simply wasn't around; international bands didn't tour here. We were part of creating a scene and laying a foundation for bands to follow. The isolation helped us to create our own identity as opposed to merely emulating bands from abroad."

Given this isolation, it was not easy to access the music that fans were demanding. Paul explained that he and his brother had a difficult time purchasing records. "In those days it was difficult finding the music you liked." The cost, scarcity and perception of the genre in the country greatly affected the music that was stocked on store shelves. Growing up in the Cape Town suburb of Thornton, Paul and his brother were captivated by the music that provided something Paul described as an "inherent rebellion," adding that "[the] sense of individuality and freedom, the visceral, chemical effect it has inside of you, it all just clicked." Yet, he continued, as a result of an overbearing church, "it was virtually impossible to see anything we liked on TV or hear it on radio. But there were a few radio shows that gave it some airtime." Artists such as Iron Maiden, Van Halen and Twisted Sister received minimal airplay. With the help of a neighbor, they discovered KISS and an airing on a local television show, *The Pop Shop,* exposed them to the "Aces High" video by Iron Maiden, which Paul described as "mind-blowing." Saving allowance money, he and his brother would often find themselves in the city center during the weekends purchasing albums. Eventually this record collection helped Francois' post-army DJ job as host of Saturday metal afternoons at the Cape Town venue Arties Cellar Pub, which was known as the place for metal in the city. The venue would not only bring together many in alternative scenes, including hardcore and punk music fans, but a host of themed nights for all of those who enjoyed "underground" music. Arties provided a space for cassette tape trading and fanzine distributions, as well as a VHS and Betamax tape circulation provided by those with overseas connections, allowing South Africans to connect with the happenings of hard rock and heavy metal outside of Africa, and catch glimpses of their favorite artists performing live.

Establishing live music relevance for local alternative music, building networks through the country and providing a foundation for how to promote and market heavy metal in Africa was much of what Paul's generation did and are recognized for in the South African rock and metal community. But what was to come now that heavy metal was established with an underground footing and apartheid had ended? Now that metal bands were to live in a free society, what steps would they take to expand the path for future metal bands? And now that apartheid was over, what were the challenges moving on?

THE WALL CRUMBLES

A dark, rather ominous, lonely warehouse with poor lighting, rusted tin roofing and a slightly fetid odor right in the city center of Pretoria on a weekday night was where the answers to my questions would begin. Not the sort of environ a foreign traveler would want to find themselves in, but this was where Van Zyl Alberts, leader of the groove- influenced death metal band Bloodbeast,[6] and his band mates Choroz, Werner, and Andrew convened for rehearsals. The rehearsal space location may have been something out of a crime drama, but, as Van explained, it was rent-free. In his mid 30s now, the long-haired Afrikaner looked the part of one of the most respected death metal musicians in the country with his goatee and tattoos. Van has lived within the South African metal scene for a while, stemming from his time as a member of his previous death metal band, Architect of Aggression, who along with his brother Anton and revolving door of bassists were continuously followed by controversy.

---

6   Since this interview, Van remains the only original member of Bloodbeast.

"We were controversial, in-your-face progressive death metal," explained Van. Cited as the godfathers of South African death metal, the band drew ire often as a result of their outspoken stand on religion, politics and censorship. The band's profile rose to prominence in 2007 when they organized the Rock Against Religion concert on July 7. "Outrage," Van exclaimed when describing the event. "We had protesters at the show. We had the whole country talking about religion." Yet the fears of a public short of embracing metal were realized. Fears of Satanism and the proverbial "kill your dog, kill your mother" stereotypes dominate the discourse of those who do not understand metal and consistently associate the genre with negativity.

During South Africa's authoritarian years, there were great lengths taken to quell the spread of metal. Adam van der Riet, a veteran of the Cape Town metal scene, explained that in the '80s, "Pretty much everything was suppressed by a stifling Afrikaner fundamentalism back then." One salient object of this fundamentalism was a book written by former police officer Rodney Seale. A staunch conservative and mouthpiece of the Dutch Reformed Church, he penned *Rock Music and the Right to Know* (translated from Afrikaans), a book that found itself in the hands of many parents and school officials. Seale's attempt to steer young minds and parents away from this music was bolstered by showing rock and heavy metal music videos to Afrikaans schools all over the country.

Apart from screening music videos, Seale would play hard rock and heavy metal music, presenting the students with the lyrical content of the acts in attempts to drive students away from this music. "He did us a tremendous favor by what he was doing. He went to great lengths to find these bands!" laughed Christo Bester of Groinchurn, as he remembered learning about new bands from Seale's speeches.

Seale's book details what he viewed as a correlation between Satanism and rock music. Assuring the reader that every rock song was a gateway to Satan, his book became a staple among church members, parents and anyone else who cared to promote the false stereotypes about metal. Rodney Seale's book has brought anguish to many in the metal community because of what it overlooked: the primary reason metal played such an important role in their lives. It stood as a voice of expression, unlike religion, that sought to achieve a goal through conformity. And for many, their church was dedicated to promoting the values of a God whom they felt was being exploited in the name of white supremacy and authoritarian control. In some ways Seale's work parallels the efforts of the Parents Music Resource Center (PMRC) in the United States. Headed by Tipper Gore (former wife of then U.S. Congressmen and future Vice President Al Gore), the PMRC attempted to regulate the content in lyrics as well as create a method that informed parents of the lyrical content contained on the records,[7] which became the basis for the now-famous Senate hearing held on the matter.[8] As in the United

---

7   The black and white "Parental Advisory: Explicit Content" stickers on album covers.

8   What made this hearing famous – apart from the musings of the influential New York group Twisted Sister's vocalist, Dee Snider, who pulled his prepared speech out of his back pocket and, as he puts it,

States, South Africa distributed a list of songs and albums that were deemed offensive. In South Africa, however, the authoritarian government provided a list of artists and records that were to be banned. The list of banned artists and songs included those who dared to speak up against the government or stood in solidarity with political opponents[9] outside of South Africa.

Recalling experiences in his life that were influenced by such fears, Van explained, "there used to be a department in the police that specialized in Satanism. If people suspected that you were involved in Satanism then, they would report it to the police and they would come to investigate you. Needless to say a lot of metal fans were harassed." Two instances that stood out during his recollection took place at the Afrikaans school he attended. The first involved his brother being on the receiving end of a diatribe insisting there could not be two gods – the result of his scribbling of *"Black Sabbath"* on an exam paper. "Because he listened to Black Sabbath, he believed in Satan" was the correlation assumed, according to Van. Furthermore, he explained his brother was asked to make a choice between Jesus and Satan before the school's administrators because of his love of metal. Another instance occurred following a school talent show in which Van and his bandmates performed

---

"shocked the committee by completing sentences" – was the testimony of folk music legend John Denver. Denver had earned a spot on the list as a result of the misunderstandings of his lyrics from his hit song, "Rocky Mountain High."

9   One such artist was Stevie Wonder, who upon winning a Grammy for his song "I Just Called To Say I Love You" dedicated the achievement to then-prisoner Nelson Mandela during his acceptance speech.

the Jimi Hendrix song "Purple Haze" and were summoned on suspicion of pedaling drugs. Similarly, Odyssey's Dean Smith remembers getting comparable treatment when the schoolmaster of his Johannesburg school noticed *"KISS"* scribbled on his backpack. "He came running at me, a Bible in one hand, and putting his other hand on my head while shouting about casting demons. Military state that country was!"

Growing up in a small town roughly an hour outside of Pretoria, former Bloodbeast drummer Werner stepped into the conversation: "Once a guy came to our school and held up a Meat Loaf record and was going on about how Satan lives in this music. These groups that would come along didn't know what extreme metal was. They would have crapped themselves. They showed a Metallica record, and my friend looked at me, yelling, 'Hey you got that'! loud enough for the presenters and his classmates to hear. We erupted with laughter, though I was laughing even harder at the idea that Meat Loaf was spreading Satanism through his vivid and expansive rock operas."

Patrick Davidson, guitarist for the melodic death metal band Mind Assault, recalled life in South Africa growing up during apartheid and how its link with conservatism also introduced him to metal. "The government had a strong tie with the white Afrikaner church and it was compulsory in government schools that there were Bible classes in the curriculum. They would sometimes screen these Christian documentary-style films in Bible class about how *evil* those bands were supposed to be. So it's no lie to say that school introduced me to metal at the age of 10 or 11 or thereabouts. Needless to say, those were my favorite classes. I don't think the church knew about death or more extreme metal in those days; they'd have a shit otherwise!"

Anton de Willars, bassist for Cape Town-based groove metal band The Warinsane, shed more light on exactly how the church tried to manipulate the sort of music the youth would get their hands on. "To say that metal was frowned upon is a big understatement. Rock and certain pop artists were really made out to be as demonic and evil as your imagination would allow. Real metal was still fairly unknown in the country and under the radar of the authorities at the time and as such not so much in their crosshairs. If they only knew!" It is what Anton proceeded to explain that left quite the impression. "I remember being given assignments at school where we had to research musicians – pretty tame stuff like The Beatles, Queen, Sting, Rolling Stones – and find and point out all the ways that they're trying to subvert our thoughts in order to brainwash us into becoming Satanists."

As the cacophony of brutality filled the Pretoria skyline, a fast-paced movement of technical, groove-oriented death metal plastered through the roofless rehearsal space that Bloodbeast was using to hone their craft. The question as to whether bands today are still divided on the issue of conservatism from the Dutch Reformed Church and how it affects rock and heavy metal was one that lingered throughout Bloodbeast's pummeling practice that evening. It was a question that I returned to throughout the next few weeks in South Africa. Some, like Alistair of the Cape

Town post-punk influenced With Dawn, argued that the Afrikaans population has "moved on from the conservative side of things." But others, such as Louis Henn of Cape Town's Megalodon, felt that conservatism is still hindering growth of not just heavy metal, but of all genres of music.

Two instances that supported his argument occurred during my visit to Cape Town. First was the cancellation of the popular music festival RAMfest (Real Alternative Music Festival) during one of its scheduled performances in Bloemfontein, a city in the heart of the country's farming region often noted for its pervasive conservatism. The second occurrence was the protests that accompanied the tour by global pop star Lady Gaga during her visit to the country. During my interview with Cape Town's Zombies Ate My Girlfriend, the Lady Gaga protests infuriated band members because of the stubbornness that they feel hinders the current state of South Africa's burgeoning music culture. Gavin, the band's vocalist, passionately expressed, "I feel rather bad for those people. Evolve!" But has the Afrikaans community moved on?

Many I spoke with felt the conservative wall had been compromised as a result of the success of the most popular hard rock band in the country, Fokofpolisiekar (Fuck Off Police Car). George van der Riet (no relation to Adam), guitarist for the progressive metal band Strident, explained that while a lot of Afrikaners think conservatively, "Fokofpolisiekar opened the gates for people to be a bit more opened minded." The Cape Town-based quartet (referred to often as "Fokof") moved their indie/punk-influenced hard rock from their rehearsal studios into the discussions of a country rife with religious conservatives. "I don't think we ever realized that we challenged the church or the government, but we definitely rebelled against the norms of growing up Afrikaans," stated vocalist Francois van Coke.

"Religion is a big part of Afrikaans culture," he continued, "because the Boers believe they had a pact with God. We did not believe in that god and weren't scared of saying it." Performing exclusively in Afrikaans, one of the country's 11 official languages, the band garnered controversy wherever they went. Their videos, their songs, their ideas seem to mock this idea of adhering to the ideals that led to so much negativity. Never shy, Fokofpolisiekar, who formed in 2003, took conservatives head on.

Fokofpolisiekar has earned the respect of many involved in the alternative music scene because of their willingness to stick to their beliefs and challenge the norm of the country's conversation, even enduring a national scandal when their bassist wrote *"Fok God"* (*Fuck God*) on a fan's wallet – an act that led to a national outrage and numerous show cancellations. But the band, despite protests, never backed away. For many protesting, this was exactly what they feared rock and heavy metal music was going to do: corrupt an impressionable youth. However, Fokofpolisiekar succeeded because the generation known as "Mandela's Children" now had a voice and an outlet. They were the right band, at the right time. They spoke to those to whom no one was listening and soared from stereos into hearts. Few artists will enjoy this sort of emotional loyalty. Adam van der Riet said of the band, "They went out of their way to break down those rigid cultural barriers, to reject the stereotypical past and embrace the freedom to be yourself, in the company of whoever [*sic*] you choose." The following Fokofpolisiekar have amassed in South Africa is incredible. Francois van Coke's commercial appeal is special. From being the object of scorn to the object of praise, his persona is now selling products in national advertisement campaigns. After seeing enough people sharing their emotional attachment, even to the point of tears, I understood that Fokofpolisiekar's legacy, music and message mattered.

Things were moving quickly for me in South Africa. I had become comfortable navigating the massive Johannesburg/Pretoria area using public transportation. The exceptional Gautrain served as a strong indicator that things in this country were moving right along. The above-ground, high-speed train connecting the two cities, and a few in between, became my "go to" when Herman was unable to meet musicians with me. Herman accompanied me often because he, too, was excited to meet the musicians who impacted South Africa's rock and metal history. I also found myself touring with a few bands in the country, including Juggernaught, over the course of a few weeks.

During one particular trip, Herman and I drove the band's gear across country toward the Western Cape, a mere 18-hour drive from the capital city that gave us plenty of time to catch up on old Skid Row and Judas Priest records, as well as some hysterical banter. All of this without air conditioning, as our bodies slowly began to melt into the upholstery of the small cab of the pick up truck. The other band members flew!

The scenery between the two cities is breathtaking. The splendid natural beauty of the country came to life as Herman and I headed west. Farmlands eased into view as Gauteng's soft hills carefully placed themselves in the rearview mirror. Towns disappeared as quickly as they appeared: small churches in the middle, one traffic light, a small general store and a few homes were all you had to form a quick memory. Hours upon hours of farmlands eventually gave way to the mysterious Great Karoo, a vast swath of arid land and cloudless skies, with the ever-ominous Swartberg mountains on the patient horizon. This landscape kept the mystery of early life to itself. Creatures that roamed the earth from its earliest periods had come and gone. Once in a while a fossil turned up here and there in this land marked by the occasional windmill, but many of the secrets of this region remain silenced in the otherwise blank landscape.

Lives were lost here, too. Somewhere on this land, behind the soft hills, the British built their concentration camps where they held women and children in order to get Afrikaners to surrender during the Boer War. Twenty-six thousand perished in those camps, many of which existed in the area I was staring at. Black Africans were taken in those camps, too, and kept separately. Even in suffering, skin color divided South Africans. Herman stopped at a post that marked where a concentration camp once stood. Prayers were scrolled in any one of the many languages spoken in the country. Perhaps in death people are united.

On this specific site, they were in prayer. We continued. I thanked Herman for showing me that spot, but silence gripped us. I kept wondering how the beauty that lay all around could contain so much horror and mystery. But, I had to let those thoughts go; the Great Karoo became an easy distraction for my mind. Everything settled down. Things became calm in my world. There was really nothing else to do but think. The road passed below us, but to our sides the world stood still.

"These mountains look scary," I said, breaking the silence. Herman just laughed – as anyone would have, I'm sure. "This is what Middle Earth must look like," referring to the *Lord of the Rings* book and film series. Herman agreed, nodding his head, reminding me that the acclaimed and treasured author of the series, J.R.R. Tolkien, actually grew up in South Africa, not far from where we were passing at the time. Staring at the Swartberg mountains and their ominous nature, I wondered if this is where Tolkien envisioned his fictitious world, where people of different "groups" lived separately, with separate languages and separate identities, and seldom interacted. I was not then, nor am I now, well versed on his works, but I could not help but think that his fantasy world was not very different from the realities of the South Africa that surrounded him. Those rocky, frightening peaks jutting out of the dry sands of the desert consumed me for the remainder of the sunlight. For as long as those mountains were in front of us, we were silent, consumed in our thoughts.

When I would break the silence, I kept coming back to this country's history. Perhaps Herman was annoyed by my insistence of always discussing the past, but that is what was persistent in my thoughts. "If there is anything that sets South Africa apart, it's its complexity," he remarked during one of my inquiries. Perhaps that is what Tolkien understood, as he was able to channel that complexity into his art, much like the musicians who make up this complicated and diverse landscape. Everyone is alive under one collective, aware of their differences, divided by forces seen and unseen, yet working together. The complications of the country came to live in everyone. Perhaps this is why the mid '90s was a crucial time in the country's creative history. All artists found a way of unleashing that complexity, with painters, writers and musicians releasing a collective frustration. Herman was right. South Africa was complicated and perhaps still remains that way. Now I had a reason to be silent. I learned so much of the country's history through academia, but was unable to understand the true complications of a nation undergoing a new identity. Music was my way of better understanding this.

MOVING BEYOND THE DEVIL

Many of those I met are not old enough to have been forced into military conscription, or remember the events that shaped the struggle against apartheid such as the District Six riots, Soweto Uprisings or the Sharpeville Massacre. Headlines and news reports from the modern South Africa often include a naive mention about a "nation still divided" or a "still fractured nation," but is it really?

Most South Africans do not frequently identify with their race before their nationality. A 2012 report states that only nine percent of South Africans identify with their race before anything else.[10] Outsiders' mentality, though, is still very much black and white. The heavy metal community understands this all too well, as voices from outside the continent have denounced South African metal as "un-African" because of the predominantly white makeup. Some critics, even within the country, have suggested that perhaps the genre serves as a mouthpiece for a continued separation between races, perhaps embraced by a young population that wishes to keep an aspect of "whiteness," or privilege, through music. This is absolutely not the case.

Rock and heavy metal have grown significantly within the past 20 years in the developing world. Metal is not the sort of genre best served forced. Quite often, the genre is discovered and adored by fans who take control of their musical taste, maintaining that drive throughout their life, without so much of a drop of conformity or a foray into the mainstream. Metal is inclusive to everyone, regardless of gender, sexuality, skin color or religion. The genre has grown globally because of its acceptance. In South Africa, however, the genre is slow in its growth.

Is culture the reason? Cultures that are steeped in history and tradition may have a lot to do with why metal is seldom embraced by black South Africans. But given South Africa's history of division, the music stood a better opportunity to be embraced by non-whites during that era as a result of heavy metal's gravitation toward themes

10   Source: Futurefacts.org.za

of struggle and resistance. Musicians in the country today will eagerly share the similar sentiment that blacks *need* to get involved in the metal community for the genre to last and grow there. The current crop of metal bands has been proactive in getting the blacks who enjoy metal to be less furtive in their passion of the music. To paraphrase the members of the Cape Town-based thrash metal band ING, the ultimate goal is to represent population demographics at rock shows, as in having 92 percent of the crowd be non-white.

Darkfiend is a South African metal promoter and the brain behind the popular Metal4Africa website, which started as a response to the growing metal communities throughout the continent and a networking forum for others in Africa to discover new artists and share ideas. Speaking with a bit of concern when discussing the bi-annual Metal4Africa festivals held in the Western Cape province, he commented, "We've reached our attendance ceiling. It is what we have to offer for local music. If only there was more penetration into the outlying areas, it could count in our favor in the long run." Pondering an ideal situation where township performances happened monthly and with a smile suggesting that it was an idea that has already been given the discourse it deserves, Darkfiend was adamant in expressing that metal in South Africa has a brighter road, and non-white involvement is vital, hinting that nothing would change the country's metal culture for the best more than township concerts.

Townships are a very strong and poignant image of the African landscape. Lines of tin- roofed homes are prominent in photographs, videos and imaginations as a standard of African life. Absent, of course, are the paved highways, shopping malls, skyscrapers and modern homes that represent the ever-changing African life. Yet, for all of the country's signs of modern progress, townships are still very much a part of life in South Africa. It is estimated that over half of the population in South Africa lives in townships.

While not in complete destitution, populations are often connected to water and power lines, and residents tend to live in communities that one must visit to understand. Not often on the destination "must see" spots for tourists, townships surround suburbs and rural areas alike in South Africa, some the result of government planning, others born organically. Townships are places where the vibrancy of culture and the tragedy of poverty cohabitate. Not typically associated with heavy metal culture, townships have become a center of music, places where traditional elements sprinkled with Western hip-hop, R&B and electronic influences have resulted in South Africa's most popular genre, Kwaito, which is often described as African-styled house music. A few rock and metal musicians confessed their pride in the genre because of the uniqueness of the music. Adam van der Riet admitted, "You won't find it anywhere else in the world. It has a very unique style and dance. Whether you like it or not, no one can deny that it is very original and unique." Stars of the genre include Mandoza, Mapaputsi, M'du

Masilela and Arthur Mafokate, who was the first to put the genre in the South African musical conversation in 1995 with the politically charged song, "Kaffir," a term that is a pejorative epithet in South Africa.

Juggernaught has experimented with this unique sound, recording a song with Kwaito artist Mapaputsi, called "Busstop!" Others, such as Cape Town's Strident, have recorded with a choir based in the Western Cape (an area steeped in traditional music). And, the now-defunct Johannesburg-based thrash band Insurrection once recorded a few songs featuring Zulu-style gumboot dances and formal drumming during the early '90s, becoming the first metal band on the continent to do so. But the possibilities of expanding the boundaries of heavy metal are endless, as other acts throughout the globe have not hesitated to incorporate local influences into their music.

Historic for its resolve, the relinquishing of apartheid ushered a new mentality as it did precedent. Cultural inclinations also flowed in the breeze of optimism, as artists were now free to work and collaborate together, as well as enter realms of discovery. However, in terms of rock and metal, the progress was still slow. "This problem has to do with conformity," stated the smoke-throated Kgame, vocalist for Under The Chernobyl Cloud, "especially amongst the youth. *Especially* amongst the youth!" I was curious as to his background, wondering how the self-professed "township kid" discovered metal and found himself shouting at white audiences in Johannesburg nightclubs.

Kgame, who was born in Atteridgeville,[11] spoke of his father's involvement in the struggle against apartheid. Eventually, his father was tracked and caught by the ruling government. "I was young, about three or so, when the cops burnt down our house with my family in it looking for my father." Captured and sentenced to nine years on the notorious Robben Island, his father became a member of the first ruling ANC party upon his release. As a township kid whose family fought against the political isolation they faced, Kgame gravitated toward metal as a result of hearing a Marilyn Manson song when he was the eighth grade, igniting an immediate connection. "Metal is freedom," he proclaimed. He paused to catch his thoughts, falling silent, looking down for a second. What he thought about, I will never know. In his opinion, the conformity and conservatism among his peers was detrimental to metal's growth into the black communities as a result of the peculiar and stifling associations that this music still retains with the occult and anarchy, something that has undoubtedly hampered its reputation and growth. "Anything with negative connotations will suffer," reminded Kgame.

Interest in this music in the townships has grown in recent years. The ever-changing, ever-growing vibrant township of Soweto is one such place. Black metal band Demogoroth Satanum, punk/hardcore act TCIYF, as well as melodic hard rockers Ree-Burth call this ever-changing township southwest of Johannesburg home.

---

11 Located west of Pretoria, the township was established in 1939 by the government as a black settlement.

Soweto stretches as far as the eye can see. Approaching the city skyline of Johannesburg, the outskirts of the township sit quietly and unnoticed as busy commuters speed by on their way to the city. Soweto, today, is a mix of everything South Africa contains. Homes made of corrugated tin sheets lined up against newly constructed homes equipped with running water, power supplies and the occasional satellite dish. Dirt roads bleed into paved ones. Schools, businesses, government buildings, restaurants and shopping centers – all form a collective that I can only describe as misunderstood. Soweto is wonderful, so vibrant and alive. It is really unlike any place I have visited in South Africa. Continuing into Soweto, it was another 90 minutes until the landmark Orlando Cooling Towers came into view. Featuring colorful murals painted all the way around, the towers have come to symbolize the growth of the township since the 1950s with the construction of the power plant. Herman pointed, doing a double take, "Jesus! They jump off of those now." As he kept turning his head toward the towers, perhaps forgetting he was driving, we both stared in amazement at what has since become a unique bungee jumping site.

Not far from the towers sat Maponya Mall. One of the largest shopping malls in the country, the very modern structure sits in the middle of Soweto as a reminder of not only this township's growth, but also South Africa's transformation. A huge glass façade greeted Herman and me as we made our way past the promenade of clothing shops to the food court where we were to meet Demogoroth Satanum's leader, Modiba. As we sat in a pizza shop –

ordering nothing but lattes and cappuccinos while waiting for a man whose text messages read, "you'll know me when you see me" – he appeared, wearing an unreadable band logo shirt featuring upside down crosses and his long dread-locked hair, clashing among the crowd of his contemporaries dressed in the latest suburban fashions. Modiba was quiet, polite and extremely intelligent. He understood heavy metal as well as anyone could. Extreme metal complimented his wit, acumen and demeanor perfectly. Modiba recognized Herman immediately and began to chat with him for a bit, trading stories as well as collecting advice from a venerated fixture in the South African music community. He turned to share some thoughts and to invite us to his band's rehearsal. But I was curious about life in Soweto, where he was born and raised.

"As a kid, most remain utterly ignorant to the flaws in society, although looking at it in retrospect, the demographic was less than desirable but we enjoyed the kind of environment we were in. Youth holds the promise of beauty. When you're young you don't give a fuck, you just play, pushing tires, playing with brick cars, building kites and things of the sort. Also, a lot of the roads in the townships were mostly dust. We would wake up in the morning, have breakfast and spend the rest of the day playing and getting our asses dirty from the sand and shit like that. Then you get your ass kicked from being out all day. It was a good way to grow up."

This township had gradually formed its own identity. Established on old farmlands as a home for blacks evicted from vibrant suburbs such as Alexandria and Sophiatown,

Soweto erupted in the conscience of the world in 1976 after the now-legendary uprising. As a result of a student protest that erupted after the government had mandated curriculum in Afrikaans, over 10,000 students marched in protests, only to have police open fire and kill 23. Since then, Soweto residents have not been shy in claiming an identity of their own. The apartheid government responded by trying to improve the lives of the residents by providing electricity as the world marked the massacre committed by the national government. "Now it's a lot more chilled. With time we've seen Soweto grow from the once brutal war zone to a place where now all people from the different cultures can embrace one another in kind spirit. We have malls and all the various establishments that put Soweto among one of South Africa's biggest cultural and tourist attractions," explained Modiba in his confident voice. Soweto is home to over a million people and is a place where all of the nation's languages converge in a unique blend of extraordinary humanity.

Elsewhere, there have been a few suburban bands who have performed in townships, notably Truth And Its Burden, Facing The Gallows and Bile of Man. Members of the extreme death metal band Bile of Man spoke fondly of their experiences. "We were the first death metal band to play in a township, we had so much fun at that show. Everyone was having a good time," reminisced drummer Riann. Keeping a smile throughout, Riann spoke well of their performance in Tembisa Township outside of Johannesburg. "It was organized by a friend. Power was connected from across the road, from some guy's house."

To their delight, the turnout was overwhelming, as fans were enthused about the assaulting, blast-beat-saturated death metal attack from the band. They laughingly recalled the unforgettable strides and left-to-right sways of their former vocalist, who performed with a rather intimidating presence and found himself looking out onto a crowd of young fans mimicking his swaying.

Facing The Gallows, a prominent metalcore band, also shared the same enthusiasm after performing in a township east of Johannesburg, Vosloorus, in January 2013. "It is alive," stated Ricki Allemann, the band's former guitarist, recalling that performance. "We arrived, and there were kids playing metal off their phones" and to their delight, Facing The Gallows were introduced to local metal band, Missiles of Doom. Others such as Johannesburg's Truth And Its Burden performed in a township school in East Rand, outside Johannesburg, an experience vocalist Ashley De Beer said he will never forget. "Kids went absolutely crazy for hardcore. They were wild – louder than the band! They were crowd surfing and they never gave a damn what people thought," reminisced the loquacious, ever-smiling vocalist. Music, especially in areas of derelict, is an escape that is unbridled. To be exposed to something new, different and exciting is a matter that will never be forgotten by those whose lives revolve around squalor and the faint hope that someday things will change for the best. Metal, for some, may be the bridge that inspires change.

But what has kept others from doing more in this regard? Is there trepidation? Are the negative perceptions of the genre still hampering the spirits of those moving it forward? "It is always going to be a marginalized community. The main crowd that listens to heavy metal is the middle to upper class white crowd," noted George van der Riet, adding that music needs to "stop being segmented. Joint gigs and tours need to happen. We have to take that leap of faith." Alec Surridge, formerly of Sacraphyx, a band formed on the heels of apartheid, explained the band's attempts in the past to get metal to the non-white population were not always met with fondness. "We wanted people of all colors to see it, but we were stamped out." Cultural stigmas have a negative effect on metal. There is a still strong conservative element in the townships. "It is definitely cultural," stated Cape Town musician Damian Rijkers. "We need to break that stereotype of 'blacks listen to hip-hop, whites listen to metal'. You see it in Africa [blacks listening to metal], but not much in South Africa."

Passionate South African heavy metal fan Wanda Ngwenya feels that a stigma attached to "white" culture from the black communities has been responsible for the schism. Born in raised in a township in KwaZulu-Natal, he discovered metal when buying a bootlegged R&B DVD near his home, only to discover the disc was filled with metal videos. The extremely passionate fan describes his Zulu culture as rather obstinate. "We need to take metal to the townships, [but] most black South Africans are so ignorant toward rock/metal." As Demogoroth Satanum[12] explained, "In the township a lot of ideas that allow freedom are viewed as the Devil's work. At one time skateboarding

---

12   The members of Demogoroth Satanum chose to be represented and quoted as a band, not as individuals.

was viewed as Satanic because in the eyes of the holy, kids who would willingly throw themselves down stairs and get hurt had the Devil in them. So obviously with music like metal and the images associated with it, it will cause people to brand you." When asked if they hid their passion within their community, they laughed off the assessment. "Music is passion. And to be forced to hide your love is alone an act of sin. That is one thing that we never did. Metal was, and still is, part of who we are. We didn't see the need to hide who we are just because it might offend the next person."

Is metal perhaps hurt by the nation's past, as a result of the genre's association with whites? Wanda explained that many of the youths in the townships "swear they experienced apartheid," yet are not old enough to have even lived one day under the former rule, conceding, "Our past has something to do with it." Demogoroth Satanum shared similar concessions, with obvious annoyance. "Anyone in our generation who still blames apartheid for their situation in life is just making excuses for being dumb. Those times are behind us. There are still those who hold grudges against others because of their skin, but we say screw them. All of them, blacks and whites. Metal, to a certain degree, forces people to look at the world they live in. It gives us perspective into what contemporary society tends to ignore and shun. Through metal we've learned to confront and question that which lies beyond what we've been told and what we're accustomed to. The free-thinking aspect of the genre and some of the ideals the music expresses are some of the primary attractions. The notion of being free to question, for example, the religious establishment, which in Soweto is frowned upon and in some parts warrant murder by burning," they explained, rather emphatically.

The acceptance of this music in the townships represents a country on the move forward, not because of a forced culture, but because the music represents individuals making a choice of how they wish to express themselves and how they wish to be seen – choices they made on their own.

"This country is still young in that respect. Ninety-five percent of the people in this country want South Africa to move forward. We are all from Africa. That work must be done together, rather than divisively," shared Riann of Bile of Man. "It will always be there. You can't just wash it away," explained George Schoombie of Sacraphyx. In many ways South Africa has moved on from its past, yet it is still an aspect that remains, allowed Durban musician Brandon Van Eeden. "It is a sensitive subject. It will always be there," he commented, lamenting the lack of opportunity that affects everyone in the country, regardless of skin color. Though not everyone agrees that the issue is that of the past, Alistair,[13] formerly of With Dawn argued, that "[1994] was a hell of a long time ago. I don't think that the previous regime has anything to with what these kids are looking at now." His bandmate Kevin Rule concurred. "This generation is so detached [from the past], they are free to make up their own minds about what goes on here. A lot of Africans are looking for change, for better things."

---

13   He has since moved to New Zealand.

For many, the issue is an economic matter. With an income disparity that is one of the worst in the world, South Africa's gap is omnipresent as you travel. Yes, the proportional representation of the racial makeup makes the division obvious, but traveling throughout the nation one sees that poverty is not endemic to one racial group over another. "After 1994, the focus was concentrated on a specific elite. People seem to be living in worse poverty twenty years [later]," noted Ricki Allemann, though speaking anecdotally. The frustrations are obvious and newsworthy as strikes and wage disputes in South Africa occur often and occasionally make international newspapers – notably the tragedy over mining wages in Rustenburg, where police officers opened fire, killing 34 striking miners in August of 2014.[14]

With an increasing unemployment rate that hovers around 40 percent, musicians in South Africa today envision a life in the country for themselves and their children. But with the reality of a high unemployment rate, low wages and one of the highest crime rates in the world, South Africans worry out of passion, as well as their love and concern of country. "People see Africa and they get put off," said Ashley De Beer of Truth And Its Burden, but "[many] don't see the great things our country does have. We want to take those negatives and turn it into positives. I am stoked on South Africa."

Sitting with Herman one evening over a few drinks, I told him what others were saying. He was moved. Herman

14   "South African Company Fires 12,000 Striking Miners" http://www.cnn.com/2012/10/05/world/africa/south-africa-mine-strike

absolutely loves his country and it was obvious in the way he presented it to me over my visit. This was a person who lives for his country. In an honest moment, he shared, "I used to obsess about moving away from South Africa, but the more I traveled, the more I realized that you have to be strong to live here. You get so much in return. Everything here has a charm." So many others in this generation also confessed their desire to move at one point for a more secure future. These aspirations of expatriation were different from those of the previous generation. It was called a "white flight" after apartheid fell. Many were fearful of civil war or violent discourse, or were just completely dissatisfied with having lost their privilege that they left in disgust. For many now, the challenges of building the country up together have been greeted by an understanding that what happened before will not deter them from pushing forward.

All of the fears espoused by the previous generation never came to light. South Africa moved forward and grew. The economy is the second largest on the continent, and it shows. And, South Africans are extremely proud of their country.

As a result of a large economy and a well-developed state, the South African music scene stands apart from others in Africa because of the unbelievable music infrastructure available. South Africans are beneficiaries of a wonderful network of print, radio and television outlets that support rock and metal artists. Furthermore, the access – unlike any other that I have seen in Africa – to elite musical equipment has allowed international touring acts to include South Africa on their tour itineraries.

"I look like I eat a lot of meat," joked the mercurial, unfiltered, unapologetic and outspokenly verbose and unique personality, Louis Du Pisani. Having once hosted his own nationally televised metal program[15] and organized of the nation's Wacken Metal Battles,[16] his hysterical manners gave way when it came time to comment on matters of effect; the bearded, long-haired colossus clutched a beer in his hand and spoke without hesitation. "There are plenty of people capable of supporting us [local acts], but they don't. People are here. They listen to the music. It is just a matter of getting them off their asses. We have too many bands here and no support. Eastern Europe has a few bands, and tons of support."

South African musicians have not seen a large return in support for the local scene, which Louis (himself the frontman of the excellent metal band The Drift), like many musicians, found to be of concern. But why did he feel that way knowing that international acts are coming through and that just a generation ago, South Africa had a massive rock and metal community. His argument was supported by the idea that perhaps South African bands sound too

---

15   Louis was the brainchild behind the *Ondergrond* (Underground) television show that aired on the MK music channel. The only animated metal show on the planet, the show featured music videos and interviews from local and international bands and was achieving a cult status worldwide until it was cancelled.

16   The winner of this "battle" is awarded a trip to Germany to perform at the legendary Wacken Open Air metal festival. Both Agro and Sacraphyx performed at the legendary festival prior to this competition.

much like their Western influences and maybe a more localized influence was needed. "Patriotism is a word that doesn't exist here. A lot of the bands here that get it right are those that sound African, even those bands that sing in Afrikaans. If you make something uniquely South African, you'll get your name out. I hate the fact that we outsource our inspirations. This music was born from conflict. If you [were] a liberal white kid in a conservative right-wing racist society, your message was going to be so much more powerful. We don't need conflict to make good music, but often conflict channels itself into art. We had it. Why don't we use it?"

The previous generation – struggling through conflict, racial divisions and authoritative government – was what made that group of South African musicians more successful than the current. They promoted relentlessly through every available underground channel, while this generation remains complacent, waiting for television shows and the crop of radio shows to do the promoting for them. Louis had a valid argument.

The aptly named Wayne Longbeard sat behind the microphones of his weekly radio show, Before The Witching Hour, in a Johannesburg studio. Weighing in on the matter of whether local bands were perhaps being complacent, he, too, never showed restraint. Wayne elaborated on the media and its contribution for the national metal scene. "I don't think radio does nearly enough for it [the local scene]. They really could do more. They really could," he said in his soft-spoken voice. "This is a niche market, the radio industry in South Africa – and that's so odd, this music isn't a niche type of music in this country. It is so skewed, it's ridiculous. I think radio is a massive thing. Radio should be doing a massive thing for South African music." I learned that evening of a quota on national acts, which radio stations usually met by adhering to the "safe" selection, defined as an already established and commercially viable local act to be played once an hour.

Responding to my questions between songs, slowly pushing the large microphone to his side while gently lowering his headphones to his shoulders, Wayne reflected on how far hard rock and heavy metal in South Africa had come along. "It is in a healthy state right now," deviating from the course many of the metal acts had conclusively reached, that metal in the country today is stagnant. Wayne reminded me that many international metal acts are coming now, "where you wouldn't see that before. A lot of fans are going for these big acts and are going to see South African acts, which they didn't make a point to see." "True," he affirmed, "metalheads are so into the music, but a lot of the guys don't support local music. But RAMfest takes a chance on them anyway." Many of the acts I had spoken to were booked to perform at the upcoming festival or had performed at previous versions. RAMfest, a South African festival called Woodstock, Krank'd Up, and the Oppikoppi Festival (the largest in the country) all are fantastic gatherings of music enthusiasts throughout the southern African region, yet the international headliners are few, as are the metal acts.

"I think we should just be patient. We are still in the infancy of having the ability to go overseas and do these things. A time ago we didn't have the opportunities that we have now," Wayne said. "There are a lot of impatient people out there going, 'maybe it's just not my time', but it doesn't matter if it is your time, because you are just helping to build the bricks for the next generation. A lot of things are very new. You have to be very patient with the whole thing."

Observations fresh after having recently arrived from a small tour of Europe and a three-city trek of the United States with his band, Deity's Muse, Wayne shared his honest comparisons between Africa and the West. In the latter there is "lots of hard work, lots of bridges being built. There are no shortcuts. You have to swallow your pride with these sorts of things. And if there are shortcuts with these sorts of things, they are few and far between. There's a hell of a lot of negativity in the South African scene, and I'm tired of it. I'm tired of the negativity because I see more positive things out of it than I do negative. I'm very positive about the whole thing."

THE INCREDIBLE, THE UNEXPECTED AND THE MAGICAL

It was time to depart South Africa. I came here with so many uncertainties as to what to expect, what I would see and who I could meet – if anyone would even meet with me. And they did! South African musicians let me into their homes, their lives, and opened up – sharing as many stories about their music and their country as I could take. I never expected this much. I traveled to the four largest cities in the country and met over 40 musicians, and made memories that will last a lifetime. Herman and his family were beyond gracious. He accompanied me on a lot of my trips around Johannesburg, Pretoria and Cape Town (using their equipment vehicle to drive me around Cape Town while on their tour. Thank you, again, Juggernaught.), and even checked up on me during a tour stop in the nation's largest southern city, Durban. He never ceased to amaze me with his never-ending stories and facts about South Africa, and extremely useful language tips in Afrikaans and other local Pretoria languages. I also had the fortune of jumping into a van with Facing The Gallows, who allowed me to tour with them so I could get whatever I needed from whomever I needed. I was blown away by the rock and metal community's generosity and support.

Other musicians kept in touch regularly throughout my trip to make sure I was taken care of, gestures that would follow me around the continent. Furthermore, South Africa gave me the confidence to continue forward.

Always a moving country, and one of the few places on earth I describe as magic, South Africa is a place I never enjoy leaving. Though it is a country still stumbling to gain traction and a new identity, there is just something about this country that stays with me wherever I go. It is a country that is learning and blossoming into something great and always is optimistic about what awaits – much like the next generation of South Africans, heavy metal musicians or not, they just know that something extraordinary will happen. Whatever apprehensions outsiders have about the country are typically forgotten after visiting South Africa. It is a nation that has always, and will always, leave an impression. South Africa is stunning. Young, ambitious, hungry and generous, there will always be something special about South Africa for me.

I had no idea if even traveling to Africa just to meet rock and metal bands would be worth the time and finances, but after having traversed one of the larger countries in the continent three times around, I could not help but want to keep going. I bought a bus ticket to the neighboring country of Botswana and kept going. Again, where I would go and who I would meet were a mystery, but the adventure of mystery seemed befitting.

Cape Town's Zombies Ate My Girlfriend performing at Germany's legendary Wacken Open Air Festival in 2016.

Photo credit: *Markus Felix.*

With Alec Surridge. Without our conversation in 2009, I doubt much of this would have happened.

With Clifford Crabb of Johannesburg's Agro.

Francois Van Coke

Photo credit: *Wayde Flowerday.*

Soweto's Demogoroth Satanum.

Photo credit: *Portia Muigai.*

Patrick Davidson, the Cape Town blogger that was the very first person to respond to my inquiry about African metal. Performing live with his band Mind Assault.

Photo credit: *Disorganized Chaos Photography.*

Juggernaught performing live in Cape Town.

With Paul Blom of Voice of Destruction and Terminatryx.

BOTSWANA

2

BOTSWANA
Heavy Metal Dreams Awakened in the Kalahari

Boarding a bus in Pretoria, I waited as the cabin quickly filled with a mix of Tswana and San, whose clicking languages and orange skin stood as great reminders of where I was heading. I waved goodbye to Herman and his girlfriend, Sue, silently thanking them for their generosity.

Eight long hours later, after meandering through the maze of pothole-ridden roads past elegant hills and quiet, we stopped. I suddenly awoke. It was now dark, late, and I was extremely fatigued. We had reached the border. A lone woman in uniform ushered me forward with a sturdy nod in the quiet, banal white building, her eyes focused on me, but only for a fleeting second. "30 days?" she questioned on the other side of thick piece of glass, only to ask before I could say anything, "What for?" "I'm on vacation," I stated mendaciously.

This rather short, quick exchange was all that we shared. Smiling, she pushed my passport through the small window and said, "Enjoy! You will have a nice time here. I promise." South Africa was now behind me once again. I stepped out the door and into the night, glancing at the memories that were now just a few feet behind me past the brown fence. I was now in Botswana.

Small, stable and progressive, this country has transformed itself from a poverty statistic to the "Switzerland" of Africa. Botswana does not deal with corruption, poverty, war, nor does the country struggle with a history of racial or ethnic division. It was dusty and quiet, but with a passion for heavy metal unlike any I have seen. Having garnered international attention for the peculiar looking men and women wearing leather in extreme heat, Botswana's metal community was different. A few bands here have made splashes in foreign ponds and have shed new light on metal in Africa as a whole, not just their country. But the adventure that came with the trip and the people that I met was something extraordinary.

THE FIRST ROCK STARS OF BOTSWANA

We met in a hotel lobby just outside the country's capital city of Gaborone. With a unique and commanding presence, he wore a nice polo shirt, pressed jeans, imported leather shoes, aviator sunglasses and had a fresh splash of cologne. Brooks, as he is known, entered the small lobby to everyone's snickering recognition and pointed directly at me, never breaking his smile. "Brooks, how are you?" "Brooks, can we get anything for you?" repeated the staff, while others looked up from their newspapers, caring little then quickly returning their gazes to the scattered headlines as he came my way. Brooks was told I was staying at the Oasis Hotel by a local heavy metal band, Metal Orizon, and came to inquire why an American had come all this way to meet hard rock and heavy metal bands in Botswana. But who was he? I was just told to make sure I met him.

After a bit of small talk, he pulled me outside so he could smoke a few cigarettes and asked me if I would like to accompany him to a radio show the following day. Brooks was a radio DJ. However, he was not just any disc jockey, spinning records and pushing play on radio advertisements, but *the* DJ who ensured this music had a home in the landlocked nation. Brooks' radio show – which aired on Saturdays from 12:10 to 1:00 p.m. – was the only rock show in Botswana's history. Transitioning between cigarettes, Brooks extended his hand and asked me to be a guest on his show before I departed the capital city for a rock concert. "You'll make history," he explained. Unbeknownst to me, I would be the first ever American on his show and, most likely, the first ever on national radio in Botswana.

The following morning, Brooks picked me up from the hotel and took me to the station in his slick black BMW. Windows down, he blasted music through the early afternoon sky, weaving through the light Saturday traffic. ZZ Top, Filter, Nirvana and Judas Priest made heads turn our way, as he just smiled along. The sheer volume of the music overtook our conversation, yet it gave me time to absorb Gaborone, which was alive with modern hustle and bustle, dotted by the occasional cranes working on the city's future. The buildings that already formed the city center were spectacularly modest – not quite skyscrapers, but for this city they were enough.

Rushing into the station, we compiled a short playlist for the show, while making sure I understood my cues. We had arrived with little time to spare. Brooks grabbed his paperwork and a stack of CDs and asked me to follow him. Walking into the studio, he locked the door behind him, pointed toward a set of headphones and quickly grabbed the microphone. It was exactly 12:10.

"*Dumelang Botswana!*" I said after my introduction. With my voice broadcasting to thousands of listeners tuning into the country's only rock radio show broadcast on one of the three government run radio stations in Botswana, I felt it was only proper for a visitor to greet in the traditional language. With his deep, slightly smoky and ever-enthusiastic soft voice, Brooks led his listeners into the realm of absolute rocking bliss for the next hour, chatting about my reasons for visiting Botswana, as well as taking phone calls from the curious about my travels, impressions of Botswana and favorite bands. Once the show was over, I asked Brooks if I could stay and speak with him a bit more, this time formally and on the record. He agreed, but asked that we do this upon my return to the United States, through a series of email interviews. Brooks wanted me to focus on the trip ahead.

Headphones off, with the silence of the studio behind me, I set out to see the Botswana rock and metal scene with my own eyes. I was asked to attend a concert by Metal Orizon in Francistown that evening and was more than happy to oblige.

Brooks drove me to the central bus station in Gaborone after the show – and after a few beers at a rather entertaining watering hole, Razmatazz. With crowds gathered around a collection of blue, 1970s-era buses that resembled boxes more than anything else, I was confused. Screams in the Setswana language were coming from every direction. Pointing every which way possible, it seemed that a million voices were dictating where I should go. "Francistown here, Francistown here," I heard. I could see a blue box already on the move with a screaming, pointing porter running along side. Brooks enthusiastically pointed me toward that specific bus. "There," he said, with a frantic pointing motion. Within a second of committing to the bus, my bag had disappeared, grabbed by a young man in a torn white T-shirt and flip-flops, as I was pushed onto the moving box. Surrounded by other blue boxes leaving at the same time to be scattered throughout the vast dry lands of the Kalahari, I glanced out the window and got a glimpse of Brooks, in his light blue polo, dark blue jeans, the aviator glasses he was quite fond of, and his trademark smile waving me goodbye.

Finding an available seat in the back, next to a quiet man around my age, I now began to worry about my bag's fate. Had someone just run off with my clothes? Was I now stuck with the same underwear for the next month? I was livid and unsure. And I had to pee. There was nothing I could do. Within a few minutes of sitting, still pondering the whereabouts of my bag, a slip had found its way into my hand, passed along by every passenger, with a number handwritten in red ink. It was my luggage slip! My bag was below the bus. About 30 minutes later, an ultra-thin Motswana,[17] wearing a train conductor's hat and pants fastened way above the waist, made his way through the bus ever so slowly collecting fare – and, also, reassuring me my bag was safe.

Assaulting the pavement and overtaking every single thing known to man that could have possibly been on that two-lane highway, that bus ride between Gaborone and Francistown marks what is likely the only place in the world where it must literally be quicker to take a bus over any other form of transportation. Stopping twice to pick up more passengers and drop off those who had reached their destination, a quiet and charming aspect of the Batswana came to life, as the windows of the bus began to fill with the sight of hands and voices of men and women peddling soft drinks, chips and candy bars – adroitly balancing their inventories on their heads – for the price you both agreed on. My seatmate, holding a bag of potato chips and a can of Coke, tapped me on the shoulder. I assumed I was to pass the goods on, but just heard, "No, no. That is for you." Without so much as a word, my seatmate purchased me a Coke and a small bag of potato chips. I was taken by his gesture. He did not accept my offer to repay him for the

---

17   Motswana is the singular noun for a person from Botswana. The plural form is Batswana.

snacks; all he cared for were the words, "Thank you." We engaged in small talk for a while. Perhaps this is what he wanted, to break the silence.

He was from Zimbabwe, returning home after some time working in Botswana, and was under the impression I, too, was a Zimbabwean heading home. I told him I was an American traveling through Africa, which made him laugh. My mannerisms had fooled him into thinking that I was African as well. I took that as a compliment. Because of its proximity to Zimbabwe, during the middle part of the 2000s Francistown became accustomed to Zimbabweans frequently crossing from the nearby border to stock up on essentials that the country was desperately lacking as a result of the horrendous food shortage that followed their historic economic collapse. Hysterically, I was asked on more than one occasion if I was from Zimbabwe.

The gesture of my seatmate buying me a soft drink and snack reflected exactly what has happened to me on every single trip to Africa: the generosity of Africans revealing itself at every opportunity possible. Without even knowing that I am actually a foreigner passing through, Africans never seem to mind helping anyone out, even strangers crossing into their frontier. This is, and has always been, the Africa I know.

I arrived in Francistown later that evening. By this point, the sun had long set and Francistown was a just conglomerate of distant, unfamiliar lights. Scattered shopping plazas and grocery stores littered the uneventful fairway. By day, Botswana's second largest city was nothing different: just a collective of shopping plazas, grocery stores, a movie theater and a bunch of pubs. Drinking and shopping seemed to be what most did here to pass the time.

During the early '90s, heavy metal grew in Botswana because of Metal Orizon, the first heavy metal group from Francistown. Metal Orizon's influence made it possible for acts such as Amok, STANE and Wrust to begin writing and recording original songs, tirelessly getting their music to as many people as possible. I was grateful to be invited to their concert late that Saturday evening.

The Mimosa Bar sits on a dusty corner of an intersection that would be easy to overlook anywhere else in the world. In desperate need of paint to cover up the dull concrete walls, this bar, on this night, was impossible to miss. Leather-clad and overly exaggerated metal fans stood outside, crowding the street, enjoying the sounds of their favorite metal bands blasting out of car stereos while excusing the debris of beer cans they left on the ground with disregard. It quickly became apparent that a large number of those fans standing outside would not even enter the bar to watch the band – they were only there to drink and listen from outside, a matter that irritated the band members and bar owner alike.

Metal Orizon entertained the audience of 30 or so that gathered around the outdoor stage (and paid their entry), under the awe of the southern hemisphere's spectacular showing of stars, for the next two and half hours. The small audience's enthusiasm remained high the entire evening as the band's flawless musicianship carried through the cool night. Drummer Selaelo gave a clinic as he jumped through his 3/4 and 7/8 time signatures, directly influenced by traditional Setswana culture. This was an extraordinary night. Most had come forward and thanked me for coming. Having heard me on the radio, a few wanted to take their photos with me and just talk about hard rock and heavy metal.

Having made the arrangement to sleep at the home of their guitarist, Gabriel, that evening, the two of us made our way to the opposite side of town to a sleepy residential area. Gabriel's home was off a main paved road, covered by dust. Not the sort of residential suburban neighborhood the imagination conjures, but this was rural Botswana; everything here was slightly off the beaten path. Barely able to distinguish what I was seeing in the darkness, the moon allowed my eyes to settle on a single-room building constructed of cinder blocks and corrugated tin roofing sitting between two other similar dwellings forming a U shape. Containing his bed, a small dresser and tea kettle, lit by one single light, his room did not have a television, kitchen or bathroom, just a toilet stashed behind some bricks a few feet away and a long drop just beyond that. (Use your imagination!)

Inside his small room, a small portable CD boom box poked out of a small clutter catching my attention, along with a small pile of CDs next to his only power outlet. Without hesitation, Gabriel showed me his CD collection consisting of a few Metallica records. None of them were bootlegs. Given his wage working as a state vehicle inspector, these records cost him a worthy chunk of his monthly earnings. These records were also his connection to the rest of the world. Surrounded by the African desert his entire life, Gabriel was now connected to millions around the world because of his favorite record, Metallica's ...*And Justice For All*. Gabriel shared his love of metal that night with a slight smile hinting at how confident he felt when those records played. Though we were both exhausted, it was that slight smile that reminded me why I had come to Francistown in the first place. He offered me his bed while he took to the floor, which I insisted he did not have to do, but he would not have it any other way. We were both soon fast asleep.

Awoken by the southern African sun blaring in our faces a few hours later, Gabriel and I, still quite sluggish, were picked up and taken to an upstart suburb to the home of Metal Orizon's bassist and founding member, Santos. Offering me breakfast and the use of his bathtub (which I seized instantly), Santos was a rather quiet and extremely modest man. He sat alone in his living room – hands joined across his thin waist, wearing only blue jeans, cowboy boots and an oversized belt buckle – waiting for the rest of the band to finish eating so that he could present me with the Metal Orizon story. In his soft-spoken voice, Santos recalled forming Metal Orizon in 1990, shortly after he and a schoolmate, Spencer, were introduced. "I knew he was listening to rock music. And I was listening to rock music (too). We had the interest to form a band and we put our thoughts together." By 1991, the band – Santos on bass, Selaelo on drums, Spencer on guitar and vocals (as well as the principal songwriter) – become the first metal band in Botswana.

Sitting in that blistering heat, scattered across two sofas with the sound of a quiet Sunday afternoon in the background, Santos, a middle-aged police officer, broke away from his timid and reserved personality to explain that there was only one rock band in the country throughout the '70s and '80s – Nosey Road – but the exposure to international artists arrived slowly thereafter. By the time Metal Orizon was forming, they were already well versed in the music of AC/DC, Metallica, Iron Maiden and Led Zeppelin. "We started playing small places in bars, then we started approaching the promoters to slot us so that people can [*sic*] see us. It really worked for us."

It worked well. As the band pushed forward, many others were now starting their own bands as a result of the influence of Metal Orizon. "Most of the guys who formed the bands were our fans," Santos offered. "Most of the bands that came after us, almost all the bands, we helped them quite a lot," added Selaelo. He and Santos were proud of what they were seeing in terms of growth, but are still reticent to believe something big will happen. "[Our scene] is growing, but there is no progress. Even those who push Botswana music should go beyond. They should be more patriotic and play more local rock. After those 50 minutes," Santos continued, referencing Brooks' show, "there will be no Botswana rock played. I think there will be more bands coming. The kids go crazy. They pose with guitars even though they don't play guitar. There is still a future for good music."

As our discussion was coming to an end, I turned off the voice recorder and we shared a wonderful conversation about our favorite bands and albums, again getting lost in the depth of the music without realizing how far away I was from the place where the memories of those records were created. They offered to show me a bit more of Francistown, but I could not stay any longer. I had to return to Gaborone, as did Gabriel, who was originally from just outside the capital city. I asked, however, what happened to the man who wrote Metal Orizon's songs and also started the band – Spencer? And, could I meet him? I was told that was not possible. Spencer passed away in 2001.

His name was one that carried all the respect in the world from his peers. The late Spencer left a small legacy and a large amount of clout throughout the country. It was a matter that still brought pain to Santos and Selaelo. Their pain was subtle, but their pride in what he did for Metal Orizon and their country was palpable. This dedication to the music allowed the band to continue after his death. "We didn't want to lose touch. We had that love of the music," explained Santos. The room quieted to absolute silence when discussing Spencer. Quite the showman and talent, he was, and is, still a local music hero, now memorialized by a statue in Gaborone. A life immortalized for everyone to see. He was the first true rock star in Botswana.

The rest of the band drove Gabriel and me to the bus station, and this time I was spared the chaos of many buses in motion at once. We boarded one together, sat in two available seats in the back of the overwhelmingly crowded bus (many people rode the entire four-hour trip standing in the aisle) and let the windows change the scenery for us. It was a great opportunity to see the Botswana countryside up close. No longer a snapshot in an encyclopedia, Botswana's landscape looked just as listless and motionless as it would in any photograph. Arid, flat and relatively calm, there was never a moment when the brown turned to green or the dust gave way. It was an uneventful ride, with the only exception being the stop halfway through the trip where we had to exit for a "foot and mouth" fence, disembarking and stepping through a small pool of water as the bus drove through another designated pool of water designed to stop the spread of disease.

It was easy to grow fatigued of the unsightly dusty earth, but instead I grabbed my iPod and shared my earbuds with Gabriel so we could distract ourselves for the ride. ...*And Justice For All,* one of our favorite Metallica records, the one I saw laying in his room, kept us busy for the next hour. I still wonder if our air guitar solos, swinging arms mimicking the motions of the strikes on the cymbals and feet tapping to the smacking of the bass drums irritated the other passengers. But no one said a word or even seemed to mind. Everything that should have been wrong on that bus ride was not as Gabriel and I were locked into bliss, singing along and smiling as the sun began to disappear.

I disembarked where I was instructed to, at the Phakalane stop. Standing alone along a highway lit by the moon, with the occasional car jetting past and barely able to make out the sign that marked the bus stop behind me, I was not sure of where I was. I just knew I was at the correct stop, and this is where I was told to wait.

Just out of the corner of my eye, a young lady approached asking if I "feel safe" waiting alone for my ride. I responded that I did, but she insisted on waiting with me. "You'll be safe," she assured me, but to make sure, "I'll wait with you." A minute passed before another person appeared. This time, it was a middle-aged man also asking if I "feel safe" waiting[18] alone. "Where is your ride?" "On its way," I responded. "OK, I will wait, too. For safety," he said. The wait lasted 20 minutes, with both of them by my side. We shared small talk, large smiles and quick anecdotes over those 20 minutes or so.

Before long, two flashing headlights caught my attention over my right shoulder. I thanked the two strangers (whose names I never got), and was on my way. I approached the car and noticed the tall, pony-tailed man eager to shake my hand. "Good to see you," said Ivo Sbrana. As soon as he noticed my two new friends, who were now leaving the isolated bench in different directions, without so much as me getting a word in, Ivo said, "Oh, they were making sure you are safe!"

FIRST FAMILY OF BOTSWANA ROCK

"Never eat there" joked the wizened Ivo in his careworn voice as he pointed to the supermarket on the right of his driver's side window. "You'll get sick. I promise!" Bouncing between jocular aphorisms and serious discourse, Ivo

---

18   Botswana is actually one of the safest countries in the world. Needless to say, their act of kindness was astonishing.

showed me around his adopted hometown the following morning, while explaining the ins and outs of Botswana's rock culture today. Originally from Italy, his father moved the family to Botswana to become one of the first doctors[19] in the country when Ivo was barely a teenager. In his weathered Italian accent, Ivo shared bits of information about Botswana, while he ran errands around Gaborone. He had called me the day after I arrived in the country, hearing of my visit from his son, and said he was eager to meet. It was impossible to resist his offer for me to stay at his home after my trip to Francistown. About 12 miles from Gaborone, the small village of Mokatse sits snug against the South African border accommodating Ivo's farm, a quiet property he shares with his brother Renato and their respective families. What brought me to the Sbranas' was their distinction of having started the first rock band in the country, Nosey Road. Ivo and Renato formed the group in 1969 as a school band, later to be joined by Ivo's wife, Delia, and friend Joseph Motupi on drums.

Mokatse is small. There was nothing around except for a few other residences that were just as quiet and barely in sight as the Sbranas'. Dust followed every car as the pavement ended long before you could hear the faint, distant sound of an engine. Come to think of it, everything seemed so distant on this patch of the Kalahari, and watching the dust settle back on the earth was a great way of passing time in this part of the world. The Sbranas had moved here a few years before from a Gaborone suburb

---

19   A hospital in Gaborone even bears the Sbrana name.

seeking tranquility. This place was perfect for quiet and ideal if you disliked neighbors. There was simply nothing around.

Surrounded by silence, the Sbrana farm is blanketed by the tranquility of rural African life. The nearest paved road took several minutes to get to and unless you knew where you were going, you would find yourself driving in circles looking for the modest gate that marked their property. Night drives were something we did for entertainment and were dotted by cattle making their beds in the middle of the road. The sounds of hyenas added another layer to your quiet slumber. If you paid close attention, you could hear the wind stirring something up before it came your way.

Showing me around his residence with his son, Juice, Ivo pointed out the new crops of watermelons, spinach and other vegetables they were hopeful for. Tall and broad shouldered, the haggard Ivo walked and pointed as our feet gave the dry Kalahari some company. Along with the paw prints from several dogs they kept, slither marks also dotted the dusty landscape from the snakes rummaging through their yield, much to the chagrin of the neophyte farmer. Nature was getting its take of their crops, too. The land engulfing the farm was flat and dry – very dry – as rain was sparse in this part of the world. It was obvious why a very large green tank stood behind the house. The tank contained water needed for their crops as well as for personal use. Sometimes a truck would come around to deliver water, other times we would have to drive to a nearby river to fetch water.

Houses contained within four concrete walls no more than about 30 feet long seemed to be the norm in these parts. Ivo's small, perfectly symmetrical, white house sat here on this patch of flat land with just a small mountain in the distance and a rock formation about a hundred yards from nowhere, with Renato's equally symmetrical rectangle off to the left of sight. I knew that the lights of Gaborone were just a 20 minute drive away, but hearing the silence and seeing the southern hemisphere night sky come to life became a part of my daily routine, as it was easy to get lost in the vastness of pitch black. I was their guest for 10 days and beyond grateful for the invitation.

The peace and ubiquitous silence was broken by the only disturbance that occurred frequently in between the brothers' homes: the sound of power chords, ripping speakers, and the cracking snare drum of Ivo's son's band, Skinflint. Just steps from their door, in the opposite direction of the crops, sat Ivo's recording studio and rehearsal room, where he not only records his band, but also various acts of random musical assortments. It was a great opportunity to see the work being done by Ivo and Skinflint firsthand as they were hard at work completing the recording of their record, *Dipoko*. Ivo explained that for a while he was the only rock engineer in a country that has a very small number of recording studios in the first place. And here I was, never having imagined myself inside a home studio that stood alone in Botswana.

My stay provided me an up-close seat to the weaving and pacing of Juice, the frantic son who was a display of nerves and raw energy as he was anxious to complete his band's new record. Juice, also sporting long hair, was quiet – very quiet and very shy. His naiveté was carefully hidden underneath his timid nature, a stark contrast to his over-the-top personality that only reveals itself on stage. Juice and I spent many evenings chatting about the vagaries of life, watching old action movies and sharing our collective passion for heavy metal music long after sunset. Waking up every morning (well, more like early afternoon), Juice would say very little as he was focused on his upcoming performance in the recording space.

After a family lunch (which was our breakfast), I would walk over to the studio with him, wearing my worn down flip-flops and often the same clothes I woke up in, pointing toward the tracks that snakes lay the night before, and watch him go through the motions of writing and recording lyrics repeatedly until his voice coarsened. A carefully listening Ivo, who adroitly balanced the operations of a farm and sound engineer, would always offer commentary and advice to his nervous son. Ivo is the complete opposite of his son. He was extremely confident in the final product and never hesitated to express how he felt about what he was hearing. After all, he had 30 years of recording experience on his son, who was still very much the tenderfoot to the world of rock and roll. Juice listened to feedback on the recording process, carefully either applying or rejecting the ideas.

What Skinflint was doing was as routine and mannered as what any band with a mission would do. The trio, rounded out by bassist Kebonyi and drummer Cassandra, Juice's cousin, were also busy prepping for an upcoming concert in Kenya, as well their local album release just a few weeks away.

The routine of their lives quickly became mine as I, too, was engulfed in *Dipoko*. There were moments where the band would invite a response from my interpretation of what I was hearing, but for the most part I was a quiet spectator. Trips to town were infrequent and an event when they happened. These trips were a way of getting groceries and other necessities, as well as enjoying the occasional stroll in a very modern Gaborone shopping mall. I would also accompany the family on trips to purchase new crops, even assisting in the planting of orange trees along with the two farm hands they hired as staff. I would always do my part in setting the table for the nightly family dinner on the picnic table just outside their front door, which served as their dining room, a dining room under the stars of Africa, without televisions, phones or any other form of distraction. Pretty soon my stories of life, past lovers, family, disappointments and joys also became a part of their lives. Dinners were a great way of sharing honesty without embarrassment. Occasionally we were joined by the rest of the Sbrana family – Renato, his wife, and Cassandra – but for the most part it was Ivo, Delia, Juice and me enjoying dinner under the most pristine night skies.

"When we started playing, there was no rock music in southern Africa. There were a couple of bands in South Africa [writing] their own songs mind you, [but] there was no rock music in Botswana. We were the pioneers in this country. We had the first recording studio, the first to put down music and market the music in this country. We were part of the birth of the music industry in Botswana," explained Renato. Early in their career, Renato admits, it was difficult, especially with a genre of music that was not convincing many at the time. "We discovered the music here, [and] were inspired by rock bands internationally. We used to buy LPs from record shops," he said. Renato reminded me that though from Italy, his and Ivo's love of rock had developed in Botswana, which is how they see themselves: no longer identifying as Italians, but as Africans. "We had one radio station, RB1, [and] we used to get 5FM [from South Africa], but it was fuzzy. It was inspiration and dedication for love of rock music for the message of change. We got inspired by that," he added. Ivo noted that this passion for rock music had always been his sole motivation to spread the music "to the people." Nosey Road was one of the first bands in southern Africa to record and release records, thus earning the name given to them locally, "the first family of rock."

It was Nosey Road's drive that led to promoters in South Africa to take note and book the band there. They even had the opportunity to support Eric Clapton[20] during his appearance in Botswana in 1989, which a beaming Renato remembered well. "It was great! We loved it!" Pointing behind him, toward his daughter Cassandra, Renato stood confident knowing Botswana's musical culture has changed for the better, and that Nosey Road had a large

20   Clapton did a rather extensive tour of southern Africa with stops in Zimbabwe, Mozambique, Swaziland and Botswana on his 1989 World Tour.

part to play in this movement. He smiled proudly as we concluded our interview on a dusty and vast lot. "We have something here!"

During my stay in Botswana, the strides made by Nosey Road were obvious. They showed many that a local band could write and record original music. This was not something limited to just South African bands anymore. The attention today has focused on a new generation of rock and metal acts in Botswana, perhaps more so than in any other African country. The rock and metal scene in Botswana today has not forgotten Nosey Road's influence, but the culture has changed significantly over the past 20 years. More would follow as the late 1990s saw an increase in the number of original bands coming into play, a period in which Nosey Road would temporarily relocate to Italy in the hopes of taking their band to the next level. By the time Nosey Road returned to Botswana, rock and metal had exploded in the Kalahari.

Botswana's introduction to metal was perhaps by accident. Radio stations from neighboring South Africa, broadcasting on 5FM, were accessible from Gaborone, a city that sits just about 12 miles (20KM) from the South African border. While the reception was not crystal clear, Batswana cited the names of Barney Simon, a popular rock DJ broadcasting from Johannesburg, and bands Rabbitt and Black Rose, as well as the metal bands Groinchurn, Sacraphyx, Agro and Voice Of Destruction as influences. Brooks' radio show also had a great influence on the spread of rock in the country. But his show did not commence until the '90s, nor did he typically play aggressive metal, instead favoring hard rock and metal that features clean vocals. Ace, former drummer of the groove-influenced death metal band STANE, credits tape trading and magazine trading from South Africa as his earliest form of exposure. The 50-something said he discovered rock with acts Deep Purple, Van Halen and Bad Company. "Tape trading. That was what we were doing." One would tell another of a band they were enjoying by passing cassette tapes around, a very simple and successful undertaking. Make a copy of an album for yourself and pass it on, much like Americans did in the early '80s thrash metal community in California's Bay Area. Odirile of the band Amok shared how studying in South Africa was "a blessing" by being able to hear and acquire more heavy metal records to pass on to his fellow Batswana. Though he indicated that it "was not really that difficult" to hear and acquire metal in Botswana, it was merely a bit more challenging.

Others, such as Metal Orizon's Selaelo, who grew up in the rural parts of the country, explained that his introduction to the genre was pure accident. "I didn't even know there was a type of music called rock. Sometimes when I passed by our neighbor's house, carrying buckets or pushing a wheelbarrow going to fetch water at the standpipe, I would hear Fleetwood Mac or Uriah Heep's music coming through the window. I would stop and sit on the wheelbarrow, have a dose of my favorite sound and then continue on my journey to fetch water." With a solid smile, he continued. "From then on, I never looked back. I loved it."

Vulture, of the death metal band Overthrust, explained that while rock was something that was listened to in his rural home, it was not until he met Stux of the band Wrust that metal was presented on a larger scale. "Stux got me into metal. I would check at his place, and he would let me hear Morbid Angel and Hellchild. It was difficult in those days. Our country was still developing, and things took much longer to get to Botswana."

Word of mouth and the dedication of the fans helped others discover heavy metal. The music was the air they needed in a country many felt was drowning in an identity crisis – at the crossroads of ancient tradition and modernity. Fans jumped on this music perhaps for the very reason that it empowered a new aspiration. "This music is freedom. It is in my heart and will never be taken away from me. It gives me the power to express myself and to believe in myself. It is a way of life," stated Dumi of Metal Orizon, who, like Vulture, could not even imagine the course his life would have followed without this music. "The music means individuality," expressed Juice. His bandmate Kebonyi also shared a similar sentiment. "Metal gives me confidence. When I listen to metal, I can do anything."

Other factors that contributed to the spread of metal in Botswana include magazines and underground fanzines that came from South Africa, as well as the records being sent back from those who studied overseas. Santos of Metal Orizon explained that part of his introduction to the music was from schoolmates who pursued degrees in the United States, United Kingdom and Australia. "Our friends were bringing us back this music: AC/DC, Led Zeppelin and Metallica."

Once a few made it a part of their lives, it was clear that this type of music found a new and passionate home in the dry lands of Botswana. This passion is unreal. It was not long before the world also learned just how passionate fans here are.

VISIONS OF RENEGADES

Though the bands in Botswana tirelessly promote their music outside of the country, to little or no avail, it was Frank Marshall's *Visions of Renegades* photo series of metal fans in Botswana that allowed the rest of the world to first catch a glimpse of what was happening in the country.

First featured on *Vice* magazine's website in 2010, the photo set started the buzz of Botswana. What followed were features on CNN's *Inside Africa* and the BBC, in the United Kingdom's daily newspaper *The Guardian* and countless other news outlets around the world. Simulacrum photographers who wanted in on the Botswana metal culture also followed, shooting for fashion magazines or for novelty. Frank Marshall snapped because of his love of metal and the country. The South African first traveled to Botswana with a metal band from Johannesburg called Rhutz for a Gaborone concert, which led to subsequent trip out of interest. It was during one of his trips that he took note of the lengths to which the local fans would go to publicly display their love of heavy metal. So, Frank began taking photographs as part of a school project, eventually landing on the pages of *Vice*. He never expected the response that followed and the curiosity from Western audiences also allowed local bands to gain a surge in attention from audiences outside of southern Africa as a direct result of the success of the photographs.

Throughout my stay in his hometown of Pretoria, South Africa, Frank met me several times to discuss the photographs and his motivation. We often listened to old Megadeth and always veered off topic. He was always honest and very straightforward. Frank has a way of finding comfort in situations where you could otherwise be uncomfortable. Often wearing a heavy camouflage jacket, black jeans and dark sunglasses, Frank was shy around others, except those he knew he could trust. He delicately explained his fears of the world judging the photographs in mockery. For Frank, Botswana's metal culture is about as genuine and passionate as any other in the world. "They don't embrace the music, they live for it," he told me in his modest voice. "The images I took provoked interest in the surface image mostly. The subjects of the portraits were sort of emancipating themselves, [saying] 'hey look, we exist'!"

Appreciating the success of the photographs, which still surprises him, Frank reminded me that while the attention on him and his subjects is nice, the focus should also be on the music. With their geographic isolation, the chances of these rockers getting exposure were non-existent before *Visions of Renegades* began appearing in global newspapers and music magazines. However, once those photos were published, all began to change. Most in the country cite the photographs as an important moment in Botswana's young metal history. What Frank did for the country has permanently changed their heavy metal culture for the best. "If it wasn't for Frank, none of this would be known," stated a confident Vulture, while pointing at a Dutch television crew standing behind us, yet another media outlet that had come to profile the metal community in the country. "Frank allowed the world to see what is going on in Botswana"

But, who were in these photographs? Referred to by many as the "heavy metal cowboys," these local fans have gone to the extreme of covering themselves in leather. Fans would also carry an assumed and over-the-top moniker to identify themselves. It was easy to see why the world was interested. Personas such as Razor, Undertaker, Demon DeadMan Rider, Gunsmoke, Coffinfeeder, Coachese and even a fan named Blackie Lawless (who adopted the name after his favorite musician) walk the remorseless desert heat plastered in leather. Jackets, trench coats, cowboy hats and cowboy boots adorn the dedicated, often with outlandish and eccentric props. One fan I met had attached a tea plate, spoon and teacup to his belt.

An exaggerated saunter is also commonly seen as a heavy metal greeting in this part of the world: one foot in front of the other, hesitant and slow, with an elongated pause between steps so the arms can be raised one fist up at a time. Their hugs are deliberately rough, handshakes tough and the high fives will leave your hands red for days. The local rockers in many ways are easy targets for mockery, yet, surprisingly, it does not happen often. And of course, they are always ready to be photographed. These leather cowboy rockers have become a symbol of good within the country for the surge of positive attention they have brought to Botswana from international media outlets. And, as I saw, they are quite the entertainers for those who gather to see their pride.

It is not quite known where and when this style began, yet many have noted that it began in the late '90s. "Some fans started showing off their love for metal by wearing tight pants and their rock gear in public regardless of the occasion. Around 1998, the unusual rock star outfit caused a lot of curiosity among the hostile members of the public, [which] I would say brought more attention to the metalheads," stated Selaelo. E-Force, guitarist of Gaborone-based STANE, reaffirmed that "some people confuse the rockers with cowboys, [but] you have to go to the shows to see what rock is about." When questioned about the origin of the head-to-toe leather style, E-Force shared the story of a specific fan. "One guy, who is a soldier, is also [sic] a real cowboy. He used to come to town with leather and all in around 2000-2001," E-Force said, explaining that the admiration for his style led many to follow suit. Though this story is one of question, throughout my travels in Botswana I was often told of a fan who would show up to concerts on horseback, covered in leather. Inquiring as to whom the mysterious cowboy was, no one seemed to know. Many were convinced this was just another fictitious fable. Others have cited Brooks, the popular DJ, as the reason behind the dress after he received a pair of boots and a cowboy hat from a friend who had vacationed in Texas, leading many to follow the style of a man who was already seen as a trendsetter. The likely scenario is just the replication of a culture they have seen in images throughout metal records and photographs, with fans embracing what they had grown accustomed to throughout their metal life and expressing their ancestral tradition of cattle farming through a style and music that allows for this sort of localization. However, my intuition feels the style was merely the result of fans in an unofficial competition toward absurdity, continually outdoing each other with even more over-the-top attire.

Most metal bands in Botswana do not adorn themselves in leather. Most musicians actually referred to a lot of fans as "posers" or, as Dumi stated, they are "misrepresenting us" by merely absorbing the style as a fashion trend instead of expressing their passion for the genre. "Most of the people who did these acts – parading, marching, demonstrating and posing – in metal outfits were not necessarily die-hard rock or metal fans, per se. Why do I say that? Some don't even know a single rock band. It was more like a fashion thing to them (being seen in full metal gear like a rock star) than being passionate about heavy metal. Metalheads were and are a small community, and almost everyone knows everyone. But, we still regard them as part of our family because [they were part] of the 1996 metal scene explosion," Selaelo allowed. Furthermore, Skinflint bassist Kebonyi says that while judged, "Metal is confidence. What is reflected by the music and the culture has been latched on to by the rest of the fans dressing in leather. [Our] culture doesn't accept heavy metal fans. The villages, the people, they all look at you." Added a proud Vulture, "People think we are rough, we are evil, we are creatures, but this music teaches us how to interact with other people. It teaches us to be free with expression, to do things on your own, and to be unique, to do things that will make you feel happy."

NEW WAVE OF BOTSWANA HEAVY METAL

There was a brief pause in my trip to Botswana as I returned to South Africa to visit Durban with Facing The Gallows and continue on my tour with Juggernaught. I returned to Botswana as soon as possible. This time I skipped the bus and was joined by Frank Marshall. My previous trip via a "luxury" bus from Pretoria was a long and drawn out affair that took the better part of nine hours and put me in the dark when it came time to seeing the landscape. The only memorable experience came from the Kalahari San who were on the bus retuning from a government sponsored "cultural" exchange trip to South Africa, which was really a banal exploitation of their culture – one the current government of Botswana was using as a way of making amends with a group of people they have pushed to the margins of current Botswana life. Their unique features and wonderful language, which contains clicking sounds, was a remarkable distraction from the tedious trip and very welcomed.

When Frank offered to drive to Botswana in exchange for the border fee and some gas money, I was ecstatic to not have to sit through nine hours of agony and children vomiting from motion sickness. As we drove from Pretoria to Gaborone in his small compact car, we kept the windows down, blaring metal out of the stereo as the soft mountains of South Africa's North West Province began to disappear, giving way to the flat, dry landscape of Botswana. It was one of those rare moments in life that will remain unforgettable. Every single detail of every single second of this drive is still seared into my memory. Everything was perfect: the weather, the drive, our conversations and, of course, our musical selection. Frank and I headed to Mokatse to pay a visit to the Sbranas, who were, once again, welcoming. An immigration officer, who wondered why anyone would visit Mokatse, held up our border crossing. We explained we had friends to visit as well as a dinner to get to. He smiled at us as we passed. The sun was beginning to prepare itself for its nightly ritual of setting, but not quite yet.

Our turn off the main highway leading to the capital provided us with a wonderful experience that moved us both, to say the least. After we turned to head toward the Sbrana farm, the pavement yielded to dust following our every move, forcing Frank to slow down to give way to the intricacies of driving on this pebbled path. The farm was in our sight, but just as the final turn toward their property began, a group of kids with ever-so-playful smiles began shouting *"Dumelang"* ("hello"), while running toward us waving their hands, just to make sure we saw them. It was a gesture and a moment that is impossible to forget. Frank and I kept the smiles on our faces the rest of the night.

This time Gaborone was no longer unfamiliar and was a welcomed site after the bouncing back and forth from the colossal cities of South Africa. It is nothing at all like Johannesburg, Cape Town, Durban or Pretoria for that matter. A rather small city, it is very easy to forget that Gaborone, or as the locals call it, "Gabs," is Botswana's capital city. Missing are the major thoroughfares that cross other capitals. No massive skyline sticks out of the ground, nor do any six-lane highways surround the city like they would in South Africa. Gaborone is a quiet relief to the organized chaos found throughout other African cities. You would often find yourself held up by the lingering cattle or the "Botswana Robot[21]," a stubborn donkey just standing put – unwilling to move – right in the middle of the road. These were the only traffic jams locals spoke of.

Gaborone is unique. Botswana is not a country that relies on Western aid or handouts. It is not a poor country by development standards; it is a rather prosperous country with a remarkable stability, both economically and politically, which is perfect for a great metal community. Gaborone is also home to the majority of the country's rock and metal bands, notably Wrust, who were one of the most recognizable African metal bands going.

Sharing a pizza at the Riverwalk shopping mall on a cloudy Saturday afternoon with Frank, frustratingly sending out text messages to the members of Wrust, we finally received

---

21   Robot is the word used in southern Africa for a traffic light!

a reply from the band's leader, Stux. He agreed to meet with us, though it seemed he was only responding as a result of my constant nagging. Stux sent ambiguous directions to his home via text, not responding to my inquiries to clarify what he meant, nor answering my phone calls. Piecing together what we could, Frank and I asked for directions from pedestrians on sidewalks, at bus stops and in roadside shops in a whirlwind tour of the city that put us everywhere and nowhere at the same time in our quest to meet the enigmatic vocalist. Though Wrust was an inactive band at the time, I was determined to meet the leader of the band whose name carried weight around this part of the world. After about a 45-minute adventure that led up and down roadways, byways and throughways, we found ourselves on the dusty road we assumed was correct and noticed a gate marking the number we received in our original text message. Looking at each other, without saying a word we both shrugged our shoulders and rang the doorbell.

Tall, thin, dreadlocked and very soft-spoken, Stux Daemon answered the door after our exhausting adventure and about three doorbell rings. Awoken from an afternoon nap (which is why he never answered his phone), he greeted me with a timid handshake, then pointed at Frank, uttering, "Marshall," in a very surprised voice. Tucked away on a dirt road in the Block 7 suburb of the capital, Stux's home was indicative of the burgeoning middle class in Botswana. Entering his spacious living room, we sat to exchange pleasantries while he inquired about my trip to southern Africa. Showing off a studio that he was building in a converted room, he gave us quick tour of the rest of his home and a bit of small talk. Stux wanted me to meet another Wrust member who was working not far away before we got into further details. Ten minutes later, yet another quiet, reserved and ironically named drummer, Demon Lord Master, sat between the vestiges of an auto accident and the salvage of another in the auto repair shop he owns with his brother to discuss Wrust, as well as other matters relating to metal in Botswana.

The band formed in 2000 and quickly solidified a name for themselves by 2002, when, along with guitarist Ben Phaks and bassist Oppy, they received a feature in the United Kingdom's *Metal Hammer* magazine, which featured them on a compilation CD focusing on global metal.[22] With graceful support throughout southern Africa, the band's groove/thrash-influenced sound and blue-collar work ethic garnered them a significant fan base in neighboring countries, especially South Africa. It did not take me very long to realize I was in the company of one of the most passionate and erudite musicians I had ever met.

"What you do – you play along to a CD or a tape, then there is a local band playing almost the same thing! That has a big impact on you," Stux stated when discussing one of his heroes, Metal Orizon. A regular at Metal Orizon concerts, Stux befriended the late vocalist, Spencer. Described as focused, Spencer would mentor his young acolyte Stux, allowing him to attend rehearsals

---

22   *Metal Hammer* has also featured two other Botswana acts: Crackdust (Global Metal Vol.2, Issue 216, March 2011), and Skinflint (Global Metal Vol.3, Issue 223, October 2011).

and recording sessions in South Africa where Stux would quietly observe and learn from his early metal idol. His time with Spencer and Metal Orizon gave Stux the knowledge and acumen needed to form his own band. "I learned a lot from them," he explained after telling me exactly what sort of impact seeing an original band performing locally has on impressionable young minds.

Discussing the sort of difficulty that the band has run into in Botswana – in recording, promoting, marketing and performing – Wrust, determined to make a name for themselves, decided to branch out and also become a part of the South African metal community. "We were playing four times a month, each and every weekend in South Africa. Their scene is passionate. I wouldn't say it is massive, but they don't discriminate. It was a sense of fulfillment, that you belong." Demon Lord and Stux would explain that the professionalism involved in the South African scene was something missing from Botswana. "When a show is to start at eight, it would start at eight." These concerts also taught the band to assume roles unfamiliar to them at the time – that of promoters. This alacrity would help them gain a business acumen seldom found in the African metal scenes. The labor paid off immensely for the members of Wrust, who found themselves on the South African label Witchdoctor Records, were asked to headline the Metal4Africa festival in Cape Town, acted as support for Swedish metal legends Entombed in Johannesburg and were even chosen to tour as direct support for one of their heroes, Sepultura. That was an experience that only humbled the band even more. As Stux recalled, "Sometimes you feel so small when you play with a big band, but you need that."

"Getting exposure is not easy for any band out there," explained Demon Lord, posturing, "we want a contract." While Wrust became the most popular band in a country that is not theirs for a small while and became the face of metal in Botswana, the reality remains that they are in complete geographic isolation. Botswana does not exist outside the plain of reality, yet it exists close enough to remind many that they are not in London, New York or Los Angeles. Record companies are inundated with social media success stories and quite often do not have an ear or do not have a clue to what is going on in a country many are not even aware exists. "As you grow older you realize it is not only about the music, but it still means a lot." As Stux and Demon Lord looked at each other, they realized the reality of their situation (in terms of musical infrastructure). Stux stated dolefully, "One way or another, African bands are always going to be one step behind." They felt the burden of their geography daily and were aware of the difficulty that lay ahead. Frustrated, Stux gave up. The musician I met was comfortable reminiscing about the days of playing to rabid fans in South Africa and recording an album that is held as one of the seminal recordings in African metal history, *Soulless Machine*. He was now living his suburban life, raising a child and playing music as a hobby with some friends in a melodic rock band called Kamp 13.

Stux and I connected instantly, and we kept in touch regularly throughout my trip and since. He has contacted me about life's joys and sorrows, as well as about what was happening in the metal world that he and I cared so much about. Frank and I left Stux's home after spending that afternoon with him knowing that we had just met someone special – disappointed that the machine of music had spit someone like him out, but grateful nonetheless we had the chance to meet him. It was a meeting that had changed so much for me. Personally, meeting Stux was the validation I needed to write this book.

But the Wrust story took an unexpected twist. Stux had informed me shortly after visiting Botswana that he was reforming the band. He said it was our meeting that led him to think about his future as a musician and his band. As he insisted, I "lit a fire under him." The feelings were mutual. He wanted to write new songs and do another album. He was reigniting the fire! Wrust released their second record, called *Intellectual Metamorphosis*, in 2013 and immediately hit the pavement with shows throughout southern Africa, once again performing with international acts in South Africa. It was also not long after I left Africa and returned to the United States that Stux and Frank Marshall sent me an email with some news. A documentary filmmaker from Italy had contacted them explaining his intentions to shoot a film on Wrust, as well as the Botswana metal scene. The film, *March of the Gods*, followed Wrust as they did something no Botswana metal act had ever done before: perform in Europe. As part of the 2013 SoloMacello Festival in Milan, Italy, Wrust made history in front of an audience that was ready to hear what the Botswana metal community had to offer. An elated Stux shared his excitement via email to me, saying it was a "Dream come true. For us it was simply the best time. The fans at the gig...OH MY GOD!" Skinflint followed suit as they performed in Sweden later that year, too. Both were steps in the right direction for the Botswana metal community and the African metal scene as a whole.

Filmmaker Raffaele Mosca remembered his spark well when we spoke about *March of the Gods*. "Everything started on the day when I came across Frank Marshall's photographs from his project, '*Renegades*' in *Vice* magazine. The unique local metalhead aesthetic spurred me to read up on this phenomenon, and it didn't take me long to realize that I couldn't but [*sic*] turn this story into a documentary." Frank's photographs had opened the door once again for Botswana's metal community. This time someone wanted the music to be the focus of a project. A delighted Frank was eager to help, explaining the film took his photographs to the next level because, as he stated, this explains "why they exist and what they stand for." And now the world would also hear Wrust, a band Frank feels "bridged the gap between contemporary metal and the rest of the world." "One of the first bands I discovered was Wrust, whose music is amongst the heaviest and most original of the local scene," explained Raffaele, "[Their] openness to collaboration, artistic quality and determination made them the ideal band to represent Botswana's vibrant subculture – they were undoubtedly ready to step on a stage outside their continent." Raffaele also documented band's performance in his native Italy as part of the *March of the Gods*. "Wrust's gig at SoloMacello really showed their potential. The audience was unexpectedly curious, excited and responsive."

But with the heavy metal world's attention being directed toward the country, why are local metal bands still finding difficulties moving forward? Referring to themselves as the "Maintainers of Brutality," the members of STANE were not shy in voicing their frustrations of Botswana metal life outside one of their concerts. "You won't find many people at the concerts," stated guitarist E-Force. For as much as they loved what they were doing, they voiced disappointment with how the local laws have greatly impacted the attendance at concerts. "It is about taking our music to the people." As E-Force spoke in a hamburger restaurant, I asked him how they could take it forward. "We don't have some [*sic*] venues where we are able to perform. We don't have the time," he said, referencing the laws that forced clubs and bars to close by midnight. "Before this law the bars used to close at 2 a.m. Even the clubs used to welcome the rock music, but not anymore. We would love to play to the people, take our own sound and play twice a month, even in the day," he lamented. "The problem is the support from the government. Most of them don't understand [that] rock and roll is all about discipline, fun and freedom," explained Vulture. He feared that perhaps the perception of the genre stood in the way of building a solid foundation in the country. "Media is not doing enough to put us on the map." For all of the attention given to Botswana by major publications and global broadcast media, the local media have remained silent.

Similarly, musicians like Juice echoed Vulture's frustrations. "The press lost the eye on the ball." Even after his band was featured on an episode of CNN's *Inside Africa* detailing the spread of metal in Botswana, Juice was stunned that the local media just passed on the stories of the local acts. Though his band benefited greatly from the international exposure, he was worried that perhaps too much would be overlooked, perhaps even risking the band being seen as a novelty. "They should have put more focus on the bands. Without the bands, without the music, there wouldn't be that image. Try and show what the bands do, what the message is behind the music."

One of the aspects separating Western and African rock and metal music is that of cultural influence. While most of their influences come from Western acts, Botswana bands have struggled with the identity of their cultural surroundings and how to incorporate them into their music. A question I was frequently asked before I embarked on my trips was whether or not African bands had records that sounded like that of Brazilian metal giants Sepultura and their album, *Roots*. The album shattered expectations by metal fans as a result of Sepultura's enlisting of the Xavante people in their ancestral Amazonian setting. The seminal album contributed to heavy metal's expanding and diverse template. Expectations of similar instances have been placed on the Botswana metal community. Why? Simply because *Roots* was a different-sounding record by a group of musicians from a country steeped in African tradition, as well as the album's percussion-heavy anthems. However, the only comparison is that like Sepultura, African bands do not come from the West.

Bands like STANE describe their groove/death metal as being heavily Western, yet, "the beat is more African than Western, [using] a strong African taste" because of their origins, according to guitarist Tx. The band, like others, has entertained the idea of local themes, as well as Setswana language performances. However, both language and instrumentation have been fairly absent in the Botswana metal landscape. Some feel, though, that first they must make metal the way they know how. "Right now we are starting to step on the roots, the elements of old school death metal. After that, then we add the cultures of ours," explained Vulture. "It's not about the culture or all that, it's just that the song has to sound good. Of course you're going try use your surroundings to influence your music, your thoughts, your songwriting, your creativity. [The song] has to sound good. If the song sounds shit, it's going to sound shit [sic], whether you put in weird traditional instruments. The song has to sound good," commented Stux.

Traditional Tswana music is typically vocal heavy, incorporating many singers instead of focusing on one, while percussion is often left out. Instead, rhythms are replaced with claps, accompanied by the traditional dancing styles *kgabo, serto* and *setapa*. Other instruments, notably the *segaba*, a violin-like bowed instrument, and the *setinkane*[23] (a small wooden box with small "forks" attached at different lengths that is often played like keyboard), also

---

23   Most commonly referred to as the *mbira* in other African countries.

complement local music performances. Often, an acoustic guitar is also infused with local music. Kwasa Kwasa, which is the Africanized rumba, and the South African import Kwaito have also found a comfortable home in Botswana. Western imports hip-hop and dancehall are also found throughout the country. Yet, the incorporation of these sounds and Tswana language remains absent from the rock and metal music being performed in the country.

Influenced by bands such as Sepultura, Metallica, Pantera and Metal Orizon, who at times plays in time signatures associated with Setswana culture (3/4 and 6/8), the members of Wrust felt the matter was a non-issue. "Most of the time I play in 4/4," stated Demon Lord Master. "It is sort of difficult," he commented, turning to Stux in Setswana, wondering if he understood me correctly. "We have songs that have elements of that, but it is not something that we focus on," interjected Stux. However, Wrust began experimenting with Setswana elements for their 2013 release, *Intellectual Metamorphosis*, on a song called "Spiral of Torture." But why are bands hesitant to focus on their tradition? "Botswana is a country on a race to modernization where one has to struggle to find elements of traditional culture," noted Raffaele Mosca. "The locals seem to be happy about this frenetic development since everyone we met had a job and led a comfortable lifestyle, but we were shocked to see numerous constructions of massive imposing buildings and an exaggerated passion toward anything Western, or more specifically American, which goes hand in hand with the rejection of the country's cultural roots," Raffaele's assertion is one that is noted throughout Africa and has something to do with the fact that essentially, every rock and metal fan is based in a metropolitan center where tradition and culture are often brushed aside for the comforts of modern life and a cosmopolitan existence, rather than traditional identity.

If there is one band in Botswana that has truly incorporated African elements into their music, it is Skinflint. The trio has taken their heavily Iron Maiden-influenced sound to include lyrical themes of African effect. While others address matters of the mundane, Juice explained how important it is to incorporate African themes in his band's lyrics. "I used to watch a lot of other local bands play. So many other bands that play metal in Africa try to sound like European or American bands. They were trying to westernize their music. Try to do something different, something original. Try and sing about our background, where we come from. Try to give Westerners a new feel, a new take on metal." Bassist Kebonyi added, "Music is all about teaching. We can't talk to people about Western ideals or about the way they are. First of all, we need to talk about our surroundings, our experiences, our African life." Skinflint records *Iklwa,* which details the life of a Zulu Warrior, as well as *Dipoko* (a Setswana word meaning *ghost*) both reflect on African wars, mysticism, tradition and culture. There are lyrical themes that have been seldom touched by others in Africa.

THE TRAGEDY OF BOTSWANA

Botswana does not fit the African stereotype often conjured by Western imaginations. Independent since 1966, the former British protectorate – spared from colonial rule – gained self-rule as a desperately poor nation. Spectators of the divisive rule of apartheid to the south, the collapse of Zimbabwe to its eastern border, a spiral into a tragic civil war in nearby Angola as well as one in Namibia to its east, Botswana sat silent, avoiding these tragic fates. What Botswana did was exhibit patience and learn how to deal with their sparse resources, notably diamonds, transforming their landlocked country into a leading economy and one of Africa's jewels. Botswana has become a well-developed nation, with a strong currency, leading medical technologies, stunning education system, and a strong democracy. However, there is one salient issue in Botswana that has tragically devastated the country: AIDS.

With the second-highest infection rate in the world, sadly one in four adults in Botswana is affected.[24] I was curious as to what the members of the metal community felt about the issue. How were they addressing the matter? Also, how did the disease, and its death rate, personally affect them? Told of the World AIDS Day concerts held every year in the country, I wanted to learn more, since it was in fact Metal Orizon who organized the very first one in 2001. In recognition of World AIDS Day, "we invited bands from South Africa, [including] Agro, with the objective of

---

24   Source: Avert.org, Also, the CIA (www.cia.gov). These numbers give Botswana the second-highest infection rate in the whole world. Only Swaziland has a higher rate.

raising awareness," explained Selaelo. Dumi, who replaced Spencer[25] in Metal Orizon three years after his death, in a rather somber tone said, "AIDS is killing us. We needed to create that awareness for all of us and our followers so that they can take the precaution of condomnising [*sic*]. At Metal Orizon shows, we try to encourage friends to use the available resources the government has put forward for free." "You can't stop people from having sex," commented Renato of Nosey Road, but "it's important for musicians to tell everyone that HIV is dangerous. It is absolutely crucial that Botswana mobilizes every sect of society to do this, and the musician and music should not be forgotten because we carry a weight with the people. We change minds. We change the message when we are onstage."

The first AIDS concert took place in the northern city of Maun, a dusty, quiet town in the heart of the Okavango Delta, where animal migrations occur in great numbers and wildlife photographers are constantly bumping up against tourists for their prized shots. Maun is also referred to locally as "Maun Rock City" for its endearing and passionate metal fans. Clifford Crabb of the Johannesburg-based band Agro, who performed at the 2001 event, recalled, "The show was well attended...thousands! The Botswana Minister of Health was in attendance and gave us his blessing, along with Miss Botswana. A wonderful experience." Yet, the success of the 2001 concert has been difficult to follow. "It was getting big, but I don't know

---

25   It was never revealed to me how Spencer died, nor did I ask. I was told by someone who requested anonymity that he died from an "infection."

what happened to it? We are trying to revive it now, [it is] very important," lamented Coachese of the Maun-based trio Remuda. "To send a message is quite important. For a long time people have been using this AIDS thing just to cash out. A lot of people have been making money from AIDS," commented Stux, who would like to see honest and focused events become more prevalent in the rock and metal community.

Obstinate and promiscuous young males in various African countries continue to believe that AIDS is a fictitious matter or that they will never contract the disease. Many may point directly to the governments of African nations for abandoning their responsibilities to protect their own people by way of prevention and awareness campaigns, yet others may point to specific aspects of populations in Africa: they are stubborn and careless or, simply put, they do not care. Extensive campaigns by the Botswana government and Western-based charity organizations have attempted to warn of the dangers and seriousness of the disease, but often such warnings fall on deaf ears. Though the government has been lauded for its sincere attempts at bringing down their numbers, this issue is still of vital concern.

One notable step the government of Botswana has taken to bring these numbers down has been to provide the necessary medication to the infected at no cost. These measures have slightly reduced the number of infants who would have otherwise been born with AIDS. I found it difficult to generate a discussion on the matter during my meetings and interviews with everyone in person. Even after I returned to the United States, I would follow up the issue of AIDS with the rock and metal community via email, only to realize that many still did not care to discuss the matter, even with the comfort of a computer screen and anonymity in front of them. I can recall the day I sat to interview Stux (the same day of a Skinflint concert) and the second to last day Frank and I spent in Botswana was World AIDS Day. December 1. So many remembrances around the world and so many people in the public eye using that day to commemorate those who have been lost. But, here I was visiting the country with the second-highest infection rate, a personal witness. Nothing was being done locally to honor the deceased. Nor was there a national discourse on the severity of the situation. It was just another Saturday.

The few who did discuss the issue of AIDS, however, realized the urgency of the situation. With a faint frustration in his voice, Vulture expressed unrestrained concern on the matter. "It is very important! We also have to do something about it as a rock community. We just don't play rock and come about the sensitive issues to just ignore and don't give support [sic]. We are also giving support in the way we can give support. This crowd," pointing around the crowded venue where we spoke, "we also want to involve them. We are also concerned. We are also having a say about the people we have lost through HIV/AIDS, and we are doing something about it. We hope that in the next two coming years the situation would have improved that people will be taking care of themselves and not wanting to get infected with the virus," stated the emphatic vocalist.

"We are also active somewhere else, that is why we have decided to get a month to do something about it. We are doing a lot. In Ghanzi [Overthrust's hometown on the country's western border with Namibia], we have an annual charity rock festival each and every May. It is called the Overthrust Winter Metal Mania Fest to benefit local orphaned kids. Usually we specialize in orphaned and disabled kids. We try to raise funds for them in the form of food, clothes, money, or we try to build houses for them to show that we care about those who are disabled in life and those who are disadvantaged in life," said Vulture, who is also one of the festival's organizers. Feeling rather confident in their endeavors, the members of Overthrust, who actually met while training at a police academy (all of them are active police officers), have taken the initiative into their own hands and trust, enlisting support from local officials in Ghanzi to ensure that their money and goods are donated appropriately.

Sadly, a few have even abused the idea and have thrown their own concerts, confusing locals and only serving as profit-making scams for concert organizers. The 2001 event had government support and sponsorship, yet as the members of Metal Orizon explained, "Everything in Botswana is difficult. More needs to be done." The overall sentiment of the music culture in the country is that of a lack of respect for rock music and rock culture. If Botswana is gaining global attention as a result of this music, why is the government so slow to respond in acknowledging the power the musicians have in fighting the obstacle that has prevented Botswana from taking the next step in becoming a fully developed nation?

It was difficult getting many I spoke with to open up about the subject, yet the few who did were honest about their views on the matter. I was still curious as to why so few would discuss the issue with me. I would quickly learn that many are afraid to talk about AIDS, as it was the "off the table" topic in Botswana. One person I spoke with, who will remain anonymous, felt there is a fear in the air when discussing AIDS. "I cannot go public since it is not allowed in Botswana to say who has died or who is living with AIDS."

I would sadly learn that a few of the rockers I had met at one of the concerts I attended (though no one in any band) had passed away since my second trip to Botswana. What from? I had to leave the matter alone. Perhaps it was AIDS that had claimed more lives and the tragedy of a nation silencing more mouths. It was between the buried and their loved ones to know. The attempt by musicians to use their music for a cause is a reminder of those who have lost the fight to this global endemic issue. The memory of not just the Batswana who have succumbed, but also everyone in the world who has lost the battle to AIDS is recognized any time anyone speaks of this disease. AIDS remains one of the greatest challenges facing humanity today, and will remain so until a generation of humanity learns about AIDS in history books as something that once was, but no longer is.

"Ke a le boga Botswana, Go siame"

Botswana reminded me often of how similar metal fans and artists are globally. At times, I had to remind myself that I was in Botswana on a journey to tell the world of metal in a forgotten place. Fans and artists had shared their passions with me, asking me if I had seen American bands like Pantera, Cannibal Corpse, Metallica, Manowar and W.A.S.P., all of which are favorites among many in Botswana. It was easy to forget where I was. While standing under the chill of the clear Kalahari night sky at a local metal concert one evening, the sounds of a few local acts reminded everyone at the event of our passion for rock and heavy metal, one that had remained strong through the years of all of our collective lives and will most likely endure.

Introduced to many throughout the local community, I eventually bumped into two American Peace Corps[26] workers who were happy to meet a fellow countryman. Wondering about the fate of the bands in this country and if the world would take what was happening here seriously, we began to discuss metal in the country when one of the two glanced over at me and observed, "These guys wouldn't last a day in America." Putting it bluntly, I thought about whether or not bands from Botswana could make it in America, or anywhere else in the West for that matter. It was something all of us were eager to discover someday. While it became apparent that musically most of the acts

---

26   A rare sighting in Botswana, considering this country's development.

were able to pace themselves with Western acts, there were still the obstacles of perception. Could a band from this corner of the world be taken seriously?

This concert, this evening, was special for many reasons. It was the celebration of this music and this country. It was also the culmination of my journey through Botswana. Frank and I would depart the following morning. Leaving the Sbrana farm for a second time after an unforgettable show of hospitality, Frank left Botswana with a strong validation of the connection he has with the country and I was leaving Botswana forever in debt to this land and its people. I am a better person because of this experience.

Recalling something that Selaelo had told me a few weeks prior – "We just want a chance. If you produce good music, there is still a future" – I felt something more behind his statement. His eyes, his demeanor, his candor told me something else. He was not just referring to his band; he was speaking on behalf of every musician in the country. Will the bands from Botswana ever get a chance to leave the continent and perform to greater audiences? Wrust and Skinflint did, but will the others be afforded that opportunity? Will they be taken seriously or judged as novelty? Every musician in Botswana felt that plenty of challenges remained. Money, sponsorship and the drastic decline in the number of venues has diminished but not destroyed the passion of bands in the country. "We dream of Metallica, AC/DC, Iron Maiden, Slipknot," expressed an optimistic Selaelo.

It was December 2 when Frank and I crossed the border back to his native South Africa. My thoughts had distracted me from the stunning scenery most of the ride home, as I was reflecting heavily on our visit. It was a quiet trip back, the complete opposite of our musical enjoyments on the drive to Botswana. This time the music was just background as Frank and I shared a few ideas and collective thoughts. Botswana was now as much a part of my life as it was his. The country was no longer a background in Frank's photographs or an old banal black and white photograph in an encyclopedia. Botswana came to life for me. I could now imagine myself there whenever I wanted to. Frank and I discussed what this country also meant to him, having spent so much time there. He shared his Botswana with me – his second home – the marvelous country that broke the stereotype of Africa and is still pushing forward. Botswana's charm was not hidden; it was easily felt and wonderfully experienced. Much like the rest of Africa, it was easy to fall into this country's stride and way of life.

I had attended a meeting with Botswana's former President Festus Mogae a few years earlier in Washington, D.C., where I had the opportunity to pitch a question to him. Instead, I chose to sit and listen to the discussion he had with the small audience on matters of development, growth and his lament of the HIV/AIDS crisis in his country. He, like his country, had defied many and became an exception in Africa. Sticking to his beliefs and passion for his people, he moved ahead during a critical period of growth in Botswana. Careful with the advice he received from corrupt neighbors, he learned from what he saw and used his insight and global networks to transform his country into a growing and formidable economy. Much like their country, the Botswana metal community is also defying expectations by taking the world by storm with their confidence, pride, and passion.

A FINAL FAREWELL

For nearly 23 years, Brooks entertained listeners on his Saturday afternoon show. He had me on his show once in the studio, and again as a phone-in guest to discuss how things were going for me in Botswana and if I was getting the necessary material to write a good book. I was honored by the gesture of his invitation and laughed with him throughout my trip as we traded text messages and short phone calls on matters of rock and Botswana. He checked up on me often to make sure things were going well.

During my stay he was more than happy to meet with me and when he did, he asked that I not record our conversation so we could have a *real* discussion. Instead, he asked that I email him after a while so we could discuss whatever I information I needed for this book. Sadly, our formal interview never happened. On July 18, 2014, Brooks Mmolaadira Monnaanoka left us.

Devastated, I sent emails back and forth to Botswana to find out what happened. All that I was told is that he died from "illness." An outpouring of emotion was collectively felt throughout Botswana. A national television station even aired a tribute to his life in media.

I can only imagine the silence that shocked rockers throughout Botswana after his death. Brooks inspired a generation. He motivated so many to pick up electric guitars and chug away until life made sense. I can remember him now leading me into his studio or through the streets of his hometown – blasting those Judas Priest records without a care in the world. I remember the first time I met him, leaning up against his car, sharing what this music meant to him and trading stories of our favorite records. But I will never forget the last time I saw him that Saturday afternoon at the chaotic bus depot. I can see him now in that light-blue polo shirt, aviator glasses and signature smile waving at me. So long, Brooks.

Brooks seconds before we hit the air.

Slaya of Gaborone's "Maintainers of Brutality," STANE.

Sbrana Farm in Mokatse, Botswana.

Skinflint crushing it live!

Photo credit: *Portia T. Muigai.*

With Demon and Stux (R) of Botswana, and Africa's metal giants, Wrust.

Overthrust's Vulture.

KENYA

3

KENYA
New Horizons in the Great "Riff" Valley

"Everything's changed," *spoke the reserved and bespectacled Lurs Rumbler.* "The audience we hoped to draw is the audience they are after," *he explained. Showing me around Nairobi's Central Business District at night, sorrow lingering in his voice, Lurs told me that the event he organizes, the annual Nairobi Rock Fest, had to be postponed as a result of the tragedy at a shopping mall that occurred just two weeks before. Terrorists from Somalia had murdered 56 people in a crowded Westgate shopping mall on an otherwise quiet Saturday afternoon. It was an act of retaliation for Kenya's involvement in their country's affairs. The grief-stricken country was still reeling from the ramifications of those fresh acts of terror. Questions and frustrations lingered as many were still trying to grasp everything that happened.*

Nairobi's rock and metal community is growing. Still relatively young, the local community has embraced all aspects of rock and has passionately displayed their love of the music. Independent since 1963, Kenya has found itself at the center of a growing region, much like the capital city, Nairobi, which grew from a village into a bustling metropolis with global aspirations. Kenya's youth have shaped their own identity and the rock community reflects this well. Rockers today have the annual Rock Fest to boast about, and other parts of the world are beginning to take note. Not bad for a generation that was first exposed to hard rock music as recently as the 1990s.

Today's Kenyans are voices of their own independence. Two weeks after the horrific attack, it was clear they were not going to allow tragedy to define who they are. Born into a country of promise and no longer a charity case, how are Kenyans today shaping their future? Not confined to ideals of ethnic groups, how has this generation shrugged away the horrors of the post-election violence in 2008 that grabbed global headlines, and what is the metal community doing to address matters?

It was a long trip to Africa's east, but landing at Jomo Kenyatta International Airport, things were the way they were supposed to be. A rather content young lady had greeted me with a smile as I approached her. "Are you on holiday, I mean vacation?" she corrected herself after noting I was American while chuckling. "Yes," I lied, for it was the other wildlife that had attracted me to Kenya: rockers! What lay ahead was comforting yet unfamiliar. Nairobi began to look and feel like an African city right away, yet my surroundings were different and my ears were entertained by Swahili, a language I had studied, but had fallen out of practice with. Getting ripped off on all cab rides, contracting malaria, eating the worst pizza ever, enduring crowded rides via matatus, visiting Africa's largest slum and earning a permanent Kenyan identity all lay ahead. This is Kenya.

Breaking the Silence

Sitting on the quiet patio off a high-rise building located in Nairobi's South B neighborhood, Marc of Ages, as he is known locally, described the climate of Nairobi's music culture during the early part of the 2000s. He sat smiling, wearing a faded grey T-shirt that had red sleeves and green cargo pants, while his right hand came up to eye level every time he spoke. It had been just a few years since Kenya had its formal introduction to rock, and his band, Rock Of Ages, began performing original compositions in 2001. Unbeknownst to Marc and his band members, by doing so they were one of the first – if not the first – band in Kenya to perform original hard rock music. Quiet and sincere, Marc described that period in his soft voice. "You could [perhaps] find bands that would play at functions and throw in a rock song every once in a while, but we were doing something full time. I would say we were the first rock proper band." Marc explained that Rock Of Ages, a Christian band, used the church setting as a place to rehearse, perform and compose their music. A proud fan of rock, Marc recalled that moment when his life changed. "Right when I was a kid, I used to love the sound of the rock guitar. I always loved powerful things when I was kid. Almost every boy loves loud stomp, nasty things, and I used to love the sound of the electric guitar because I could hear that tone, that was cool. And I could hear these bands playing that same fuzz tone: that overdriven guitar sound. It was the guitar that drew me to the sound."

Through our conversation during a lazy Sunday afternoon, Marc jumped between his life and his musical inspirations. I was curious as to how, not that long ago, his band had formed and how this country would have its first rock band just in the beginning of the millennium. "When I was growing up, rock was accessible, but it wasn't a style that was really widely accepted. There was some programming on TV. We watched Bon Jovi, Def Leppard, Poison, but I could also hear some of my favorite bands: Petra, Stryper, White Cross. Those are the guys we used to listen to." But according to Marc, it was not until later that his band had its first formal introduction to rock. "We had the Nairobi Rock Fest in 2009. That brought in other bands and developed shock waves throughout the Kenyan industry [sic]. Even the tabloids were talking about it; the mainstream newspapers and electronic media were talking about it. So I could say the impact was made then, in my view, in 2009."

Rock had only catapulted into Kenya during the late '90s with the introduction of a local radio station, Capital FM. Before that, rock was limited to a small part of the playlists on Voice of America and BBC Radio. But with Capital FM launching a strong mix of Western music, the wheels were set in motion for a sort of revival of music in Kenya that for the first time would cease to infuse local tradition, language and culture. Now the music would be more focused and directed toward a new mindset. Many in Nairobi will point out that before the late '90s, there were places to see and hear rock, but it was in such small numbers that those who were loyal to the music were hard pressed to find others with the same interest. Of course, Kenyans had known about the genre long before the '90s. Acts such as Elvis Presley and The Beatles were getting airplay on the radio during the post-Independence era, but the foundation for a rock culture from this period was never fully realized.

A few Kenyan acts even released records overseas during this time, notably Sal Davis, whose records could easily rival anything released in America. Much in the vein of the Rat Pack, Sal Davis was based in Europe for most of his career, because, as he stated in a 2011 Capital Television interview, "how many records could you sell in Kenya!" Other acts such as Slim Ali and The Hodi Boys, The Cavaliers Band, Question Mark, The Ashantis, Kelly Brown, Daudi Kabaka[27] and Matata were also performing what was known as rock n roll at the time, but today could be interpreted as cabaret, pop and funk. Though not rock, these acts point to an alternative music culture running

---

27   Kenyans refer to many acts from the '60s, '70s, and '80s as *zilizopendwa*. The term means "to be liked," but musically would fall in line as "Oldies" or "Goldies" with American audiences. The acts often performed in English, with exceptions, of course, but never achieving much success. Yet, they were vital in laying a foundation for music that broke expectations from East Africa.

parallel with Western music simultaneously in East Africa, showing that Kenyans kept a westward ear early on. And much like alternative music artists today, those artists struggled to turn people away from traditional music for their brand.

"Unlike southern Africa, where local music was always supported, local music [in Kenya] took a different dimension. Kenyans never really liked local [rock] music. There may have been rock fans, but no rock scene in the sense that people congregate together and listen to rock," said Knord, a local rock and metal DJ.[28] "In terms of radio and wide scale exposure, 1998 was the year Kenya was introduced to rock. Before [then] there was no rock scene." While rock began to break the dam, the flood of metal had yet to flow. Knord shared that those who had grown up in the late 1980s and 1990s used Western movie soundtracks as a starting point, as a few films, notably the highly successful *Terminator 2*, provided prominent exposure to this music. Some would also discover heavy metal through marketplaces selling bootleg compilation CDs that had names such as "Top Hits" featuring popular songs from Europe and the United States, introducing many to acts such as Metallica, Guns N' Roses and Nirvana. But it was in the 2000s through the increased accessibility to the Internet, and a specific radio program, that heavy metal would find its stride.

---

28   In the greater Nairobi music scene, DJs are not exclusive to radio stations. Many, including those interviewed in this book, are contracted to play music at local clubs, much like the European dance and techno scene.

In 2009, a radio program called Metal to Midnight, started by Shiv Mandavia and his metal-obsessed friend, DJ Switch, hit the Nairobi airwaves. "I don't know if anyone did it before us," explained Shiv in his heavily British-accented English. A fourth-generation Kenyan of Indian descent, Shiv had spent a decade of his life in central London, where he discovered and fell in love with heavy metal. "Metal to Midnight came about when I got back into Kenya and I couldn't find any metal. I had to find an escape or introduce it into Kenya, which had never seen it or heard it before."

Airing between 10 p.m. and midnight on Tuesdays and Thursdays, the show played a collection of new and old heavy metal, including extreme metal. "I approached radio stations to bring up the scene in Kenya," said Shiv, but the "issue we had locally is that having had no background on metal or rock at all, and having had an extreme music just slapped on their face was quite shocking."

Reflecting on the program, Switch – in his mellifluous made-for-radio voice – recalled, "Through that, the cult movement grew. We started having overnight shows [and] used to have debates as well." The debates, as he recalled with a smile, were to engage the listeners to see who was out there: "Metallica versus Megadeth" type debates to enlighten the spirit of the small metal community, assuring fans they were not alone. "Heavy metal was on the radio in Kenya, a conservative nation. The articles [in the press] concerning the scene became a tad more positive, more metal bands emerged, and people had little fear of discrimination when it came to doing extreme music. I believe it was the biggest leap for extreme music in East Africa."

MARCH FROM THE UNDERGROUND

"It is a medium to transcend yourself, to redefine yourself on your own terms. The main thing for me was having that transition of energy," commented the Nairobi-based Xenostate. Without realizing it, during the early part of the 2000s Xenostate and his bandmates in Class Suicide were beginning to construct a piece of history in the East African musical landscape; they had formed one of the first original heavy bands in the region. Though he never describes the music as metal – opting instead for a tag of mostly punk/hardcore – he was extremely modest in his explanation of his band's history and his role in laying the foundation for what was to come. "I got an interest as soon as I got into high school. Nirvana, whatever was playing on the radio in the States, is what we heard. We were just playing Nirvana and just wanted to be loud, but then we shifted to punk and hardcore." Though other bands were active at this time – Point of Vertigo, Haggis, Impish (also featuring Xenostate), Navarone, Bloodshed, UETA and M2O – it was Class Suicide who many credited as the band that was the catalyst for launching heavy music into Nairobi.

Born and raised in Nairobi to American parents, Xenostate would divide his time between Kenya and the United States to attend university. "I was so determined to come back and keep feeding this thing. It got to the point where I was obsessed over it – always returning to Kenya with suitcases full of musical equipment (and other accessories that were easily at his disposal in the United States), instead of clothes. I was always worried it would die out," he explained in his quiet home in the Western suburbs of Nairobi. "A lot of people thought I was crazy." He was often told that "there is no way people were going to listen this music," yet this pessimism was the springboard his bandmates needed to push forward. Much to their delight, and to those who were there to be a part of the first Class Suicide show, "There was a massive response! It was like we were taken over by spirits. It took on a life of its own from that point!" Class Suicide drummer Kwame Bonsu also spoke of the lift that his band helped provide for those seeking more. "We had a very faithful following. Even people who didn't love or even know what rock is were actually very excited about it, because it was the first time to see what they were hearing on TV and on the radio." Recalling many of the early performances, "We were playing a lot of gigs in local bars, clubs and a couple of gigs at an underground parking lot," Kwame said. "The difficulty was getting people to come to the shows. You had problems going to the 'white' bars, people two generations older saying, 'What the fuck are you doing'?" Xenostate recalled with laughter.

"The young folk were puzzled, and the old folk were horrified," added Bloodshed's Wanjiru Gichaga, speaking of that early period. UETA's Jaaz Odongo recalled, "It wasn't very 'Kenyan.' Most people were surprised a scene actually existed and were more fascinated by the culture around it."

"The biggest challenge was ourselves," Ross Patel remembered of that time. As the leader of the band Navarone, he and his bandmates were also coming into the scene just at the early stages of this movement in East Africa. "There weren't many rock shows, so it was hard to get a reference for what to do. The first rock show I ever went to was also the first time we performed. We got to know the other bands and there were regular Kenya-punk shows." Detailing their rehearsal schedule, Ross continued, "We worked hard daily for a show that happened maybe once a month. It never felt like too little. Getting from crap to decent" was the ultimate goal. It was this nostalgia that prompted an emotional and honest recollection from Ross. "That was the happiest time of my youth, the Kenya-punk scene, discovering and playing music with my friends."

For Ross, like Xenostate, the effort was not something from which they would realize results immediately. "Slowly, more and more people started to come. I think this kind of thing appealed to people. It was a community. It was Kenya, and that spirit in the scene that was half of it," explained Ross. He would later move to Los Angeles, unsure of what was happening back home, if anything was happening at all. "I think something was going on that maybe I didn't notice. By the time I got back [2013], there was a rock radio station, an entire frequency on the FM devoted to rock music in Kenya! The scene didn't die, it expanded! It's a validation. If nothing else, we did something worthwhile.

Maybe we never got famous. But if we inspired anyone, that is the best."

"A lot of it is owed to the first generation of rockers who made that effort when there really was nothing to stand on," said Mukasa Namulanda, bassist for the band M2O. "We were not aware of any rock scene, and all we wanted to do was to jam on songs, learn new songs, improve on our guitar skills. The principal motivation was just to play rock songs we liked for fun," he said, unaware that an underground metal scene was kicking up in Nairobi during those years. As his band entered the scene, they would learn that others also shared the same passion and energy. "After our formation in 2005, we got an invitation to attend a rock concert – probably in August 2006 – and we were surprised that there actually were other rock bands in Nairobi. At that concert, we discovered that there were quite a number of bands well advanced in their music, even with albums out."

The foundation was now laid for the small and intimate Kenyan rock and metal community. The realization that this music could be written, recorded and performed in Kenya became very, very real for a new group of aspiring musicians able to build from this foundation and carve a niche into their Nairobi – a blossoming and exciting city.

SWAHILI-TONGUED DEVILS

Victor Chweya, one of the guitarists for the hard rock band Parking Lot Grass, had come to pick me up at the apartment I was staying in on a quiet Sunday morning so I could watch his band rehearse. Very thin and youthful – it was hard to believe he was in his late 20s – he had his "in the early stages" dreadlocks and, with a straight face the entire drive, spoke in modicum and chose his words carefully. I was happy to meet Victor, and eager to meet his bandmates in Parking Lot Grass, the band that is garnering the most attention within the local rock and metal community, so I could get a better understanding of how this scene was progressing from the previous generation's efforts.

Victor and I found ourselves stuck in Nairobi traffic – an unreal experience that will leave you thinking twice about traffic jams anywhere else in the world, trust me! Car on top of car, within arms' reach of shaking the hand of the person in the car next to yours, we used the time for small talk about life and Kenya.

This slow pace also provided me a better opportunity to see Nairobi's city center under natural sunlight. A modern city skyline with newly constructed skyscrapers peeking out from behind the stone-colored, block-style colonial era buildings, the scene is a reminder of how things once were and a promise of what is to come. Nairobi is very cosmopolitan, with hints of despair – reminders of the underlying poverty scattered about. The streets are filled with opportunists and optimists crowded together in an unrehearsed play of organized chaos. Far busier than the sleepiness of Gaborone and significantly toned down from South Africa's mega-metropolitan city centers, Nairobi carries a very unique charm. The traffic, however!

After a turn off a main road, near a local private airport, Victor guided his compact sedan down an unpaved, rough road leading to what appeared to be a slum. Pointing to his right about 20 seconds later, he directed my eyes to a locked and gated junkyard where we would be entering. The remnants of wreckage and scraps of any number of cars littered the derelict setting. Unlocking the gate, we moved along to the facility's office, where the rest of the band was waiting. Small amplifiers and a dilapidated drum set dotted the room – the sort that any Western musician would just disregard, but the standard of equipment that was the basis for this band's existence. I sat next to that pieced-together drum set on a small stool leaning against a wall. The band offered me a Coke (a generous offer) as we discussed matters of effect.

It was mid October, and the band, which formed in 2008 after being introduced by mutual acquaintances, was preparing to make Kenyan rock history: they were off to Germany the following week to perform with local German hard rock bands as well as another from Africa, Angola's Before Crush. With excitement, Parking Lot Grass – rounded out by bassist Amos, drummer Ronjey,[29] vocalist Dan, and guitarist Alistair – shared their joy. "We are privileged. We are the first ones to start this, so that others realize we exist," elated Ronjey. "Just knowing that someone out there has heard your music and thought it was nice is a good thing," added Alistair. What made their German trip special was the validation it was providing for many in Kenya's rock and heavy metal scene.

---

29   Has since left the band.

Bands like Parking Lot Grass have an ambition that is difficult to break, but, of course, they too, like the other modern rockers in the country are facing challenges and obstacles that few – if any – artists in the West will never have to confront.

"There are people who think that rock is not African, not Kenyan, so there is no point in us playing this music. There are conservatives that think it is evil music," lamented Ronjey, whose thoughts are not exclusive. "Our first interviews were: is rock music demonic? Why aren't you wearing black? Do you worship the devil?" stated a frustrated Jozie of the long-running rock sextet Murfy's Flaw. Saidimu Keireini, of the local alternative rock band Dove Slimme, shared that many in the rock community have at times dealt with a negative perception. "Everyone thinks you are a devil worshiper." The roots of that mentality are perhaps born in culture or through the local press. "Most of the press is bad press. They would say orgies were being done, blood drinking. It was bad. And anytime anything bad would happen, we [rock and metal fans] would pop up," added Ruto of Last Year's Tragedy.

Timely reflections, these comments were perhaps best complemented by a local event that was garnering a lot of headlines at the time of my visit. A cargo ship that arrived in Kenya's second-largest city, Mombasa, containing a shipment of Halloween masks somehow led to a national scandal and was bombarding headlines. The press was crazed, and a government minister, Omingo Magara,[30] was

---

30   http://www.standardmedia.co.ke/?articleID=2000095602 "Bizarre Cargo at Port Not Mine, says Omingo Magara." October 15, 2013.

forced to address the media over the "suspicious" cargo that many felt was his as a result of the peculiar connections to Satanism and the occult. Innocuous Halloween masks had driven a populace into a peculiar frenzy; imagine now how the rock and metal community was viewed given the imagery on many of their favorite bands' T-shirts.

The Magara incident, which came up often throughout my trip, allowed rockers to discuss what many felt highlighted how being perceived as "different" is viewed in Kenya. During a Saturday afternoon shopping trip, I was even asked to leave a store in a posh shopping mall, Yaya Center, because of a "disturbing image" printed on the back of my hooded sweatshirt. Laughing my way out of the store, it was this perception of being different that I now understood first hand. This would not be the last time my hooded sweatshirt, of the American band Darkest Hour, would give me trouble in Africa. However, this incident pushed my curiosity. It was clear rock and metal had an unfortunate perception. But what if musicians here could take this music and infuse with local traditions? Could that help to change the perceptions of those standing outside the periphery?

"That's Western music," mocked the jovial and gregarious Saidimu, as a few heads turned in our direction in a downtown Nairobi café. The guitar player and vocalist of the alternative rock band Dove Slimme was more than happy to discuss why many felt rock and metal had no place in Kenya. What was surprising to hear was how the identity of many performing the music was being challenged. The

Kenya of today has 42 different ethnic groups and 67 spoken languages, dominated by Swahili and English. Yet one aspect of modern life that many shared with me is how far they have moved on from the idea of ethnicity and the pride that they have in their Kenyan identity, which is a cosmopolitan association.

"We have to put in mind that we are culture raised," noted David of Last Year's Tragedy. "The older generation still has that [tribal] mindset," added his bandmate Mahia. Though, it must be noted, Kenya's rock and metal community is centered in Nairobi exclusively, which is most likely what factors into the embrace of cosmopolitanism. Also, the idea that many have of a modern Kenyan identity is perhaps going to be reflected in their musical sound as well. But for many rock and metal musicians in Nairobi, questions are being asked. Should the music represent more of Kenya's tradition? Or, should their music serve as their distinct voice?

"We have the culture, why don't we do it?" questioned DJ Switch outside of a crowded Nairobi nightclub, as the topic came up with many standing around taking in the cool night air. Genres of music, including hip-hop, dancehall and reggae, have all found a home in Kenya, but have shielded inclusions of local sounds in their music. Kapuka, Genge, Taarab, Chakacha, Lingala[31] and Benga are also genres of music found in Kenya, many of which are infusions of the East African region and other borrowed sounds from around the African continent. For many rock and metal cynics, the genre's lack of inclusion

---

31   Also known as Soukous.

of local traditional music is exactly why many remain skeptical this music belongs in Kenya. Some musicians felt that adding more of a Kenyan flair to their music would boost the potential of what the local rock and metal scene could provide.

Local metalcore musician Douglas Kihoro, of the band In Oath, explained that an infusion of culture is what Kenyan bands need to craft their own identity. "Our culture is unique, and incorporating it into our music is the only way to make it stand out. Bands should embrace who they are, where they are from and the cultures that come with [them]." Guitarist for the local metal band Cause of Death, Nina Mort, agreed. Rather direct and straightforward while puffing her way down a cigarette, she commented, "We need to adopt our culture into our music. Perhaps make something new, something fresh, something people would want to listen to." In her honest delivery she continued, "I wouldn't focus on being like everyone else internationally," just before extinguishing her cigarette.

"Africa has a lot of cries and greatness. Whoever molds that into the modern rock sound, that is going to be the band that enters consciousness," noted the loquacious television personality and poet Tony "Smitta Smitten" as we sat in a rather unique setting for a conversation on the topic of rock and metal in Kenya: a casino. Discovering the music in the early '90s, through Metallica's "Enter Sandman," Tony shared with me that Kenya is a nation that is obsessed with Western ways. "The British were very clever," he stated. "We were left with a fantasy of the West," questioning as if this had something to do with

Kenya's Western mindset. Though he felt an "African" sounding metal act could possibly be perceived as a novelty, Tony concluded that a band with a more African feel could be well received. "If a band could figure it out, it could be exciting."

However this music is received, there are many who feel the music should not be compromised; it is rock and heavy metal, a sound that is already recognizable, with bands having already achieved success from all corners of the world. So why change the dynamic? "We are African. What we contribute, we contribute as Kenyans. The way we view music and the way we shape it, it is not about being 'Africanized'. Whatever we make automatically is African," stated George Gikaria, bassist of the alternative rock band Claymore Project. "We'll do our thing the way we know how to do our thing, the way we do it best," added vocalist Muthi. The band's drummer Rai continued, "I think the music can help someone look past where we are from."

Perhaps the most inclusive manner of Kenyan life through rock and metal music is to be found in the lyrics. One feature that is noticeable throughout the Kenyan rock landscape is the inclusion of Swahili, a language that is fairly common throughout the country and is one of Kenya's official languages. Though there have been smatterings in various corners of Africa, the usage of the language by a few is a step forward in creating an identifiable mark through their music. Bands such as Dove Slimme and Parking Lot Grass have featured the language heavily, though not exclusively. One reason why is to not exclude international audiences in their vision. There are a few musicians, however, who remain skeptical as to whether or not the Swahili language would be advantageous in advancing the scene forward.

"It has two sides: It would appeal to some, but the majority of the people who listen to rock understand English. The majority of the listeners would relate to the lyrics if [the music] was put out in a language they were more familiar with. If we add Swahili, it would be for the song, not to appeal to anyone," said Rai, with the understanding that his band did not want to succeed just in Kenya, but elsewhere. "I wouldn't want to do anything that would interrupt our creative process," commented Muthi. "I also don't think adding a little Swahili would jeopardize an international breakthrough. It is quite a dilemma on our end."

"There needs to be a way that people can access the music. That is why we put some Swahili lyrics in our music, in order to bridge that cultural barrier. We have to accept that Swahili is a national language. More people speak and understand it than English. Singing and writing in Swahili crosses that social divide that English creates," stated Alistair of Parking Lot Grass. Furthermore, "you hear a song that is fully in Swahili, now you can actually relate to what the guys are saying. For someone to say that metal can't be metal if it's in Swahili is very shallow and demonstrates some level of ignorance."

This theme of cultural inclusion was already frequently discussed around the African continent by other metal musicians, yet what was perhaps discouraging the musicians was that fear of being seen as a novelty in Western eyes, an aspect that every musician in Africa wanted to move beyond. It seemed that too many around the world had already chimed in on the matter and wanted "African" sounding bands. And here, in Kenya, one of a few African nations with a predominant black-African dominated rock and metal scene, the arguments were no different. Why was this argument falling only on black Africans? Was this the reason a cultural burden existed within, and outside of the nation's borders: to accommodate the uniqueness of their situation? According to Rai, "there's always a negative, sad to say, but there's always this negative stereotype about black [people], even in some things, like this is a 'black sport'. Personally, I want whoever listens to music to come out of that shell. Just listen to the music. We need to represent who *we* are." "Our music represents ourselves. A lot of people appreciate hearing that, what has been there for us at the forefront has been real for us. We don't want to play anything as a gimmick," added Stan from Last Year's Tragedy, positing that the truth in music is in the heart of the performer, not their geography.

It was ironic to walk around Nairobi distracted by the comforts of my Western life, only to be focusing on conversations that questioned whether or not a culture that was slowly slipping away should be forced into rock and heavy metal songs in order to appeal to Westerners. Metal fans all over the world were already buying records from bands based in non-Western countries, and even Western nations whose musicians grew up speaking languages *other* than English. But this is what a few found puzzling, including rock musician Jaaz Odongo, who asked, "We have a generation of Kenyans that have grown up citizens of the world, so what is their culture?"

This culture is exactly what is at the center of this renaissance: A natural, organic confluence of ideas and energy creating music that is defining a generation. "That very natural melding is representative of what Nairobi is like as a city – the coming together of different influences in a natural way," noted Jojo of Murfy's Flaw. It is that convergence that has allowed Nairobi to flourish and has allowed for the rock and metal community to discover the music as a collection of shared ideas based on their modern lives in a growing nation, unlike the country of their parents and grandparents.

It was during the conversation I had with Alistair of Parking Lot Grass that I understood why so many were reluctant to include traditional music in the metal and rock scene. Our conversation was over, the tape recorder was shut off. He had asked me to turn it back on. He was not sure he wanted to say what he was about to, but he was honest and direct. We stood up, about to leave the room, as he locked into my eyesight, with one foot out the door he was holding open. "The world is getting smaller. We can't localize rock too much. Then we stop being rock; it will become a different genre. As much as we want to identify with where we are from, we can't do it too much without changing what the music is. If you mess around with it too much, it becomes something different. We have to create that balance and be listened to anywhere in the world."

"CHOCOLATE CITY, WHAT A PITY"

A remarkable and splendid symbol of the organized chaos found in Nairobi is their public transport system of independently owned, though government regulated, shuttles and vans known as *matatus*. Though I rode them quite often as my chosen way around the city, I frequently pondered whether the vehicle would even make it to the next block. Cheap, you would fetch a ride to anywhere from 10 to 30 shillings (less than 30 cents) by standing on the roadside and just raising your hand at a conductor hanging – literally – by one foot and hand on the vehicle catching whatever he could, asking for riders in a rhythmic cadence. A system of taps on the side of the vehicle by the conductor informed the driver that he needed to stop, while a pat on the shoulder of the person in front of you would prompt them to pat the passenger in front of them, continuing until your prompt to disembark reached the conductor. No fancy cable or button was needed to indicate a desired stop. This system is flawless.

From the outside, these vehicles do not appear to be such a great idea, but once you get used to the rhythm of the taps on the doors, the screams of the negotiating conductors, the honking of the drivers and the routes of the vehicles, you are sadly mistaken to miss out on the ride. Many are adorned in bright colors with flashy signs and slogans painted on them. Some are even equipped with dance-club-type stereos and lights, and a few I rode had disco balls! I sat next to a nun from India on one particular *matatu* that blasted reggae non-stop, so loud that it was nearly impossible to hear her even though she was elbow-on-arm close. Another *matatu* I rode had its engine stall out often. Passengers would have to exit the van and push start the vehicle, as the driver nervously attempted to turn over the engine. Much to our relief, a sound that riders never took for granted – a functioning engine – would roar us back into the *matatu* as if nothing had ever happened.

Running on and off a moving *matatu* was also a common sight: passengers jumping off vehicles moving at about 20 miles per hour on busy streets, with a few even running behind one to catch their ride. There were instances where *matatus* were pulled over by police, while the passengers (familiar with the routine) would exit the *matatu* without protests. I was informed that this was just business as usual. A police officer would enter the *matatu* in the front passenger seat to "inspect" the vehicle for functioning seat belts and licenses, while the empty *matatu* would speed off, passengers scrambling to jump on the next one they could. This intrusion was apparent on the busiest routes and typically a manner of collecting a bribe from the driver, only to be returned to another spot, where the police officer would force his way on to the next *matatu*. Yet despite the madness and chaos, *matatus* are a prominent and charming aspect of the city and very difficult to pass up. There was one particular *matatu* ride that remained more memorable than all others, and it was not because it was the first one during which I was able to utilize the front seat next to the driver (finally!). It was because of where I was heading.

I had awoken on this particular Saturday morning after spending the previous few days horizontally laid out because of what I thought was a fever. The pallor, lightheadedness, hot and cold feelings, and profuse sweating that I was experiencing actually turned out to be far worse. After a rough few days of not feeling well, Lurs' brother, who was convinced I needed to see a doctor, took me to a hospital. After spending hours with a tube running fluid into my arm and two blood tests later, I was given a prescription to fill. Lurs' brother, a medical student at the time, took one look at the prescription with the sort of elation he would have had after getting an "A" on his test: "Ha, malaria! I knew it!" I had malaria? "Shit," I mumbled. I would continue on after two more days of lying in a bed, suffering through what I can best describe as the most unpleasant run between hot and cold, lucid nightmares and an odd craving for orange soda. It was pure hell. When I had the energy to get up, just a quick turn in the bed sheets allowed me to see puddles where I was laying. I was paler than the paper this book is printed on and still covered in sweat. No energy, no drive and no will. I moaned, complained and was experiencing pure misery. Every mosquito was condemned to eternal damnation. Word got out of my illness and musicians would text and call to ensure I was OK. The concern was flattering, even when it came to paying for the medication. A few had taken it upon themselves to pay for the medication and even help with the hospital bill. After a few days, I carried on with a new definition of humility.

Even though I was still weak, sweating and extremely laconic, I had confirmed my plans for that Saturday and felt well enough to fulfill them. I was not going to miss the opportunity to see a place that I had longed to visit. Situated just a few miles from Nairobi's city center, Kibera stands in stark contrast to the large shopping malls, skyscrapers and suburban homes that surround the area. It is Africa's largest slum. The trip had been organized through acquaintances and was led by a local with clout named Foxxy Loxxy. I was told to take a *matatu* to a nearby shopping mall and wait to be met by a few others who would accompany me. Meeting up with two others, we took another *matatu* about one quarter mile to a specific corner where we disembarked. Just then, Foxxy Loxxy greeted us with an ultra-large smile. Thin, with dreadlocked hair held back by his oversized sunglasses, he greeted us with what could be best described as an infectious personality, the sort that pulls you in instantly, which was comforting considering the amount of trust needed for a trip into the labyrinth of poverty that stood before us. "Chocolate City, what a pity!" he proclaimed with confidence, never allowing his smile to trail off. Foxxy's words hit as we finally stared over Kibera, and he explained that the name "Chocolate City" was a reference to the rooftops, that as far as the eye can see were all rusted in a mess of chocolate-colored tin.

One of the first things to grab my attention was a railroad line that runs through Kibera. Surrounded by vendors selling everything from chewing gum to "imported" shoes, the rail line serves as a reminder of Kibera's origins. As a favor for their service and loyalty to the British army in the early 20th century, Nubian soldiers were granted land for their efforts in the forest just outside Nairobi. The area grew informally throughout the years, with the Nubians being deemed "detribalized natives" by the independent government as a result of not being recognized as Kenyan, thus being excluded from owning land on "Native Reserves." The growth of the railroad brought commerce to the growing village that was now becoming an important city, bringing many rural migrants in search of labor, who in turn would start to pay rent to Nubian landlords. I was told that many people still move there daily in search of work in and around Nairobi, adding to the population of well over a hundred thousand people. Regardless of the claims that perhaps over a million people call Kibera home, one thing stands out when standing on the hilltop overlooking the slum: it is massive.

Navigating your way through the Kibera labyrinth, careful where you are stepping, it is impossible not to be taken aback by the poverty and lack of resources. A maze with no end is what it appeared to be. Raw sewage was rampant and the lack of proper drainage had made a visible tear through the earth that was impossible to ignore. The odor was unbearable. Makeshift bridges constructed from what looked like scrap wood were in abundance, as were the careful steps in tight squeezes that were just around the corner from one path to the next. This was not my first trip to a slum. I had visited one in Langa, South Africa, just outside Cape Town, but Kibera is different. The stark contrast still consumes my thoughts. Langa residents had access to standpipes, sanitation, paved roads (on which someone had deliberately tried to run me over) and electricity – things noticeably absent for many who reside in Kibera. This place could easily be best described as miserable. I often wonder why places like Kibera are romanticized. Poverty is not a mindset of optimism; it is a place of misery, a place where day-to-day is increasingly difficult. Places like this suck the soul from those who wish for dignity and leave very little for the empathetic. Reflecting back, I admired Foxxy Loxxy for his enduring smile and realistic vision. He was born here, raised here and most likely will end up dying here. Even in death, he will probably never leave.

I saw human feces everywhere, yet kids were not bothered; their games continued, with trace smiles. Many children would stop and wave with a smile, pausing to greet us with a "How are you?" The English classes they were taking, most likely from an NGO-funded school, were paying off, as the greetings poured in around every corner. The smiles were impossible to ignore as their stares poured in at the camera; they desperately wanted to be photographed and many were quick to pose. I wondered how long it would be before they grew to lose those smiles. After all, their parents were never smiling, just staring.

Malaria had taken a toll on me, and I needed constant access to fluids. Yet, carrying a bottle of water around the desperate was an insult. One man stopped Foxxy while pointing at me, shouting, "*maji, maji*" (water, water). I was careful to explain that drinking from my bottle would not benefit him. I was unsure of what I was carrying and was careful to not pass this infection. As I walked away, feeling terrible, I contemplated turning around and giving him the rest of the bottle. But the idea of passing on any infection was driving me crazy, and it would be devastating if I did infect him. I had access to a great hospital and the finances to pay for the medication. He did not. Foxxy said it would be OK if I kept moving, but a part of my body that was not infected felt as if it was getting sick now as well: my heart. I had denied a thirsty man water, a moment I still reflect on in disgust. How could I do this? It still does not feel right. My humility turned to disgust and embarrassment.

Leaving Kibera, a local NGO worker pointed to a few buildings on our left in abhorrence, uttering that some "awful things" happened in 2008. What she spoke of was the atrocious ugliness of late 2007. The atrocities came as a result of a presidential election in December of that year when incumbent President Mwai Kibaki, representing the Party of National Unity (PNU), ran for re-election opposed by Raila Odinga and his Orange Democratic Movement (ODM). Before all the ballots were counted, Kibaki claimed a swift victory. However, for many, the results were not accurate. In what was deemed by observers as a manipulated election, Odinga and the international community questioned the validity Kibaki's actions. This disregard for democracy was the catalyst for violence. Unnecessary and stupid, things took a quick turn for the worse. It was as if a match were lit and tossed slowly into a large pile of gasoline – exploding on impact, igniting a devastating display of inhumanity for the rest of the world to see. The white buildings we stared at as we finished our walk through Kibera stood silent. But the stories that those walls could share were what rattled me, as was the idea that the very spot where I stood could have been where someone took their last glance at the Earth's blue sky as they exhaled the thoughts of why their life was coming to an end.

"AND THE MASKS CAME OFF..."

"We suffer from something far worse than racism; we suffer from tribalism." The words that exited Switch's mouth froze me. The associations that Westerners have with Africa and tribe are common and often generalized. Yet, for many I met with, the idea of tribe is something that is very real and haunting. The horror of 2007-2008 left many inside and outside of Kenya speechless, and it still remains difficult to discuss. Most of the violence occurred outside Nairobi in other provinces, notably the Rift Valley, while some of the worst violence occurred in slums throughout the capital. Whether the result of criminal gang activity, economic frustrations or ethnicity, it was a moment that forced Kenyans to struggle with the ramifications moving forward. Having endured attacks by foreigners – including Embassy bombings in the 1990s by al-Qaeda – and the Westgate attacks by Somali militants – Kenyans found the 2008 violence especially difficult to comprehend. This was neighbor killing neighbor. This violence left over half a million displaced and over 1,100 dead.

For some, the violence got too close. "Where I was in Kisumu [a city in Kenya's west], it was three days of hell.

These guys were passing by the house and threatening us. They almost attacked us, but some members of the Luo tribe stopped them, saying we were not bad people, as we had lived in Kisumu for over 20 years." Wemo Kitawa sat quietly, reflecting on those events while the rest of her band looked on. A rock vocalist, formerly of the alternative rock band Koinange Street Avengers, she was one of the few who opened up with a personal experience five years after the events that shocked Kenya. "I am from the Kisii tribe, and the Luo, who were an ODM stronghold, believed that part of the Kisii community voted for Kibaki. In Nyamasaria, in the outskirts of Kisumu, where the majority of the Kisii people stay, houses were torched down and looted," she lamented.

Parking Lot Grass' drummer, Ronjey, was another who spoke of seeing the violence up close and personal. Detailing his experience over that period of time was not easy. Yet, the soft-spoken drummer sat four feet from me on his drum stool, sticks in hand, eye to eye, reflecting on a day that he will never forget. "I had spent Christmas with my mom at her house. It must have been around the 26th or 27th. I had decided to go to church and play drums, since I was bored of the election stories everywhere." Warned by his mother of the reports of violence in various parts of Nairobi, Ronjey proceeded anyway because, as he stated, "it seemed quiet." Upon reaching a familiar spot, he took notice of the lack of *matatus* but continued walking until he reached another spot where the vehicles were known to pick up passengers. "Upon reaching the t-junction [the spot where the *matatus* would normally be waiting], there was a big crowd shouting and carrying all kinds of crude weapons from clubs to machetes. I walked fast, trying to seem cool, because I knew what they were about; they were supporters of one of the two feuding political parties, and I was on the wrong side by tribe." Though he never told me what tribe he belonged to (nor did I ask), his day would quickly become one he never forgot about.

Determined to disappear from sight, Ronjey explained that he came across another group that had barricaded the roads.

They were profiling everyone on foot or in vehicle. Seeing that I wasn't from the same tribe as them, they asked if I was escaping to Kibera. I said the truth [sic]: I was going to church that was all the way in town. They looked at me for a moment before their leader instructed me to avoid Ngong Road [a busy road through Nairobi] lest I get hurt, so I went on to Riara Road parallel to Ngong Road. On reaching the back gate of Nakumatt Junction [nearby], there was another group, and the moment I got there, a dark blue Saloon was trying to speed by from the Kawangware side [the opposite road]. They intercepted it. Inside was a man, his wife and three kids. The man had blood sprinkling from behind his right ear. They roughed him out [sic] and hit his genitals with clubs and metal stuff to the horror of his family, also shouting and threatening his wife. All this time I had gone numb and was just standing there motionless and emotionless. A white Land Cruiser came from the other direction with some Catholic nuns, and they quickly intervened. The attackers left as the nuns attended to the man and his family. I went into zombie mode and just walked all the way to town. The city center was a ghost town; not a street urchin, police or bird was there. I thought it was cool for a second, then fear gripped me immediately. I walked toward the largest street because I was getting paranoid and thought that if someone was to kill me, maybe someone else would see if I was on a bigger, more open street. So I walked to where some close friends lived, [and] there I stayed throughout the mayhem until things came back to normal.

"It was sad to see that certain things we thought we had overcome, especially the tribal issues everyone had seemed to forget, was thrown back in our faces. [2008] just brought back the fact these divisions that we thought we'd cross still exist. It will take a while to forget," lamented Ronjey's bandmate Alistair. Jozie of Murfy's Flaw remembered those events with frustration. "I didn't even realize I had a tribe until 2008. Suddenly, all that you were was someone of a given tribe. I guess it made people feel stupid," she demurred in disbelief. "Your neighbors – who you play with, who you pray with – are throwing you out of your home, wanting you dead. So suddenly you realize that all you are is stupid. You are not equals in society, you are just some idiot that believed in peace." Douglas Kihoro of the metalcore band In Oath spoke of the incidents as a wake-up call to the reality of Kenyan life and the unspoken aspects of what is real for so many. "Tribalism is one of those things that has been with Kenya and, at that point, that's when people actually acknowledged it and the fact that we had to deal with it and not just shrug it off like every other problem." Certain that Kenya will not be the same for a while as a result of the atrocities of the post-election violence, he felt "it set Kenya back years. Healing is a long process, and I'm positive is still hasn't reached that level. The easiest thing has always been to pretend things are okay, but it's not. It's never been. The sooner we accept it, the easier it will be to change. It happened because of our flaws, and only we can change that."

"Before that time, we never used to think about something like that. But after that we saw that this shit could happen to us." The members of Last Year's Tragedy grew silent when discussing the matter as their drummer, Stan, focused his somber tone, confessing that in his Kenyan upbringing he may have grown too comfortable in viewing his country as a quiet one surrounded by conflicted neighbors: Rwanda, Ethiopia and Somalia. He realized that the horrors of other African countries had now hit home. He continued, "For us, as a band, it opened our eyes. We started seeing things differently: Don't take for granted the kind of peace you have in your country." The ease at which neighbors were ready to kill neighbors "happened so rapidly, that it reveals the how thin the veneer of civility is," added Xenostate.

Recalling the events of 2008, Saidimu was extremely honest about the disappointment of seeing his city and country turn to violence. "Suddenly, all your shared experiences are meaningless. You no longer had a name. You became 'those people'. Shocking to find it in a very metropolitan Nairobi, the masks really came off. Tribalism is a monster lying dormant within so many." The otherwise jovial and gregarious guitarist, now focused, his tone now somber – smile fading momentarily. "The worst part: I think people haven't really learned the real lesson from that period in time. It very well could happen again."

The atrocities that occurred during this period have made many in Kenya think closely about their identity and what the term "tribe" means to them. When I met with Christian and Gabrielle, brother and sister members of Void of Belonging, in the South B neighborhood of Nairobi, I asked them about the incidents and what they meant to them. Sitting in the hallway of their extremely modest home, they were quieted by the topic of the violence. Christian explained, "The post election showed us tribes are important, but tribalism isn't. Are we really trying to identify each other? The most important part is being Kenyan." The moment you start relating to tribe, he added, "you limit development. It's wrong." "What happened after the post-election violence opened our eyes to the stigma around," noted Robin of Claymore Project. "People having all these thoughts was a reality check of what's going. Now we are very aware of it, very careful of it." Ronjey contacted me after I had left Kenya, wanting to add to the discussion we had that day at the junkyard office where Parking Lot Grass rehearsed. "Before this incident, tribe meant nothing to me. Afterwards, I have been very sensitive to what tribes say to one another. The more you think about how, why and where tribalism came about, you find it with the founders of our country." He was alluding to politicians in Kenya who expose tribal lines for political gain, yet kept quiet throughout the incidents.[32] Ronjey also questioned whether or not his country could ever heal and learn from the tragedies, lamenting that "children are taught this vice by their parents. You realize that it's something that will never end."

Even those in the Kenyan population who are not affiliated with tribes, such as the European and Indian communities, watched in horror as their neighbors and community dissolved. Sadiq Karim of upstart metalcore band Moment of Silence recalled those events with dejection. "I remember a lot of despair, agony and sadness in the country. People were at hard times. I know a family that lost their son at the time," he remembered, as quietly the moments became very real again. Shiv Mandavia spoke of the incidents, recalling another similar instance his family confronted head on: "Obviously, being Kenyan it does affect me. I live in this country, and any imbalance in this country directly affects me. We have all been involved in situations that have been life threatening within these political imbalances." Inhaling from the cigarette in his hand, beer in the other, he stared down at the ground for a second before continuing. "I myself, when I was 7 years

---

32   At the time of my visit, the sitting Kenyan deputy president, William Ruto, was on trial at the International Criminal Court at The Hague for his role in plotting violence against Kikuyus in the post-election violence. Many have also named current President Uhuru Kenyatta (son of the nation's first president, Jomo Kenyatta) as a key figure in the violence as well. The local rock scene put much of the blame for the violence on key politicians, even showing me a caricature spreading throughout the message boards and social media sites of the country's leading politicians in unison flashing their middle fingers back at the country. In April of 2016, the ICC dropped the case against Ruto.

old, there was a *Saba Saba*[33] rally and people stormed into our house and burned everything in the bottom. My grandmother had to hide me upstairs. Being in Kenya, these are things you have to face and they do affect us." Like so many, Shiv found solace in heavy music.

The freedom that heavy music had provided for those I met was their ultimate escape from the confines of tribe and their awareness of a new identity. In Oath's Christopher Yagami shared how music helped him cope with the atrocities surrounding him then. "I was actually pissed off at the time." Seeing his grandparents lose their home, his parents move after getting a couple of death threats and – as he explains – watching in disappointment as "two of our leaders chose to frown and watch their country burn itself to the ground," heavy metal became what he needed. "Music is reflection and empowerment; it is the ability to change a mind or create peace. Music is still helping me deal with it [post-election violence]," explained Douglas Kihoro. "Music helped me cope, in a huge way," he said, continuing, "I doubt I'd be where I am if it wasn't for music, metal to be precise. People say metal makes people violent, but it calmed me down, made everything better." Reliving the post-election violence in their thoughts, both Chris' and Douglas' reflections were obvious: if not for

---

33   Meaning "Seven Seven," *Saba Saba* refers to the events on July 7, 1990, when Kenyans took to protesting a dictatorship and fought to usher in a multi-party democracy. Many of Indian descent were targeted as a result of a politician's views against the Indian community. Kenneth Matiba, a vocal leader against the lack of a democratic institution, promised to remove Kenyans of Indian descent from the country, often inciting violence toward the Indian community in the country, which his followers would act upon.

metal, they would have not been able to escape mentally. "If in 2007, some people who I know now were affected met in the street, we wouldn't have the same mindset. We'd be afraid of each other, afraid of what the other can do to you. But I met them through music. We healed together and healed others together. It's the most amazing thing to be united by something so unique!" exclaimed Douglas.

"The tribal thing is not in our DNA. It is superficial," commented Marc of Ages. "What is inside is not Kikuyu, not Luo. These are socialized perspectives. Music is a powerful forum. The current generation realizes this." They are brought up in the same schools, neighborhoods and social realms, especially those from the cosmopolitan comforts of Nairobi life. Bands have taken to addressing their ills by grabbing the past through songs and moving forward from those events. "We know there are things wrong in Kenya, but we've moved on. We have a song about the dark moments from the violence, but we can only move on," commented Murfy's Flaw drummer, Vikki. "In my lifetime, I never thought I would see that before, that state of chaos. I thought, 'what is Kenya turning into'?" said Sam Kiranga, who took out his frustrations through songwriting for his band, Koinange Street Avengers. David, of Last Year's Tragedy, explained, "We share multi-culturalism in Kenya. We make our music to enlighten people to see we are one." The band channeled their frustration into penning a song called "Tribute To Anarchy," in order, as Dave described, "to get people past the bullshit!"

Though the events are in the past, many still remember and reflect on the horror story that occurred in their city, in their provinces, in their country, and to their family, friends and neighbors. It is hard to travel throughout Nairobi and not come across someone who will tell you those events did not affect them. They affected everyone. For most, those events also shifted their birth-given "tribal" identity to a cosmopolitan one, bringing their rock and metal identities into focus. The terms "rocker" and "metalhead" now carried a new weight for some. "Society is calling on you not to change. Kenya is a really, really superstitious place, [but] being a metalhead, it just shapes you into something different. It's a whole culture in itself," shared Leon, one of the guitarists of metal band Mortal Soul. Bandmate Peter explained that heavy metal made him feel "less like other Kenyans," elaborating, "it sort of separated me from a lot of people. There is individuality there. Metal is all about tolerance" – an aspect the rock and metal community has grown to understand all too well. "Years later, you can hear the effects of 2008," stated Saidimu. "People are now talking in the rock scene about the corruption, they're singing songs about national unity, they are talking about it. That is what rock is, voicing those kinds of issues with passion."

This long-needed discourse is what could perhaps bring about an inclusion of tradition and culture into the rock and metal music in the future, as well as a better understanding of their multicultural nation to the rest of the world.

From the Strength of Desire

Kenyan rock and metal musicians today have realized so much with so little. Today's bands have presented themselves, with or without the support of Kenyans, out of a pure love of the music. As the second generation of rockers they are building this movement all on their own with aplomb. With a small base to build on, they have established a shift in the local musical paradigm and have changed the conversation of what being Kenyan actually means.

Kenya's Generation Y is unique. Mostly because many were not keen on associating with the legacy of ethnicity, they are more comfortable being identified as Kenyan than anything else and they are willing to push this message forward without hiding who they really are. Though there are plenty of challenges ahead, one goal that many local rockers want to see through is building the local community to the level where it may influence others in East Africa to follow their lead and build up communities of their own, much like their South African counterparts who were able to influence rock and metal communities in neighboring countries. Rock and metal scenes have remained silent in Rwanda, Tanzania, Burundi, Ethiopia, Somalia and the Democratic Republic of Congo, with a small community in Uganda led by the progressive rock band Threatening and the doom metal band Vale of Amonition.

But some feel that the Kenyan rock scene is struggling to realize their potential or even that the metalheads lack the drive to succeed. "In the region, rock needs to be bigger than what it is and that is why we need to be serious. It is only going to spread if we are serious about it," posited Kwame. The local rock and metal community is growing, but with hesitations from the local populace. "It has a lot to do with the perceptions," noted Ruto. The music suffers from not grabbing the same reach and access as other local genres do, and radio stations are hesitant to promote local rock acts.

Throughout my trip, I listened to local rock stations pushing well-known international artists, but no local acts. The local newspaper *The Daily Nation* features a segment called "The Rocker" in its supplemental magazine *Zubqa* and a few others take to promoting the music in clubs, yet the promotions remain minimal. Promotional activity has been focused on social media more than anything in Kenya. The region features a strong Internet community as a result of the government's push to connect the country. A direct result of the strong connection to the Internet is widespread downloading, which is how just about every single rock and metal fan in Africa is able to get the music they want. If they wish to buy music, heavy import and shipping charges would be added to the inconvenience of purchasing music from Europe or the United States. As DJ Knord asked, "If we did not have file sharing sites, then where would we access some of this music?"

But with this global connectivity comes global aspirations. Their unlimited access to music has allowed them to thrive in the already global community. "We've grown to make metal and hard rock available in a couple of years," said Switch, "but I still think we can do better in time. We can still do better, but I'm not sure. One thing about Kenya, we are trend people. As long as metal is as strong as it has been, Kenyans can still do it."

"I couldn't imagine it could happen in Kenya," said Mahia of Last Year's Tragedy. The sentiment was shared by many in and outside of the Kenyan metal community, as eyebrows raised when even mentioning this music in Kenya, much less outside of Africa. But what is next? What will the landscape of alternative music sound like in the future? "It is a sensitive time in our scene. The current bands have the responsibility to push it or kill it," commented Douglas Kihoro. "We have the opportunity to be a Metallica, to influence the next generation, so we have to carry that," added Tim Aubor of the band Moment of Silence. "We have inspired metal bands to come out," stated Ruto of Last Year's Tragedy. He was tapped on the shoulder from behind during our interview by Xenostate, who, speaking to the members of Last Year's Tragedy, reminded them, "guys didn't know it was possible until you were out there." There was much to be learned from his comment, considering those band members were once regulars of Class Suicide shows. Today, they are seen as one of the leaders of the heavy metal scene by many fans in the country.

"Metal is an ever-so-growing genre. It just doesn't stop growing, and that's why we are so dedicated," commented Shiv Mandavia. But there remains a major obstacle for many: support.

One reason for this that I noticed traveling through Africa is money. Rock and metal are live genres where money is required to attend shows and support acts. Rock and metal have attracted mostly middle to upper-class fans in Kenya to form bands, primarily because of the costs of taking up an instrument and recording. As a result of the large class divisions throughout the country, it is easy to see why so many may be dissuaded from forming or joining a band. Former Bloodshed member Wanjiru noted, "growth is limited, as rock music is seen as something that only some of the upper-middle-class to upper class enjoy. It is viewed as something suburban and rarely does it appeal to the population as a whole."

DJ Knord observed that at one point he was irritated by the notion of an unflattering truth: elitism in the local metal community. But, as he noted, "a lot of the new-school metal era comes from underprivileged homes." They are ready to get jobs – however menial – earn a living, and enjoy their lives as metal fans. He continued, "They represent a growing majority. They will define the face of Kenyan rock scene in years to come!"

"A main thread that permeates through all these bands is a strong appeal of common experience across divides of all kinds. Music is an expression of common cause across humanity," commented Xenostate. Ronjey noted that rock and metal really have the potential to make fans view the world around them in a different manner: "This music gives you the freedom to just be you. It is connecting people." "It unites us," added his bandmate Amos. "It gives us the idea that we can play outside and share ideas within the same context."

"Africa now is the target worldwide. Africa is the next big thing. It is going to bring in much bigger influences in the future, and I think metal will be a much bigger scene in Africa, and, hopefully, with the influence of the local culture1," stated Shiv. His comments got me thinking what would happen if I were to return to Kenya in a few years to follow up on the metal scene. The local rock and metal scene has changed so much in the past 10 years in terms of growth, as has Kenya. Behind an extremely literate and computer-friendly youth culture pushing the surge, Kenya is looking toward a bright future.

The rock and metal community understands this well and is also moving forward, without hesitation. "We don't have promoters who come and go. It's us doing it," noted Robin of Claymore Project. "For us it is a dream come true," said an excited DJ Hue Skills. "It's awesome. It is really awesome." In 10 years, "it will be something else, I promise you!"

Kenyans, as much as fans in every corner of Africa, are about taking their scene to another level, perhaps also changing the mindset of what Africa is supposed to be. "According to the world, metal is not African. That's not the case," reminded Switch. The optimism exists for so many, not just in regard to the growth of the rock and metal community, but also for Kenya as whole. With another Nairobi Rock Fest looming (which occurred a few months after my visit), another foreign band coming to perform and the ever-growing optimism that rock and metal would get two feet firmly on the ground in Kenya, things are looking up for this wonderful place.

We sat on a nightclub deck overlooking the city on my last night in Nairobi. I wanted to reflect and share so much with everyone who I had met during my time in the city and thank everyone once again. For many, it was the first time having a proper discussion on the rock and metal scene in Kenya, and the first time an outsider had spoken to those making the scene move. The faces of those gathered beamed with optimism.

Smiles and pleasantries consumed that evening, with members of the rock and metal community soaking in the experience as much as I did, chatting without a recorder in their faces about life and their country as well as the music we love.

But I would never forget that night for something else, something that moved me. Their way of thanking me for my visit and their way of reminding me I was always welcome was displayed by the humbling gesture of localizing me. From now on, while in Kenya, I would be called Njoroge – a common local name, but I was OK with that. I could not stop smiling. With a local name I was no longer just welcomed; I was now one of them.

I had entered Kenya a few weeks before as an American and was leaving forever a Kenyan.

NJOROGE ALISEMA "KWAHERI"

I had grown quite fond of Nairobi in such a short period of time. This was a unique experience for me, as I had to learn to navigate through the city on my own in a short period of time. The South B apartment I had been staying in was near the local shopping "center" – a derelict street of decaying storefronts and desperation. I would walk, or take a *matatu*, to the South B center daily to fetch breakfast, check my email and buy more cell phone minutes. The block-long shopping area was constantly clustered with foot traffic and cars trying to navigate their way through with two slums nearby and another more modern shopping mall a few blocks away. And I was always safe. No one ever hassled me.

I quickly became familiar in the South B shopping center and locals also became familiar with me, asking away about the affairs of America and American life in general. I was always treated well.

Desperation, however, was never far way. On a trip to buy a local calling card, I remember seeing two young boys staring into a small diner with big eyes. Barefoot, with rags on their slender frames, they paced back and forth anxiously waiting for the right moment. When that moment came, in just a matter of seconds they stormed in to grab customer's leftover plates off the counter and ran out. No one chased them, nor did anyone reprimand them. I suppose locals are just used to this hopelessness.

Nairobi is different. Yes, it has its chaos and its disorder, but that is Nairobi's rhythm. It may not be like New York's or London's, but as a traveler, I prefer it that way. The city became a permanent part of me, not just for the music. I saw the best of a city that many are only able to define by its worst moments. Nairobi is more: It is alive with so much creativity, so much diversity, and so much energy.

Kenyans were kind enough to help me along the way. Members of bands checked up on me after my hospital visit. Many even offered to pay for my malaria medication, which I politely refused. I was taken into homes and offered meal after meal, even if that would have been a financial burden. Switch even organized a night at the Nairobi IMAX to see the recently released film *Through The Never*, by the legendary Metallica, where I was able to meet more fans who shared how much heavy metal meant to them.

This is what heavy metal has done: bring us together.

It was all smiles as I once again entered the airport. The immigration officer was just as pleasant as before. I explained my trip, my malaria, getting ripped off on taxi rides, my disdain for local pizza, as well as my new name, Njoroge. The jovial, middle-aged man smiled and inferred why I was given the name. He explained that I was now welcomed as family, not as a tourist. I was doing something right, he said. He smiled at me thanking him in my so-so Swahili, perhaps assured of his interpretation and understanding that I had accepted Kenya in my heart before I had even arrived. I had a seat and shuffled through my backpack, putting on the bracelet of the Kenyan flag Mahia had given me the night before. Grabbing my boarding pass and sitting among the quiet crowd, I waited for the announcement to board the plane. I was off to Madagascar.

The reality of Nairobi's Kibera. Ironically, 'Africa's largest slum' is just a short distance from some of the more affluent suburbs.

With extreme metal musician Douglas Kihoro. Not long after this photo was taken he looked at and me and told me I was not looking well. Little did I know I had malaria.

With members of Last Year's Tragedy, Parking Lot Grass, and Class Suicide.

With Marc of Ages the day after I visited the hospital.

With Peter (L) and Leon (R) of Mortal Soul.

Just a snapshot of Nairobi's legendary traffic. A short trip easily took hours during rush hour!

Two great friends I made during my trip to Nairobi, DJ Knord (L) and DJ Switch (R).

MADAGASCAR

4

MADAGASCAR
Metal in the Forgotten Continent's Forgotten Country

"You are under sanction," she said quietly, as to not be heard. "Sanction?" I asked. "Yes, you don't have your yellow book," she explained. "It was stolen," I lied. Having never been bothered to show proof of vaccinations at any African border, the lack of my yellow book on my trip never even came to mind, but here I was faced with a small, yet fixable, problem. "How much?" I asked. "Twenty," said the over-confident immigration officer. I reached into my bag and handed $20 and watched this woman – with her hair pulled back, thick glasses and broken English – slide the banknote into her pocket as she handed me back my passport. Sadly, I think I was the only person to be asked for my vaccination record, as many others got stamped in and continued. This was the first time I had paid a bribe in Africa, and this was the first time I would face a language barrier, which is most

likely why I was "sanctioned." My inability to speak French was exploited before I even entered the country!

Madagascar is a place of intrigue. Sadly, many know of the country only because of an animated film of the same name and its association with happy animals. The reality is, of course, a stark contrast. Madagascar is indeed an ecological wonder, with over 90 percent of the nation's trees, other flora and fauna completely endemic to the island. However, the nation is one of the poorest in the world. An overwhelming amount of Madagascar's 22 million people earn below $2 a day.[34] *Political unrest has also fueled so much anguish among citizens in recent years. In 2008, a coup d'état left over 100 citizens dead as government soldiers opened fire on protesters. The international community has shunned the country's political climate and the citizens even more so.*

Musically, I was stepping into a surreal rock and metal scene that has found a comfortable place in Madagascar. For over 30 years, the evolution of metal has occurred because of the foundation laid by many of the nation's seminal hard rock acts, many of which are still active. I was stunned to see videos of bands playing in front of thousands of people. Madagascar has embraced rock and metal unlike any other African nation.

Many challenges face Madagascar's rockers. An uncertain political climate, an economy in peril and a language barrier have kept the music scene isolated. Terrible infrastructure also restricts so many in the nation

---

34   Ninety percent of the population earns less than $2 dollars a day. Source: World Bank.

who endure random power cuts, a feeble water supply, and a lack of workable equipment for rock and metal bands. It was here in Madagascar where I learned to redefine the term "passion." So many rock and metal bands in the world say they perform for love, yet there is always an ulterior motive: success. Bands in Madagascar have played for 30 years without any attention outside of the island. They perform with antiquated equipment, derelict conditions and frequent power cuts, undeterred because of their true love for this music. Metal's passion is very much alive in the land of baobabs and lemurs. This is Madagascar.

IN THE LAND OF KINGS...

Stephan's voice was weathered for his young age, just 21. He sported an Afro hairstyle, a pronounced piercing on his lower lip and a heavy metal band T-shirt. It was a bit of an anomaly for many here in Madagascar, wearing T-shirts that were not sold out of third-use stands from charitable donations. He had just four T-shirts, but he wore them proudly. Unemployed, he relied on the generosity of his friends to keep him sheltered and fed. Like so many in the country, he was desperate for work, but at the moment he had found temporary employment for the next few weeks: translator. Originally from the southern city of Tolagnaro, he came from Tamatave in the country's east to Madagascar's capital, Antananarivo, to greet me at the airport.

Stephan Moustaffa would be my voice for this leg of the journey, my translator in a country where few spoke English. A unique soul in a country of intrigue, his non-Malagasy name stood out, as did his personality. Bouncing from city to city in search of employment, he had come to the capital city to help me out, after finding out about my work. He reached out to me several months before and was adamant in lending his services. Given the economic situation in the country at the moment, he had the time, as well as the ability to speak English. The remarkable story of his knowledge of English is that he learned it from listening to heavy metal. He was curious as to what his favorite bands spoke of, so he taught himself the unofficial language of the genre. His English was not perfect, but it was as good as it got in this corner of the world.

It was a Sunday afternoon. Antananarivo, Madagascar's capital city, was moving at a quiet, yet steady pace of business, with hawkers and beggars crowding into the already tight sidewalks and thoroughfares. The roads were filled with stalls selling everything and anything, sharing the already narrow lanes with mini buses (like in most African cities), mopeds plowing through the sea of vehicles and pedestrians, and beige taxicabs whizzing by. These taxicabs were unlike any I have seen. Citroen 2CVs, or "umbrellas on wheels," were brought over by the French colonizers during their rule and are still serving their purpose – somehow! These odd looking vehicles have become sacred to auto enthusiasts with a hankering for the nostalgic, most likely because of their use in the

James Bond film *For Your Eyes Only*. Running on diesel and desperation, these ultra-thin vehicles could be better described as an aluminum beverage can on wheels. Yet, they were an efficient form of transportation and a rather affordable way around. The humor always came when the driver would shut the engine off to "cruise" down hills and the occasional stops, after what I assumed were stalls but were really grabs for the back-up fuel can in the trunk. Quite often, drivers would negotiate more fuel as the rate, but, nonetheless, these rides were wonderful ways of seeing the city.

The "City of the Thousand" is a stunning collective of hills with homes built seamlessly on top of each other. The colonial European style homes distracted the eyesight from the narrow and complex stairways connecting streets to alleyways – and what felt like even more stairways. Stephan was eager to show me the city, as well as share the exercise that came with the adventure. As exhausting as walking through Antananarivo ("Tana" as the locals call it) became, it was a fantastic introduction into the labyrinth hidden from plain sight. It was on this first day that we made our way near the historic Lake Anosy – a man-made lake with a walkway and statue in the middle known as the *Monument aux Morts* – to meet someone.

The text message said he would be meeting us by three o'clock at Lake Anosy in the center of the city. At just a few minutes past, he showed up. Clean cut, wearing a green T-shirt, faded jeans, designer eyeglasses and casual brown shoes that would have cost a small fortune in this part of the world, Markus Verne approached us with a sharp smile hinting a slight laughter. "Edward," he smiled. I was excited to finally meet him after about two years of correspondence. An anthropologist, he had visited Madagascar four years before from his native Germany to do fieldwork on traditional Malagasy music, only to discover the depth and size of the local rock and metal community, which become his primary focus instead. He immersed himself with many of the local "old school" rockers in the country during his research and became another member of the scene. Accompanying him was his dear friend, Njaka, guitarist in the local symphonic metal band Hope Era. Together, the two of them would join Stephan and me sporadically throughout Antananarivo during the next few weeks as Markus, fluent in French, would also help translate.

"IT WAS THE WISH OF GOD..."

The man sat patiently in the grasp of the sunlight shining through the sliding door opposite his chair, waiting for me to arrive with a drink in his hand. He was rather timid and wore a nervous smile. It was a Sunday and he was wearing his finest jacket and hat, as he had already attended his local church service. His shoes were worn down and haggard, but they were his Sunday best. He stood up when I walked in the room, though I was slightly embarrassed by the gesture. I, too, was nervous meeting him. I was told he was to be called Newton. The room was tranquil and the respect for him was such that no one dared to interrupt our discussion. The breeze blowing in sounded like thunder as we began our conversation.

The band Newton had formed in 1981, Balafomanga, was highly regarded as one of the first – if not the first – rock band in Madagascar. "I played with my brother, then I started Balafomanga. We [heard] this music on the radio and on cassette tape. The first time I heard this music, it became my life. I wanted to play drums, so I built a drum set from plastic," he said with a slight chuckle. "It was the wish of God. The Bible says that Christ is the rock, then we started to love the rock."

"The first time, it was strange for people to get our stuff," he remembered. Recalling very, and I mean very, quietly, he added, "the young people can get this music easy, but their parents didn't really get this music. In the '80s, there were not a lot of people who would go to the shows, but after [a few] months, there were a lot of people." Balafomanga's style is not that of hard rock, nor a heavy metal band sound that was common to the period. "We were rock and roll. Chuck Berry!" he explained.

"They were famous at the time. They played at a festival for all genres," added his friend Jonah, in whose house we were meeting. Himself a rocker, Jonah formed his band Inay in 1985 on the heels of what Newton and his band members had instigated. Balafomanga's name came up often during my trip through Madagascar. So many musicians in Madagascar mentioned Balafomanga as one of the bands that allowed rock bands to have a template, a model for how it was possible to write and perform original rock music in a country that had yet to experience this on their own. After all, meeting modern rock and metal bands was absolutely pointless without grabbing a better appreciation of those who laid the foundation for this generation.

Other bands whose names were cited as pioneers in the Malagasy rock and metal community include acts such as Tseletra, Kadradraka 2000, Maingoka, Pumpkins, Test and Black Jack. Others, including Kazar, Kiaki, Green and Iraimbilanja, also played vital roles in the formation of Madagascar's rock scene. The early 1980s was a fractured time in the nation's political history, which correlated directly with the rise of the rock scene. Madagascar had a feeble beginning as an independent nation. In 1960, the year of independence from French rule, Madagascar was introduced to the *Charter of the Malagasy Socialist Revolution* led by Didier Ratsiraka, who presided over the country for a combined total of 26 years.[35] With strict anti-Western views, it was hard for many to gain exposure to this music, much less form bands. However, once the socialist regime began to see an easing in the 1980s, rock moved in. "The musical tendency here in the country, [in] some parts here, especially in the big cities, they listened more to hard rock. In 1982, there was Balafomanga, Tseletra and Maingoka, then came more. Harder bands came shortly after that," stated Mao, the loquacious vocalist of long-running act Lokomotiva. When I asked him why this

---

35   He led Madagascar from 1975 to 1993, and again from 1997 to 2002, after the impeachment of the President, Albert Zafy. During the Zafy administration, Ratsiraka was exiled and living in France. He would return to a life in exile in 2002, only to return in 2011 to Madagascar, where he currently resides.

music started inspiring a few to grab some instruments and write rock songs of their own, he responded in his perfect English: "You can see the disappointment in everyday life," he said, pointing around the area outside a posh home. "With this sound, we let people feel energy."

Formed in 1983, Iraimbilanja came from rural Madagascar and joined the thin scene of rock bands performing original music. "In 1980, it was difficult to find someone to play the music that you like. Very difficult," recalled Papaya, sitting next to his brother and fellow founding member, Niri. "It was more easy for us. We were at home and were three brothers who like the same music." He added, "We grew up in a musical family. Our father is a saxophonist, and he played jazz." With the assistance of national radio, as well as dear friends who worked in the shipping industry, the brothers were introduced to rock music. "When I listen to this music, it is in my blood. I'm touched by this music; it is in my heart, in my brain. If you like something, you love it. If you don't like it, you don't. There is a smile from the notes, and my ears and my heart. It's rock!" explained Niri. "When we started in '83, there was no metal in Madagascar. And now there are a lot of metal bands. It shows how much the young adults have it in their blood, because they listen to this music," he added.

Not long after forming their band, struggling to work and write without proper equipment, the band members kept their dedication intact, doing something that had not been done in the country. "We had been working on acoustic instruments, and then we did rehearsals in studios where there were instruments, and the recordings we also did in studios. It was after this, with the first successes [*sic*], when we were touring in Madagascar, that we were able to buy the proper instruments," shared Niri. Success came in the form of a song called "At School," which became a hit song on national radio in 1985, allowing the band to obtain proper equipment through their mariner friends traveling to Europe and the Americas. Their success also allowed them to expand their audience. "We had been playing at the National University, each year from '85 to 2000, that was how we recorded," boasted Papaya, explaining how they recorded most of their early music in a live setting. "We played each year at an open-air location to about 8,000 fans." The band has also performed in France to the large Malagasy ex-pat community, a strong reminder of how special this music is to so many in the country.

With the formation of these bands, the Malagasy population was being exposed to local rock music across their national airwaves. Aspiring musicians now knew that performing and writing original compositions was something that could be done in their country, as there were other bands joining this first wave of rock in Madagascar. "We've lasted because we love this music," stated Lallah, drummer of the long-running act Kazar, which formed in 1984, just after Balafomanga and Iraimbilanja. He continued, "It was not hard to find people to play this kind of music. We knew of people who loved rock music and those who could play this music." Short, thin, with long salt-and-pepper hair, the absolutely charming Lallah recalled the energy of the period well. Though working as an electrician to earn his keep, music is the driving force behind Lallah's life. His early love of the music inspired him to cut up cardboard boxes to mimic a drum set, an instrument that he would patiently learn to play throughout his band's rehearsals once a week until 2008, when he was finally able to get his own drum set and practice as often as he wished.

Since 1986, Kazar has recorded and entertained in a country with restrictions on infrastructure so limiting that it is amazing that they are able to record and promote their music at all. As he explained, "it isn't easy to make music in international standard, even for popular genres here. No valid recording studios, no adequate material, not a [*sic*] producer." With derelict conditions engulfing them, the band headed to France, where they self-produced their first album in 2001, ironically called *Two*. The album was done at the home of Lallah's long-time bandmate and original member, Milon. Influenced by the classic, progressive and aggressive Kazar, careful to include Malagasy rhythm and melody in their sound, has transcended a generation as they still enjoy a level of popularity among rock and metal fans.

"All the metalheads thought we did something good. We really didn't know how we sounded; we just played what we played. It came from our hearts. Almost all the people say we are a thrash metal band, but we never knew we played thrash metal," reflected Lallah. Though the local reality of finding sustainable employment interfered with much of what the band wanted to accomplish (sending primary composer Milon to Paris), the band, like many of the founding acts, remains active. "We are so happy. We are still a band, and we want to continue," he relayed.

"Starting a band in 1985 in Madagascar, we had nothing. It was so difficult, no guitars," recalled Ragasy of the band INOX. Huddled under a garage roof in the middle of his city recording studio, sipping on cold beers in between a few cigarettes, the positive and ever-smiling musician spoke well of the early years. Short and wavy haired – and always wearing a leather vest, leather pants and cowboy boots, and very much fitting the persona of what many idealize a "rocker" to be – he spoke without hesitation. He began playing guitar in 1975 after hearing the music of bands like Deep Purple and Black Sabbath on the radio. "We had Radio Madagascar. They had a one-hour emission of rock and roll a week. That was it." He expressed that he was happy I was able to visit him and was anxious to show me many photos from the era, including one from the early 1980s that features a very young Ragasy playing rock in his neighborhood alongside a band and a small audience. The others in the photo would later form a band called Green while he formed his own project, INOX. After his time in rock bands, Ragasy turned his focus to raising his children, who now perform in their own band, also named INOX, to this very day, as well as running a recording and rehearsal studio appropriately called INOX Studios in the city. I would visit his studio frequently throughout my stay in Antananarivo and run into Ragasy often, as his role in the rock and metal community was prominent. He provided places for musicians to rehearse and would not only lend his second – and third – generation equipment for live performances, but also run sound for shows as well. Among one of the many times I ran into Ragasy was a live performance of the enigmatic and vivacious singer Nini.

Extremely confident, the long-time vocalist of the band Kiaki (pronounced "Key-ka") greeted me at a dinner hall that doubled as a venue in a western suburb just outside Antananarivo. Wearing a Nirvana T-shirt and a wool cap (it was a chilly Friday night), Nini was more than happy to invite me to his band's concert in Fianarantsoa that coming Sunday. On the map the place seemed close enough, but as I would soon learn the trip took seven hours on what was the worst bus ride I had ever endured. Stephan and I woke up the following morning on about two hours' rest and headed to the local "bus station" to fetch a bus. The fare was extremely affordable, like most things were for an American in Madagascar, but the process was chaotic. Buses filled the dusty lot as a sea of people slowly emerged over the next few hours. Stephan and I snuck in a nap in the back seats of the bus (which was really just a large van) that we were told was the one taking us to our destination. Awaking about an hour later, what we assumed was go time was actually just the beginning of a multi-hour ordeal that became a test in patience. "Once the bus was full," became the standard refrain. Frustrated, I watched the scenes play out in front of me as I constantly asked Stephan, "What did they say?" And he kept telling me, "Just five more seats to fill, and we can leave." "Four more." "Three more." "Two more!" "Wait, that couple is leaving and getting on another bus. Four more... again!" Another 20 minutes passed before, finally, about four hours after we arrived, we were ready to depart.

But first – and by this point I was beginning to see a breaking point in my patience emerging – I was told the driver and his friends had to tie all the bags on the roof! Thirty minutes later we departed. At last! A defeated Stephan and I shared my music player, listening to the fastest and angriest records I had on my MP3 player. The driver apparently had no idea what driving reasonably was about. He took every sharp mountain turn and high pass as if he were in a race. The ups and downs of the stunning scenery, though, were remarkable. Passing rice paddies, farmers at work and random farm animals hugging the road as the passed by, the mountains came to life and the places in between were no longer strange. Families, collectively plowing fields or tending to animals, snuck their heads up and waved to the passers-by. Madagascar became more than a crowded capital city in a matter of minutes.

The potholes were another story. From time to time, the bus would slow down to meander around massive potholes. It was peculiar how random these patches of irresponsible management were, but roads are often the reflection of a country's political management – which, in Madagascar, is completely destitute. And, of course, somewhere along the highway the women seated in front of us vomited. I could not help but laugh at the twists the day kept throwing at the two of us.

Fianarantsoa was different than Antananarivo and lacked the 18th century architecture. The roads here were terrible, the weather shit, but the views were spectacular. We were now in a higher-elevation city, surrounded by some of the most beautiful forests I had ever seen – and which I would soon learn more about, as they became a topic of discourse among the rock and metal community. We met Nini and the rest of Kiaki the night we arrived, and the following morning Nini was eager to sit and discuss things with me. "We've been playing for [nearly] 30 years. Not heavy metal, but rock music," he explained in his broken English. "The first time I heard rock and roll – Iron Maiden, Scorpions and Johnny Hallyday [the "French Elvis"] – I wanted to be a singer. And then my dream came true." It became apparent halfway through our interview that Nini became more than a singer in a rock band; he became the voice of a generation.

Choosing to take a quick break from our interview, we left the venue where he would be performing that evening and walked to a roadside stall for a cup of coffee. Not long after we began to drink our coffee, while discussing our favorite Iron Maiden records, a small crowd gathered. The rumblings were enough to make Stephan smile. "What are they saying?" I asked, as Nini greeted them. They had gathered because they were in the company of a rock star. Later that evening, I saw him surrounded by young and old alike for photographs and handshakes. One mother even encouraged her two children to go on stage while he was performing so she could take a photo of her kids with Nini in the middle of Kiaki's set. (To be honest, the way this band's music was cherished, I am surprised Nini even bothered singing. The crowd took over from the very first note of every song.) It was clear that rock in this country was different than anywhere else in Africa. Nini shared his pride in just how far this music had come in the years since he joined Kiaki. "We had one radio [station] in 1986, only one. We have a chance to have our track on RNM [Radio National Malagasy] in 1986." He explained that during that period, the only radio station in the country would accept submissions from a few local rock acts, mostly because it was being performed in Malagasy – not French or English, but the national language. "So," as he continued, "now we have lots of radio and television." It would not take long before Kiaki and the other bands from the early '80s became household names in Madagascar.

"It was Apost who played the first metal. It is us who started metal!" interrupted the otherwise silent frontman Abasse, standing against the corner of a kitchen counter with a lit cigarette, gleaming smile and one leg propped on the cabinet behind him. Wearing his jean jacket over top a rock T-shirt (which is all he ever seemed to wear), leather boots and long hair falling behind his thick frame, Abasse waited for me to look his direction to make sure that I understood what he said. His claim was a subjective one, yet delivered with the confidence he needed to set his band apart. Abasse's bandmate and co-founder Radessa sat and spoke quietly, merely nodding affirmatively at Abasse's statement as the other band members followed along with slight smiles. The band had just rehearsed a few songs for me, about six in total covering their almost 30-year history. Radessa explained Abasse's pride-filled claim.

"In the beginning, we started the band with one guitar. He was singing," Radessa said, pointing to vocalist Abasse, "and I was humming the bass line and the drums with the mouth. With that one guitar, we started to compose a whole metal song and the rest was done with our mouths." He started making the noises, simulating a drum set and bass humming that had everyone laughing. "We didn't have any materials [equipment]."

Also long-haired, the thin and quiet bassist sat recalling the beginnings of his band, which formed in 1986 but made a name for themselves in 1988. Radessa remembered every detail with precision, as if he had been waiting his whole life to share this with someone who would listen. And for the next hour I did. "In 1986, we had a concert and we would prepare in the way we described, singing the songs. We did rehearsals every day for the concert, but only one single time did we rehearse with actual instruments. We played five songs in '86, and it went well." Continuing, Radessa recalled that it was not difficult to put together a band during this period because interest in the music came to life. "There were bands that were writing their own songs," he stated.

Radessa and Abasse shared their earliest memories of this music with Stephan, Markus (who translated this interview) and myself. "We were little, but we had this music on vinyl and had a nice collection. Since we were little, we were listening to Deep Purple, Jimi Hendrix, and in the '80s we listened to heavy metal: Metallica, and German metal band Accept," allowed Radessa, adding that, "There were still these French around, but after independence they stopped selling these records. We had relatives abroad and they sent these records in. Every time Van Halen had a new record, we had it. Same with Loudness; we knew about them, so we had them." "There were always families abroad sending these records, cassettes and vinyl," reiterated Abasse, explaining exactly what this music meant to them. "It is in our blood. It was special; it really touched us," Radessa echoed, "There was other music around. We enjoyed James Brown, but it was metal that touched us." It would not be long before they were able to touch others with their music.

When Radessa and Abasse spoke with me in their rehearsal space, I noticed that things with them were different. At one time, Abasse had owned his own bar in Antananarivo, which today serves as Apost's private rehearsal space and a personal escape he shares with his close friends. Entering can be ominous: a quick knock on the door and a peephole opens, careful to not let just anyone in! Once you enter, the remnants of a bar gone by greet you. The stories, the sorrow, the arguments and the joys that once sat on those bar stools were but memories: they now stood empty, as did the coolers and taps. We were led to a small room behind the main bar through an ambiguous door, hidden from sight and opening up to a full rehearsal studio. Original (not knockoff) Marshall half stacks, a full imported drum set, as well as a top-of-the-line PA system stood in front of me, leaving Stephan speechless. Everything that so many musicians in the country had dreamed of ever seeing was at Apost's disposal. Why? Because of their labor! Forming a band in this corner of the world using your mouths as instruments behind a voice and an acoustic guitar proved that Apost was extremely passionate about their craft, as well as extraordinarily dedicated songwriters. And that craft paid off for them.

During one visit to Apost's studio, of which there were plenty, a group of local musicians and acquaintances had gathered to relax and share in conversation and music. On this particular evening, though, something spectacular happened. Every person stopped at once, interrupting his or her conversation and mirth to begin humming a melody in unison. Markus interrupted me also, grabbing my arm slightly and pulling me in closer excitedly and whispering, "Oh, are you hearing this? This is probably the most famous song in Madagascar." The song being played, hummed and sung along to was "Apokolipsy." Written by Apost in 1987 and recorded during a live performance on a radio station, it was the only version they had of the song until they were able to release their first record in 1999. "At that time, there was a single television and one radio station in the whole of Madagascar," Abasse remembered. "Technically, it was still the nationalist/socialist system. It was there where we recorded it, at the one radio station. It was recorded all at once – live – and they screened it and broadcast it, and it became a hit," remembered Abasse.

To say "Apokolipsy" was a hit was being modest. The song was still so relevant years later that even young up-and-coming rock and metal acts in the country are adding it to their repertoire. The money Apost had earned from the song allowed them to reach larger audiences as well as to invest in the proper equipment that left Stephan speechless every time he walked into that room. Abasse smiled. "It seems to have touched the people. A combination of the lyrics, the melody, the sound of the riff. As a package, it really touched the people. Young and old have listened to it. Even at weddings they were playing that song and dancing to it [because people were touched by it] and so on. It was everywhere for a while." The "sing along" friendly verse and chorus were something remarkable, as the room only got louder with voices in unison. The heavy sway of the back and forth rhythm made it a catchy and easy song to remember – remarkable, considering when I asked what the song was about, Abasse responded, in a louder volume now that the room was in full sing-along, in one of the few English words he knows: "doomsday!"

Apost was one of the bands that surfed in on the wave of Madagascar's newly discovered love of distortion. With a new generation of Malagasy rockers attuned to what was going on in the West, sporting T-shirts (most of them knockoffs) of international bands and constantly referencing current acts from the West, I was surprised by how many never forgot about the efforts made by those who came before them from their own country. In most cases across Africa, many of the younger bands were learning about their country's rock and metal history through me, surprised to learn that it existed before their focus on this music came into view. In Madagascar, however, young bands often cited their country's early acts as influences, as a result of the first generation of bands' passion – remarkable, considering these acts were formed, composed and performed during a time of anti-Western political and economic peril. Not that the economic situation in the country had actually improved much during the past 25 years.

Markus explained to me during one of the interviews I was conducting that a small change in the political situation in Madagascar was the break that rockers needed. "There was a socialist period and metal was hidden. From the '70s to that point, they listened to metal, but there was no actual metal played locally. But when this broke down, money came in. They had very anti-Western politics at that point, and then they couldn't go on with that because they needed money from France and from the West. Then politics changed and these guys [we were in a room with members of Apost] started,[36] and then the other bands started to play their music. So [the nascence of rock and metal in Madagascar] is clearly related to the political periods in Madagascar," he explained. The end of the socialist regime came in 1992 when the Third Republic of Madagascar came to light. Money was coming in, but for many the prospect of getting out of poverty was not going to change. After spending several weeks in Madagascar, you wonder where the money went, if it went anywhere at all.

The topic of politics came up often in Madagascar. This music, for some, served as the means to voice the concerns that many youth felt needed to be expressed. Though some completely avoided the topic, others were

36   Markus reiterated that "the World Bank and the IMF forced Madagascar's second republic to open up during the first years of the 1980s, and a few years later the first metal bands emerged on Madagascar's scene."

not shy at all. Throughout South Africa, political discourse was unavoidable, yet in the case of South Africans, many were pleased to be discussing these matters publicly. In Madagascar, however, the discussion quieted down and grew uncomfortable at times. At the time of my visit, the country was in its first year of a new president. Hery Rajaonarimampianina had been sworn into office in January 2014, the first elected leader after the heavily publicized coup in January 2009 that saw then democratically elected President Marc Ravalomanana ousted by political rival Andry Rajoelina,[37] then mayor of Antananarivo. Things took a tragic turn when members of the Presidential Guard fired upon supporters of Rajoelina in February 2009 while they were protesting in front of the Presidential Palace. Initial reports were that 38 protesters had been killed, though, sadly, 150 protesters were killed. Things in Madagascar were not looking good, and musicians were insistent in telling me what life in Madagascar was really like during this period – and is still like for most of them.

LAND OF DOOM

"We won't write about politics; we don't want to go to jail," uttered Erichi of the band MetaMorphozed. I remember the exact look the rest of his band leveled upon me after he spoke in his broken English. The quiet that fell within those four walls from Erichi's response triggered a look of

---

37   At the time of his seizing power, Rajoelina, a former DJ and rock fan, was 35 years old.

discontent from the 10 young eyes glancing back. What did he mean? Was he serious? Or, did I just put everyone in the room in an uncomfortable situation by bringing up politics? Markus had advised me that these topics were not totally off limits after I mentioned my intention to bring up political issues. "They are afraid of publicly talking about politics, not about politics per se," he explained. "They just want the country to function, and most of them don't care much if Ravalomanana or Rajoelina is president. They want politicians to leave them alone and care for the country. There is not much going on in the sense of our [the West's] left/right divide. Yes, they are fearful. Money is getting devalued constantly, and they fear Madagascar will decline again after some 10 years of promise and prospering." If I wanted to discuss the political situation in Madagascar, like I had learned discussing ethnicity in Kenya, I would have to proceed cautiously. Stephan, like Markus, had encouraged me to continue asking political questions, just not in public.

"We want to talk about revolution," affirmed the unapologetic front man, Eddie, of the Antananarivo garage-rock band Dizzy Brains. Polished in his demeanor, the tall, thin and well-groomed singer had an honest personality. He wore maroon jeans, designer shoes (imitations), a fashionable sweater and a scarf wrapped around his neck. He never held back. While his band was not metal, their homage to bands like the Rolling Stones, White Stripes and MC5 stood out in the Malagasy scene. It was this raw energy that caught my attention. Led by Eddie's raspy throat, the band presented me with a video for a song called "Vangy" over lunch one afternoon. The lyrics, which were translated for the video in English and French, were a clear stab at the system. The song included the lines: *"they say Madagascar is prospering, but it's clear demagogy...wanting power and glory is the source of all our discord...they let us die of hunger if we are Gasy like them... Not surprising this country is dying a little more each day."* I asked the band members about the brutal honesty of the track. Eddie responded, "We want to write similar lyrics in all of our songs. We don't care if the government stops our music, we will continue to sing about poverty and misery here in Madagascar, which is a big part of all our lives." Stephan and I could not help but notice that the members of the band belonged to the comfortable class of Malagasy society, but their aplomb to send their message was going to continue undeterred. It became obvious why: In order to get to the Dizzy Brains' rehearsal space, we had to walk through some excruciating poverty.

Madagascar is home to the worst poverty I have seen in Africa. Even in other corners of Africa I had visited, nothing was this bad. On this particular walk to meet Dizzy Brains, we had to turn down a set of stairs directly adjacent to a dumpster near the café where we had just met the band. This was the sort of dumpster you would see outside of commercial buildings, typically picked up and collected by a specialty truck in any developed corner of the world. Not here. What stunned me was the number of children that popped their heads out of the dumpster as we walked by. I had no idea what to do. The overwhelming fetid odor that came from there nearly floored me. Yet, there were kids – all toddlers – rummaging through the litter out of blistering desperation. Many of these kids followed us, dragging smaller ones behind them, all of them barefoot – their feet heavily calloused and infected. Stephan indicated that they might be orphans and have no one to care for them. The malodorous clothes they were wearing would be theirs until they grew out of them, likely passing them forward to the next generation of poverty. Knowing that these children would likely never escape this poverty is an everlasting heartbreak.

Every walk in Antananarivo, as does any trip to any city, town or village in Madagascar, paints a grim picture of poverty. Everything I saw around every corner was another reminder of just how things are here. People disrobing next to puddles that filled in potholes after recent rainfall to wash the clothes they had on their back is another image that remains prominently embedded in my mind. Rivers, too, were places of defecation, bathing and washing clothes. Defecation was seen throughout the sidewalks and streets as many simply "went" wherever they could. This was not the first time I had seen people defecating on the street. Earlier in the trip, I had seen a man in front of a Cape Town nightclub just "go" in broad daylight, as well as fecal matter laying about in Nairobi's Kibera. But to see it in a city to this extent was something else. Certain locations in Antananarivo were worse than others, as people made their homes everywhere and anywhere without shame. And life just seemingly continued for the rest of the population.

Nary sat on the edge of his bed in a spacious third-floor bedroom inside his home. A mariner by trade, he finds solace in the few months he spends at his home. Fluent in quite a few languages, he was more than happy to get into life as a metal musician with the long-running act that he and his brother formed years ago called Black Wizard. With an ode to classic Black Sabbath prominent in their sound, Black Wizard had gained a respectable fan base over the years, something that Nary was thankful for. Yet, there was one instance still burning in the back of his mind that he wished to share.

"When I write a song, I talk about everything in Madagascar. For example, when you go 100 meters from here," he said pointing out his window, "you see the worst place in the world. When I go past there I am crying. The situation of the population there I cannot believe. I wrote this song called 'Land Of Doom'. If you go past this place," he emphasized, still pointing, "you will cry. The lyrics ask to pray for the nation today, because this nation is going down." Nary reached over toward his computer and played a video the band released for the song. A live performance, the video is interjected with clips he took from a hand-held camera of the place he was referring to a block away: a sewage canal, straddled by derelict homes on both sides, an undesirable and dreadful poverty, just one block away from his home. "When I put this music on the TV, policeman arrive at my gate asking, 'Why you show this [sic] to everybody'? The movie of the song I make [sic] is showing everything in the city, and they don't support it." Everyone in the room stopped what they were doing. Nary said he has never forgotten that day. The incident, which happened a few years prior, was still fresh in his mind. Police had come to knock on his door to tell him they did not appreciate the imagery of his band's video. "[If] they come today, tomorrow I take my ticket and come back in a year," he said, showing me his passports, indicating the ease with which he could just leave the country on a whim, given his profession. "I'm talking about the real situation in Madagascar."

"As you have seen, the system here is very restrictive," spoke Mandiby, bassist of the thrash metal band Beyond Your Ritual, who was present during the interview with Nary. Doing their best to communicate in English, the members had grown frustrated by the poverty and politics in the country as well. "It is like a bottle: the top is very small and not everyone can pass through. When we were at school, we were told we were the future of the nation, but the people of the older class have seemed to block our way." He paused for a minute to collect the right words, noting that he worked in the country's finance sector and was concerned by the lack of money in the pockets of the working class. He continued, "We were always taught we were the future of the country, and we wanted to engage in modeling the future. But you can't get through. We chose metal to circumvent that. You can be a part of talking of the future."

"Through our lyrics we convey that we don't like our politics. We are against our politics. We talk about life and society," explained Miobula, guitarist of the band JonJoRomBona. Their unique sound and style separates them from many others in Madagascar. A heavy metal band with a traditional flair, the members were excited to host me and discuss matters of effect without trepidation when reviewing their political situation, especially the 2009 coup. "We wrote a song called "Aleoko Ho Faty" ("I Prefer To Die") about the 2009 coup d'état. The politicians here dislike everything about this country. It looks like they shelled their own country," Miobula shared. "We send the messages of the misery in this country," added the band's percussionist, Niove.

Many of the country's young acts, part of what could be described as this new wave of bands coming of age in the Internet era, are taking proactive approaches in addressing themes of frustration. "Society makes you oppressive," commented the alternative rock singer Naday. "If you don't have money, it is very oppressive," he added. For many more, it was a way of directing their anger in a healthy manner. "We have a track, '7', that talks about the [2009 coup]," stated Faniry of the thrash metal band Soradra. Remembering the day of the coup as he sat across from me, holding a drink, he never lost eye contact. His pauses were deliberate, as were the words in his reticent English. "The following day, I went to the place where the killing happened. It was… it was not Madagascar," he remembered with clarity. Asked whether or not there was ever fear in composing anti-government songs or if the government was even taking notice if anyone was writing songs of the sort, he replied, "I don't know and I don't care. Fuck the government! We write what we want," he spat out. "The politicians here just steal the money from the people and get off," added Emmanuel of the extreme band Nocturnal Mortum.

"The situation is supposed to be expressed by our music. The stranger should know about our country," stated Haja, the extremely shy drummer of the Tamatave deathcore band A Skylight's Severance. "We put these lyrics in our music for the metal community. We want the world to see what life in Madagascar is really like," he added. Toky, vocalist and bassist of the death metal band Samar, hinted that it is difficult for him to keep a positive attitude in Madagascar. After watching Samar rehearse, I asked Toky about a song that stood out for me, "No Salvation," that featured lyrics in English. "'No Salvation' is about our leaders and how they don't care about other people," he explained. "They think that they are leading the people in the right, but they are not. If the priest wants the people to pray, what is the sense in a song like 'No Salvation'? Are people supposed to be saved? We are very angry too! At the time of [colonization], French people would spit on Malagasy people. The French would rape our women." His bandmate, guitarist Bob, sat quietly beside him nodding his head up and down in agreement. The middle-aged guitar player remembers the colonial period well and was certain that the current government had taken its cues from their French colonial masters.

Kaltz, guitarist of the Antananarivo band Sasamaso, sat quietly, lowering his whispering voice even more so when discussing his frustration with his country's politics. "There are so many things we want to shout. The injustice, it is definitely about injustice. In [mainland] Africa, things are more civil. Here, injustice rules." He expressed how this music has allowed him and his band members the opportunity to speak about the issue that would otherwise be left untouched by other genres in the country. Sasamaso came onto my radar by way of their video "Fariseo." The clip found its way into circulation through Western message boards and metal blogs, raising a few eyebrows around the world in the process, given the lack of awareness of metal in Madagascar. Discussing the video, Kaltz recalled, "our prime minister from colonization has a tomb in Tana,[38] we chose this grave on purpose because 'Fariseo' talks about fairytales. [Politicians] are famous for not being honest, not being truthful. It was a statement to talk about these politicians and how they say things they then won't do and so on."

During one particular conversation on the matter of politics and its effect on music, Markus shared that Nini of the band Kiaki was once approached by the president (though, I was never informed which president) and was asked to write and perform on his campaign's behalf. When I asked Nini about this a few weeks later, he confirmed it. "Yes, he wanted us to sing only during the campaigns, but we were not to talk about politics. We have performed in front of a lot of people, but we never spoke [*sic*] of politics," he said, explaining that the idea was a bit bizarre. One day you are the singer of a rock band, the next you are

---

38   Rainilaiarivony is the prime minister he referred to. Ruling from 1864 to 1895, he helped the nation transition from a monarchy to a constitutional state and was responsible for making public school education in Madagascar mandatory.

answering a phone call from the president being asked for songs and performances in order to help "the cause," something that the band never did so as to not ostracize their fans. However, what this conversation with Nini shows is that rock is viewed in a different light for so many in Madagascar and their greater cultural scope. Being asked by a president shows just how much validity this music has in Madagascar, more than in any other African country. It has become a part of their culture. But why has their culture not become a part of their music?

"Rock IS Our Culture"

Culturally speaking, the nation of Madagascar is unique as a result of its isolation. Their cultural evolution has been brought about by the contributions from those who have inhabited the island for thousands of years now, the collective known today as the Malagasy. Musically, the country expresses itself with its own collection of sounds and instruments, which have been noticeably absent from most of the speakers of Malagasy rock and metal fans' stereos. "There is rock, and there are only tropical things. People are divided," explained Tamial of the experimental Antananarivo band Djannat. "I wanted to mix it all together, so we mix Malagasy and rock, just the rhythm [not the instruments]," he continued. The band prides itself on being able to mix various types of rock and metal music together with a traditional sound, yet they are not alone. JonJoRomBona is also working at building a unique sound in the Malagasy metal community. "We are patriotic, and we are not shy about it, thus the reason for infusing our culture into our music," explained bassist Sol.

One thing I noticed from looking around the room of their living space (three members lived in the same house) was a percussive box in the corner next to one of the members, Niove. The instrument is known as a *cajon*, which comes from Peru. He introduced himself as the percussionist of the group, but explained that the *cajon* was an instrument he was experimenting with, as he typically uses the *tembe* in the band. "The *tembe*?" I asked. In agreement, he nodded his head back and forth understanding my surprise. I had Stephan explain that the instrument is associated with West Africa, yet here in Madagascar I was surprised to see the instrument being embraced. "The *tembe* works with Malagasy rhythm," Niove explained. He went into more detail about how the band wanted to incorporate Malagasy instruments, "but no one knows how to play the *valiha*, or *sodina*," a type of flute made from bamboo or a light wood that is synonymous with traditional Malagasy music. "We do play *valiha* songs with our instruments, and the *tembe*," shared guitarist Miobula.

The *valiha* they referred to is a stringed instrument made from bamboo and strung with wire held in place at each end. Ornate, the long-tubed bamboo instrument is carved with symbols of Madagascar, decorated by the tuners that keep the strings in place. The *valiha* is also a symbol of Malagasy music, as it is the most recognizable instrument in the country. I saw *valihas* everywhere I went and even purchased one at a local watering hole for the ridiculously low price of one U.S. dollar. Tuned to a major scale, the *valiha* is one of many chordophones that make up the sounds of Madagascar, which are a fusion of its ancestral collective: Southeast Asian, African, Arabian, Austronesian and European. The music varies between regions and within the various 18 ethnic groups in the country and was quite remarkable to take in.

One night, we were treated to an impromptu performance of the *valiha* by a local musician. With the sounds of restaurant around us, noticing that I had purchased one, he asked to see it to show me how to tune the instrument as well as offer a quick lesson. Once he was done tuning the instrument, however, his lesson turned into a performance, literally quieting everyone around us and emitting a sense of ease as this instrument's sound came alive. It put a smile on the faces of everyone, including the extreme metal fans gathered at the table. Njaka, Markus' friend, whom Stephan and I met on the day we met Markus, silenced every single one of us with his virtuosity. Having once traveled the globe performing in a world music band, Tarika Be,[39] he was used to soothing audiences with the *valiha*. Njaka told me that he had left Tarika Be and the touring life behind for a new pursuit: heavy metal.

Now performing in the symphonic metal band Hope Era, Njaka confessed it had been years since he had touched

---

39   In 2001, Tarika Be was named one of the 10 best bands on planet Earth by TIME Magazine. September 15, 2001. "Best Bands: And Our Winners Are..." by Rhett Butler.

a *valiha* and apologized for the interruption. I was told that the Malagasy believe the instrument can be used to channel spirits; regardless, the sounds coming from Njaka's fingers were a pleasant relief from the beloved sounds of pounding bass drums, gut-filled vocals and aggressive guitars. Stephan could not put down the *valiha* after that evening. He wanted to replicate that performance, but, of course, it may take years to come. When I asked Njaka about Hope Era's noticeable absence of any traditional music featuring his talent, he explained, "Hope Era doesn't care about Malagasy tradition. We respect it, but we just play metal." Pondering his responses, he asked me to turn on my voice recorder once again, itching to add something else. "I play this traditional instrument like a guitar; I love this like I love metal," he clarified. He also detailed that in the future they could perhaps compose songs with this mixture of metal and Malagasy tradition, as it was an idea they have been entertaining. Hope Era was not alone. There are others who are also hoping to push heavy metal and hard rock into new boundaries. Though, like elsewhere in Africa, not everyone is in agreement about this inclusion.

"If you play rock, don't mix it," stated Nini emphatically. Nary of Black Wizard explained, "if you mix it [traditional music], I don't like it. If you make it this [mixed] music, it is not metal anymore," he laughed. The reason behind our laughter came after he hypothetically guessed what the bands would sound like if they incorporated a prominent type of music in Madagascar known as *tropique*. Though its roots lie in the Caribbean, *tropique* is popular throughout Africa's Indian Ocean islands. "It is so difficult to mix

Malagasy culture with a metal song. It sounds bad," added Joss, guitarist of the power metal band Allkiniah. One of Joss's contemporaries, Rija of the band MetaMorphozed concurred, "It is really hard to combine [the two]."

Speaking with Lallah, as a scene veteran, he shared his views on this aspect that many of the country's musicians are back and forth. "Bands here shouldn't think that rock is from the outside. They should think that rock is another part of the culture." As he sat clutching a beer bottle on a restaurant balcony overlooking busy Independence Boulevard, Lallah continued to speak as if he knew what questions I would ask next. "We don't believe in mixing things up," he shared in reference to his generation of rock bands, which never featured infusions of traditional music and rock. Lallah, always straightforward, reiterated, "Rock is our culture, too!" It reminded me that this music was not introduced by the French, nor forced on the Malagasy, but introduced organically. Many of the first-generation bands had dismissed my inquiry as to why they did not infuse tradition, or even contemplate the idea, which on its own stood as their response. Perhaps the most fitting comment on the matter came from Balafomanga's Newton, a waterfall of insight. "Rock music started here in Africa, with African people. The blacks in the USA started to play the blues, and then it started overseas. Rock is coming now to the African people. It is our culture. It is not Western culture or European culture. It is our culture."

"THEY THINK WE ARE ON DRUGS!"

Coincidentally, there are two aspects of locality prominent in Malagasy rock and metal: language and themes. All of the active bands that formed in the '80s perform exclusively in Malagasy for the simple reason that the acts are extremely proud of the cultural attachment to their language. With its Malayo-Polynesian roots, Malagasy is the favored language of the 22 million people living on the island. French is still spoken well by the "colonial" generation, and moderately by younger Malagasy. Confronted by the need to push forward, the youth are anxious to learn English as a means of connecting their music to the rest of the world, yet almost all perform in Malagasy. "We think it is more important in Malagasy, because we are Malagasy," shared Mika, vocalist of Allkiniah. I asked him if he felt that performances in Malagasy were hindering this band's progress. "We have had lyrics in English, but there are Japanese bands that sing in Japanese," he argued, positing that if certain bands can break internationally in their native language, why should the Malagasy omit an aspect that makes them comfortable?

Young acts such as Anathema perform in English for the sole reason of better marketing their music to an audience outside of Madagascar, something that hindered the previous generation, as Ragasy reminded me during one of our many run-ins. "Speaking Malagasy in our lyrics is not helping us though when it comes to marketing our music overseas," he said. "We would like to be an international band and play overseas, especially in USA and France," explained Mouma, vocalist of Anathema. Others, including the members of MetaMorphozed, argued that the Malagasy language just does not work with aggressive metal. "It is hard to sing in Malagasy when it is metal music," explained one of the band's vocalists, Rija. Co-vocalist Erichi added, "Compared to lyrics written in English, it doesn't do much with that metal feeling. It sounds a bit weird." "Sounds strange. Metal in Malagasy?" chimed in drummer Matt as his band chuckled. But like the members of other bands, MetaMorphozed has international aspirations. "Bands in other countries have brought their own signature with their songs [in English]. So it would help us market if we performed in English," concluded Erichi.

One band I came across that had been in existence for quite some time and used the English language was the hard rock group Vatofant. Formed in 1988, founder Ndriana has kept the band afloat throughout the years through passion and most recently recruited his two oldest sons as band members. Ironically, he did not speak English well. Perhaps one of the kindest people I had met on my trip, Ndriana happily hosted Stephan and me for a few days at his home in Fianarantsoa, where he was gracious enough to show us around his hometown. "I perform in English because I have a lot of respect for where the music came from, though sometimes I perform in French, too. The new generation should put Malagasy lyrics first. We have to take care of the Malagasy people first and then the other countries," he explained in his very tranquil voice, which was calming to hear considering his ominous stature.

I have continually given thought throughout these trips to Africa as to what is behind the lack of traditional influence or cultural sounds in the continent's rock and metal communities. Quite often, I return to the same conclusion: rebellion. Most of the bands in these countries – with the exception of Madagascar and South Africa, which are made up of acts from differing generations – are composed of young musicians who want nothing more than to redefine their identity through this music. But what it is about heavy metal and rock that lend them to an identity shift away from the local? This metal and rock identity follows an unwritten set of norms, like any other subculture. But, metal and rock have found subtle ways of becoming local in the various African countries, mostly through hints of language and themes. At the same time, though, this local metal community was still holding back. Was there still something in their way? Stephan shared that Madagascar, in his view, was extremely conservative, and he was made to feel unwelcome in some places because of his proclivity to wear black T-shirts with heavy metal band logos, and facial piercings. But for Stephan, like so many others, this was how he felt comfortable.

"Metal is not welcome in Madagascar. Maybe because of the Malagasy culture? Malagasy culture is the opposite of metal culture; for people, metal [to others] is Satanic music," explained Faniry. Tsilavina of the metalcore bands Set and My Funeral Song explained that "people's religion, Christianity and Catholicism, changed the mind of the people and became [*sic*] narrow minded." The problem, he said, are the religious leaders who have taken advantage of a nation whose population is not very international and the interweaving of politics to faith. According to Joss of Allkiniah, "Religion here is political; it helps them get money. If there is something wrong, they talk to the people. For example, 'Look at the metal fans, they wear black'. So many people trust them." Tsilavina explained that he and his friends, who are all in bands, have a different approach that could perhaps assuage their situation. "We began to change the new vision of metal with white clothes and short hair. The new look!" he says laughing. Though, I did notice, with the exception of a few, the stereotypical "metal attire" was absent throughout Madagascar, mostly as a result of the cost of the metal T-shirts. Most of the T-shirts were homemade or bootlegged versions shipped in and sold on street markets. Misspelling of band names, inaccurate album covers and lyrics scrawled on the back that had nothing to do with the associated album on the front were common mistakes found on these shirts. But the Malagasy metal fans who were fortunate to own a few did not care. They loved those shirts as much as they love the music and those bands.

Perhaps it is this trepidation by the non-rock/metal commoner that has hampered the reputation of this music for many and, thus, the rejection of Malagasy culture in the music. "The people here are so afraid when they see a guy or a girl in a black shirt. The religion has told them about what is good and bad, and that is why people think that rock is a bad thing. They will blame rock and roll," explained

Ndriana. "Because of the religion, people were afraid. They were scared of talking about reality," stated Claude of the band Aowa. His bandmate Setra added, "This is a really Christian country. They are blinded by religion. It's like the Middle Ages here. People are frightened that 'you can't do this' because we go to hell. It's always," he paused for a few seconds, resuming with a shift in thought. "Actually, it is a fear dictatorship here that continues to manage. The most intelligent here understand things and get out of the system, but people are really stubborn. 'You play metal'!" he said, imitating the mocking tone. "And they associate it with Satanic ideology, or really bad things."

Stephan and I had a first-hand encounter with this perception at an Antananarivo corner store. Sharing a few drinks with the members of JonJoRomBona, we found ourselves surrounded by a few local youths who were taken aback by the way Stephan and I were dressed, but they had taken particular umbrage to my attire. My sweatshirt, (which many joke is part of my uniform) of the American band Darkest Hour, features a "demonic goat" across the back, which, in reality, is a caricature with exaggerated horns and "arms" spread wide open with a motionless grin across its facetious face. It became the target of their rage. This same hooded sweatshirt got me booted from a store in an upscale shopping mall in a Nairobi, Kenya, because an employee had taken offense to the image on the back. Now, confronted by a few men – and separated from Stephan, the only person who could speak on my behalf – I was cornered and unsure of what was happening. This happened quickly! I had just bought a few bottles of beer for the members of

JonJoRomBona, clutched them in my fingers and turned around to the angry faces of these young men. With my back to the sales counter, the clerk went to fetch the owner. A few others were holding back Stephan, who was shouting across the room, "They think you are a Satanist!" The men, assuming I was French, were confronting me in French, accusing me of coming to Madagascar to spread Satanism. Our situation probably was not helped by the store's radio playing the American thrash metal band Shadows Fall, which the clerk had agreed to play for us off of Stephan's phone (likely because of the amount of money I was spending there).

Once they realized I was not French, they allowed Stephan to translate for me. I explained my reason for being there. In the end, it was agreed that I would be left alone and that I could enjoy my trip to their country on the promise that I would not spread Satanism – a promise that I kept! But the instant, on-a-dime reaction to my attire supporting one of my favorite bands and the manner in which Stephan presents himself were strong indications that an intense "rock and metal music is evil" mentality permeated this country. Even within the *Internet* youth.

"When people hear the distorted guitar, people think it is the devil's music. They still think about the same thing they did about a thousand years ago. I just want them know this is not the bad music they are thinking about." The words of Antananarivo musician Rado came clearly and without pause. He spoke passionately while surrounded by his band, Heavy Hell Stomp. "I don't think how I dress should be the topic for you to judge me. I think it is just matter of what I love to wear. I would like [people] to understand that this music has its good, too. They think we are on drugs. It has to take steps," he confessed. "I hope, as we are all dreamers and great [optimists], I hope we are a part of this change. This is the music that allows performers to truly share their feelings and to commence a dialogue about the matters affecting them most. Our lyrics [are] about changes, not revolution, not destroying anything, but changing things," he added. The appeal of this music to some was directly because of the honesty it welcomes, as was explained when two of Stephan's friends came to visit from Tamatave. "The lyrics of the band Kreator, I like their lyrics because they talk about misery, war, and chaos," shared Stephan's friend Hary, speaking of the German thrash metal band. "In my country, this misery is everywhere." Poverty, politics and the pessimism of a future in peril allows many to feel at ease within this music's expressive nature.

A few have used their lyrics to delve into exigent social issues of Malagasy life. Romeric, the quiet vocalist of the extreme metal band Nocturnal Mortum, explained that his music has helped him express his frustrations with a matter he holds close: the environment. "We talk about someone who robbed the tomb, because the politicians here export precious trees called 'Pink Tree[40]'," as the look on his face became one of frustration. As Romeric decried, seeing the trees leaving his home city of Fianarantsoa was like watching someone rob a tomb. "These kinds of trees

---

40   It is widely known that a prominent guitar company uses the wood from this tree, on the verge of extinction, to construct their instruments – ironic, considering how coveted their instruments are to many Malagasy performers.

are expensive, and that is why the politicians export them. Just like that! Because not many people know about them." A fan, who was sitting at the table behind ours, glanced over (as if he were going to argue with Romeric) and intruded in a staunch manner. "Some people here do the traffic of the 'Pink Tree'. Some people give the money to the politicians from the tree [*sic*][41]." Nini of Kiaki also uses his platform to address environmental issues. "We talk about the Malagasy culture that cuts and burns trees.[42] Malagasy should not do these kinds of things." When I asked why this was common, Nini said he was unsure, but "we have a habit to burn [*sic*] everything. You can't see these animals without Madagascar," he added, referring to the ubiquitous symbol of the country, the lemur.

Madagascar receives a lot of positive attention for its ecology, notably because of its unique biological diversity. Roughly 90 percent of the flora and fauna that exists in Madagascar are endemic. But on the drive to Fianarantsoa, I would spot smoke plumes in the distance and the horror of a black, charred earth staring back at me. As Stephan and I took in the scenery that Nini had described, I could not help but keep noticing pockets of black surrounded by the remnants of dead fauna. The process of slash and burn in Madagascar is known as *tavy* and occurs because of the level of poverty throughout the country. Farmers convert forest, topical or not, into rice fields by burning

---

41   This voice came across clearly on my voice recorder, but I am unable to attribute this quote, though I know this person was sitting behind our table and listening to the interview. The response was in English.

42   A practice known as "slash and burn."

everything down, which in turn releases nutrients into the soil that allow for a natural fertilization for the rice crop. The land is left fallow for a few years after harvest so the process can be repeated. However, most of the time dismal vegetation, or scrub grass, grows in its place. A typical forest can see signs of life 20 years after a good burn, yet that is not the case in Madagascar, as signs of tavy are everywhere in the countryside.

Deforestation in Madagascar is a crisis in its own right, but it also heavily threatens the furry and curious primates adored by so many around the world: lemurs. Their home is being destroyed. An effort by the Malagasy government to protect much of their native land was in full effect, but many still did not understand – Stephan included. It was during an off day that we were able to see lemurs first hand, even touch them, and learn just how valuable they are to the country, which is the lemur's indigenous home. The animal was now a symbol of the desperation of a nation. Yet, many Malagasy are oblivious – unaware of what they were doing, or if they were, they did not care. Everything, as they saw it, was a food source, even the precious lemur. It was hard to blame them. The country is remarkably poor. Food, however you could get it, was necessary. Speaking with members of bands in Fianarantsoa (much closer to the lemur's natural habitat), Stephan now saw how protective members of the rock and metal community were of their country.

IGNITING THE FUTURE

In many ways, Madagascar's rock scene epitomizes everything about the famed *do-it-yourself* approach that many within this genre hold sacred. It was up to the Malagasy to build rock and metal from the ground up, completely on their own. By estimation, at the time I was in Madagascar there were over 60 active rock and metal bands. Every type of band existed within the spectrum, from the black metal of Lagasy to the hard rock of Vatofant. I learned of festivals throughout the country and that a few acts, notably the first-generation acts, draw extremely large crowds. One band, Green, showed me a video of themselves performing in front of an audience of 20,000, well over 25 years after their formation. Madagascar has the largest and most passionate rock scene anywhere in the African continent. And, the musicians have displayed a passion that is unlike any I have ever seen. One thing that stood out, much like the Apost story about starting the band with nothing but one guitar and their mouths, was that many of the musicians were playing their instruments for the first time when their band would hold their inaugural rehearsals. Many musicians also joined a second or a third band in order to keep up and improve their skills. Musicians, defying their circumstances, go about writing and performing regardless of what is available to them. Malagasy musicians play, like most Africans, out of pure love for this music. Would they like to find success in Madagascar? Would they like to find success outside Madagascar? Do they stand a chance on international stages? Only time will tell.

Throughout my trip, I met passionate fans and musicians who want to see this music grow in Madagascar. A few fans went above and beyond to make sure this happened. One young fan, Romy, saves up his own money and organizes the Distortion Festival every two years. "Metal fans have a solid and strong spirit, a solid and strong mind. Poverty isn't an obstacle for the love of heavy metal music," Romy stated, adding that the situation incites a better life. A child of poverty, struck at age 11 by the death of his father, Romy and his siblings were raised by a mother who used the little she had in a country that had little to offer in the first place. The optimism that drove him out of poverty came through his love of metal, music he now shares with others through Distortion Fest and a radio broadcast. He created his Distortion radio program, which started as *Radio Des Jeunes* (Youth Radio), to counter the largess sought after by radio stations to play metal. It was probably the first pirate radio station in Madagascar, or, as Romy called it, "phony radio emission." Run by his partner, Dina, and himself, Distortion was the outlet needed to play rock and metal in the capital and now airs for one hour on Wednesdays and Saturdays on national radio. "The broadcast is necessary to inject metal into other people!" he elated.

But for Romy, the heart and soul of his passion is the Distortion Festival. Held in Antananarivo every two years, the festival is one day of sun up to sun down rock and metal, bringing bands from every corner of Madagascar, connecting them to an avid fan base. At last count, the single-day event drew over a thousand fans. Romy and his partner work tirelessly to not only promote, but to also fund the event. There are no sponsors, no backers of any sort, just their own pockets from their day jobs. Romy earns a meager Malagasy wage – pays rent, buys groceries, helps his family in any way possible – and always manages to save up the two million Ariary[43] it takes to fund this event. "The festival is a great way to introduce new acts, as well as showcase the long-time acts. Last one featured 20 acts," he shared. The festival was born from the fact that so many rock and metal acts had been overlooked. "Metal culture doesn't have the support other musical cultures do. We make a lot of sacrifices, but I am very proud of our work." Romy loves this music! His motive is to merely promote this music in Madagascar. After his father's death, this music was very much his healing process and in a way, this is the least he can do for the music that his given him so much in return.

"Where can I park?" asked Phil Ralijaona, as he called to tell us he was on his way. Stephan was baffled. No one we had met had their own car. We were taken by surprise. Phil drove himself in his recent model BMW and had taken an early day from his job to visit me. This was a rare sight for me, now accustomed to Malagasy norms, and an unfamiliar sight for Stephan: someone driving their own car, a newly released iPhone 6 in hand (not a knockoff either, the real deal!), a freshly pressed shirt and tie, and an imported record collection that he boasted may have rivaled mine after we shared a few stories. This was not indicative of the Madagascar I had grown accustomed to seeing.

---

43   Roughly 800 American dollars.

The soft-spoken construction manager, who was overseeing new gas station projects around the country, was also the host of a metal program on a local private station, Radio Antsiva, 97.6. Every Saturday evening from 7 to 8:30 for the past 14 years, the show has played the currents of metal and rock from overseas and Madagascar. "When I was 9 or 10, I heard this music. There was one radio station in Madagascar, and I heard Black Jack and Balafomanga. But before then, I never heard bands from abroad. It was when I was in high school that this guy told me about AC/DC and Helloween. I started doing this because I like music and wanted to share it. For example, my favorite band is Dream Theater. If I don't share, I listen to Dream Theater myself." Phil explained that this music for him is extremely special, notably for the feelings that it invokes inside of him when he listens, indicated by the smile on his face when he spoke at length about his favorite bands. But he did acknowledge the trepidation of Malagasy society from his experience with phone calls and emails from a segmented Malagasy public incensed that this music was being heard on their airwaves. "The problem of rock and metal music in Madagascar is that it is not the culture from here, it is the culture from 'yours'. I try to explain every day that it is not like this, especially the drugs, Satanism. It is getting better and better, but 10 years ago it was very different to talk about this here."

Phil is a person who unquestionably loves what he does. He made it absolutely apparent though conversation that he cared greatly for being able to play this music for an eager audience and even possibly introduce this music to a new audience. It was through radio transmissions that the first generation of rockers was introduced to the music. "There were guys before," he said, referring to a voice known as Metal Native.[44] But as he reminded me, early on, "rock was passed on the radio, 20 years ago, 30 years ago, [though] 90 percent of the music was from Madagascar or France." Now the music is a mix of international and local, which he feels is important to continuing the legacy of rock in the country – letting the next generation know that it is possible to craft a musical identity for Western ears with local roots. "I'm happy that there are many bands, but I tell them to find your personality. Eighty percent of them just copy, and that is not good. One band I appreciate is JonJoRomBona. You know they are from Madagascar! In Europe, they have their own personalities: Gothenburg[45] heavy metal, British heavy metal. But here in Madagascar, we have to find our own personality."

Many rockers were quick to place blame on the media for not doing any work on their behalf, but repudiations of their statements were brought to life by the tireless efforts of the radio personality and even a television show that airs with great success called "Rockshow." Many of the acts I interviewed have performed on the show. Another group promoting this music in the country is the three-person

44   I heard a lot about the mysterious "Metal Native." It appears he was the very first person in the country to play heavy metal on the air. Repeated attempts to track him down left Stephan and me empty-handed.

45   Refers to the Swedish city that is synonymous with the "Gothenburg Sound" as a result of the tremendous success and influence from the melodic death metal bands produced from the city. Notable acts include In Flames, At The Gates, and Dark Tranquility.

collective known as Once Radio, broadcast from Antsirabe, south of Antananarivo, on RDJ for one hour every Sunday. "All the bands here, we really want to play them on the radio show. Our objective is to promote all local bands here," said Michael, one of the young voices of the show. "There is a lot of rock and metal here in Madagascar, and there are many talented bands here," he expressed. Joined by his peers, Mialy and Mick, the three of them were more than happy to come to share why they put on a radio show for free. They do it because of the passion they have for the music, as well as the reputation they hope to change, explained Michael. "There are a lot of boys and girls that like metal and rock, but many are aided [*sic*] by those who think that people who like rock and metal are Satanists. So, many of the rockers are underground. We want to make this to show another point of view of rock and metal music to the people. We want to show that this is not evil music, that this is another kind of music like pop, or electronic. It needs to be accepted."

Like Romy and Phil, the Once Radio group supports the efforts of their rock and metal community tirelessly. No one is paying them do this, nor is anyone sponsoring them. It is all done for passion: an effort rewarded by the hopes that maybe one new rock or metal fan will emerge from their labor. I asked Michael how long he planned on doing this. The only one of the three who spoke English, he confided that he never sees an end to this labor of love. "They're [the early bands] still playing music during long years [*sic*]. It is a little difficult for them, but it's their passion." Like those early bands, he wishes to play this music on the radio "until the world knows they exist here!"

After meeting the "radio collective," it became clear that Madagascar's rock and metal community was different. It was here that in some way I reconnected with the reason I love this music in the first place: its honesty. Sharing stories and music with new and old fans alike, I beamed like a teenager the whole trip. Maybe Stephan had something to do with my injection of youth, but it more so came down to my reason for visiting this country in the first place, that untamable passion and joy that only heavy metal is able to provide its fans. Their work, labor and effort in getting this music on the radio and in festivals were, perhaps, the change in discourse their country needs. For them, rock and metal is the optimism that many in the country lost years ago.

The Unforgettable Country

I really did not know what to expect when I set out on the search for bands in the world's fourth-largest island and the ecological wonder that is Madagascar. For the most part, this country has kept itself quiet. But what was it that made this desperate country unique and wonderful? The Malagasy were at ease in sharing the wonders of their nation with a complete stranger. It became obvious I was the first outsider many had ever spoken to or had a conversation with. As one musician had told me, so many American metal bands occupy their lives, yet they have never actually spoken to an American about metal, much less anything else.

But Madagascar is more than its music. It is also a tragedy unfolding in front of your eyes. The worst poverty I had encountered would be seared into my mind forever. I would not want to mislead anyone into thinking that poverty equals complete despair, but it resembles something extremely close to a complete loss of hope. The people of Madagascar were beyond charming and made me smile more times than I can count. The Malagasy never once made me feel like a stranger crossing a new frontier, but rather like a guest touching, feeling and experiencing a new air. Everything grew familiar quickly. The same peddlers I passed daily on my walks – trying to sell me everything from shower heads, shoes, chewing gum and even a set of hair clippers – grew friendly and smiled upon passing. One specific child recognized me after our first encounter, as we kept frequenting a location in Antananarivo's Independence Boulevard. He quickly learned that I would give him spare change quietly, so as not to attract others. No more than 5 years old, he always smiled and was ever so grateful with his *"merci beaucoups."* I did give money to those in need often, mostly mothers looking for that day's meal. Children often were too fatigued to beg for money after spending the whole day searching for food scraps, so I would tuck money into their hands as they lay quietly on the streets, only to watch them open their eyes to thank me.

Stephan and I had grown very close during my trip. We learned so much about each other in a short amount of time. Our habits, routines and flaws were exposed to each other soon after I arrived. He was with me every step of the way. Our morning routines of him fetching bread and coffee for breakfast, while I prepped a few buckets of water for bathing were soon to be behind me. There was no hot water where I stayed, and baths were literally out of a bucket. Fill the bucket, heat a little water on the stove (if there was electricity), mix the hot and cold, wash, rinse and repeat. I would bathe like this in Madagascar in every single home I slept in. No flushing toilets (you would have to dump a bucket of water into the toilet to "flush" it after use), sparse electricity and our constant battles with mosquitoes would make us laugh more than we could expect. Also, a running joke throughout the trip was his striking resemblance to a well-known Malagasy singer. Nearly every day, more than a few times, too, people would yell across the street to grab his attention. One day, a group of schoolgirls was curious enough to follow us to an interview we were doing with a death metal band because they thought Stephan was "him." He just laughed it off casually (though worried that this resemblance would make him a target for thieves as a result of the singer's wealth). We laughed a lot. He was even a great sport about me trying to convince locals that he really was this singer, providing that innocent charm brought to life by his ebullient smile. Stephan became more than a translator in such a short time; he became a close friend.

It was time to leave and I had to bring myself to throwing more memories into my backpack. I left Stephan a CD of his favorite group, the American death metal band Carnifex, and made sure the whole neighborhood screamed with us one last time. I had no idea how to leave Madagascar, or even if I could. All of these countries were growing on me in a way that drew me closer to the land and its people, but Madagascar was just a bit different. This was a special place.

Stephan was going to return to Toamasina on the day I was departing. I knew he was distraught. During one of the interviews we were doing, he received the terrible news that a relative had passed away, and Stephan was not the same for days afterward. We spoke about his relative's death, which helped him cope. I promised him I would send him money to go to the funeral, which he could not afford to attend. I gave him money to buy a ticket home, to see his friends and call his family in the south of the island. I wanted him to know that he was no longer simply a friend, but a brother. Catching a cab to get to the airport in front of the apartment I rented, he negotiated a fantastic rate for me, as he was off to catch a bus home. I gave him some more money, as well as a hug that only a dear friend could provide. Thanking him again for being my voice, my guide and my confidante, it was tough saying goodbye. The little Citroen taxi turned around to catch the road that led us to the airport, driving right past Stephan as he walked to the bus station. He turned his head my way, smiling and waving. I smiled, too. The taxi driver would stop few blocks away to refuel. As he exited the vehicle, I could no longer keep my composure. Tears exited uncontrollably. I think the taxi driver understood why.

One of the first things Stephan said to me when I stepped into his world was that Madagascar is a "forgotten country," but he was mistaken. Everything that I experienced became, like Madagascar, a part of me. Nothing from Madagascar will ever be forgotten.

The airport was once again in front of me. This time, the border guards were not looking for money, but for an answer to a question I found difficult to provide on the spot. "How was your stay in Madagascar?" "It was good," I responded quietly, still wiping away what tears remained from the drive. I smiled, sharing the story of how I touched a lemur and enjoyed the scenery throughout the countryside, though I was concerned that the Malagasy were destroying the country rather quickly. The immigration officer smiled back and said, "Glad you enjoyed your trip. Sounds like you had a nice time." An understatement if I ever heard one. He stamped me out with a subtle reminder of time spent and handed me back my boarding pass. I was off to Mauritius.

With the members of Apost after a long night.

With Lallah of Kazar.

A glimpse of the treeless Malagasy countryside on the ride to Fianarantsoa.

With Markus and Njaka of Hope Era.

The gregarious personality that is Nini of Kiaki during a concert.

The very first person in Madagascar to reach out to me, Rado of the band Sasamaso.

The hardest working metal fan in Madagascar, Romy.

Black Wizard's Nary showing me his guitar collection.

Stephan and I relaxing during a rare evening off.

Stephan

MAURITIUS & REUNION ISLAND

5

MAURITIUS & REUNION ISLAND
Taking Flight in Africa's Paradises

"Do you have an invitation letter?" asked the assertive immigration officer. "Where are you staying? Who are you staying with? Do you have a phone number we can call?" He pressed more. Apparently "vacation" was not the answer he wanted. I knew this was going to be something I would not enjoy, but the next 15 minutes had me jittery. I was forced out of the line while an immigration officer rummaged through the notebook in my hand, curious as to my intentions. Had he seen more than I wanted him to? Had the immigration office observed that my notes and contacts had shown more than a vacationer's notebook? Now what? Was this the first time I would have to fess up my true intentions of visiting a country? I was called forward and committed to my plans of being honest. I was tired and morose after leaving Madagascar, so honesty was flowing through me. I had not dared cross the line of truth because I lacked the proper paperwork, visas and work permits to work as a "journalist." Thankfully, after a while and a few nervous rings, a local contact answered the phone and told them I was there on vacation and spending time at their residence. The condescending look on the immigration officer's face was all I needed to grab my paperwork and briskly walk away.

Though small, Mauritius' rock and metal passion was carried forward by an eager few hoping to get the island on the map for something other than its beaches. Rock and metal have had a precarious relationship with this isolated island for over 30 years. Some bands, such as Feedback, had amassed a sizable following and were able to perform to thousands, while many today stare at empty rooms with the hopes of someday making a difference for the next generation.

Mauritius' reputation as Africa's most developed nation and most stable democracy can also be deceiving as well. Sadly, the mistrust in the country's political system became widely apparent, as did the distrust in local law enforcement. Economists have long lauded this country's growth, but the prevailing wages among locals remained low and many were eager to leave. A remarkably diverse nation, Mauritian rockers were faced with a few challenges, notably the terrible reputation this music has in Mauritian culture. But how would rock find a stable home if many were looking to migrate? How difficult was it to actually be in an alternative music band from a nation associated with wealth and stability? And what was life in Mauritius really like behind the picturesque coasts?

Just a short distance away from Mauritius sits Reunion Island, a French department with an African musical identity. Bands on the island were not shy about their unique history, embracing the island's sounds with joy and unrestrained passion. Though isolated, their dedication and remarkable support became a story of legend – one I needed to see for myself. With an insatiable curiosity, I had to make the short trip over to Reunion to meet those who were the talk of Mauritius, as well as their island's musical landscape.

AN OCEAN AWAY

It was difficult to put Madagascar behind, but I had to. The flight to Mauritius was just a little over an hour, and I had to get my mind ready for another frontier. Everything was planned accordingly, but arriving with the feeling of unease after leaving a part of my soul in Madagascar was not expected. It was hard for me to get excited about landing in Mauritius. The small Indian Ocean island was the farthest east a country lay in the greater picture of Africa, as the mainland was 1,500 miles to the west. It is easy to see why so many friends of mine had a hard time finding the country on the map. "Where? Never heard of that place" was the common response. "Just keep looking!" I would explain.

The island's only airport was one of the most remarkable buildings I have ever seen in my life and was immediately different than anything I had grown accustomed to in Madagascar. Newly constructed, the building – with its marvelous entryway, scenic indoor waterfall and wonderful accessibility – was a great indicator of just how far Mauritius had come in the past 20 years. A well-built, unshaven, focused man in a tight-fitting grey shirt, loose-fit blue jeans and Adidas shoes poked around the arrivals area clutching a cell phone in his right hand. "Edward?" he asked in a really smoky voice as he approached. "Yash! Nice to finally meet you," I responded as our hands met, with what was most likely a look of confused relief on my face. A local metal musician, Yash had offered to pick me up at the airport, as well as show me around the country during his free time. The ride from the airport, along with a friend, proved to be just what I needed to change my dyspeptic mood from the flight over from Madagascar.

"Sit up front," he commanded, as he pointed toward his black sedan. Polite in his intent, Yash was a bit on the serious side, oftentimes reinforcing an explanation with a short story in order to make sure his intended point was succinct. He never spoke ill of anyone or anything, nor did he ever want to appear to be caught giving in. Yash was the consummate gentlemen in his hospitality and demeanor throughout my trip, often calling to make sure I was doing well, meeting people and eating "good local food." Asking if the drive was long, he responded, "Mauritius is small; you'll see it in no time." But first, we had to make a few stops.

Explaining just how small the country was during my first 20 seconds into the trip, we stopped to collect a man waving on the side of the road just outside the airport entrance standing next to a suitcase. A friend of Yash's, a flight attendant returning from a day's work, he jumped in the back seat in his pressed uniform. The two of them took turns (I still wonder if this was all a comedy script they rehearsed beforehand), telling me about the language that they were speaking, Mauritian Creole.[46] English and French were also spoken by Mauritians – even a few Asian languages still floated around – but Creole was the language spoken by nearly everyone. A quick and brief lesson in the profanity of the local language by my guides had us all in laughter, as they were just eager to welcome me to Mauritius.

The small island – visited by Arab and Portuguese explorers, settled by the Dutch in the 1600s, administered by the French in the 1700s after the Dutch left and later lost to the English during a war in 1810 – has been independent since 1968. Most of the population was of Indian descent, Hindu mostly, which is obvious in the religious customs and cultural practices. Tamil also had a presence, as did the descendants of Arabs, Europeans and African slaves brought to work the sugar cane fields. Mauritius is a diverse nation, by every sense of the meaning.

The island is also famous for bird lovers, as it was once home to the ill-fated dodo bird. The large, flightless bird with a small, rounded beak and rather cartoonish body did not last long after the arrival of man, a direct result of the fact that it could not escape its hungry captors. The bird's

---

46   Like any Creole language, the first speakers attempted to replicate the sounds they were hearing from their French masters in the plantations. Varying from the sounds of their masters' French, Creole was spoken by the majority of the slave population to each other. By the time the British arrived, Creole was well established.

image was everywhere. On the national crest, banknotes and road signs, perhaps the bird stood to remind the people of the island to take flight: prosper and look forward, do not be weighed down by your handicaps. Or perhaps it was just a funny-looking bird that made people smile.

About 10 minutes after picking up Yash's friend on the side of the road, I was informed that we were in the middle of the country. It was odd, as all I had seen was high grass on both sides of the well-lit two-lane highway. A random building appeared in the distance, but for the most part, there was not much around. The land was marked by soft hills and a mountain lit by the moonlight – barely visible in the distance to my left – a stark contrast to the skyscraper-lined business districts in the heart of Port Louis, the capital city. The airport on the southeastern tip was now off the screen of the GPS my hosts had turned on, as again they collectively laughed showing me exactly how small Mauritius actually is. Part of the Mascarene Islands chain that includes Reunion Island and Rodrigues, the country stretches for 38 miles between the island's northern and southern points, with 29 miles standing in the way of you getting from the beaches on the easternmost and westernmost points. The country also includes Rodrigues Island, 350 miles to the northeast, and the small Agalega Islands 600 miles due north, both of which hold permanent populations.[47]

---

47   The population of Rodrigues is roughly 42,000, while the Agalega Islands have a permanent population of just 300 people – and zero rock and metal bands!

Yash, giving me a brief explanation in the country's geography and history, was also doing his best to teach me how to swear in Creole. "This is what Mauritians do whenever we meet foreigners – we teach them to swear first!" Laughter ensued as I fumbled my way through words and phrases I was glad I never repeated to anyone. As I watched the high grass ease into residential and commercial areas, I was told we had one more person to pick up. Preoccupied with locating the address, Yash drove around a neighborhood in the freshly settled twilight, asking me if I remembered how to say what I was just taught for their amusement.[48] We pulled alongside a home off a busy road where a tall, bald man in a red T-shirt and backpack was waving us down.

Thibault de Robillard opened the back door and climbed in tapping me on the shoulder saying "aloe" as I turned around to acknowledge his presence. The extremely soft spoken, quiet and pleasant personality was amused by my newfound ability to swear in Creole. Thibault was highly revered in the Mauritius rock and metal community; it would take no more than another day to realize just how important he was and what he meant to every rocker in the country. We had driven another few minutes on a wonderfully smooth road, on par with any highway in the West, to find ourselves in a shopping plaza near an eyesore of a building along the highway that looked like a giant American football. I was told it was an eco-friendly building, but it lacked much friendliness to the eyes. All

---

48   Since my trip, I have forgotten how to swear in Mauritian Creole. Now Afrikaans – that I remember!

the lights, highways and the modern fare I was accustomed to in the United States felt so distant from the Madagascar I had just seen 90 minutes before. Looking around, I was in a country that was unlike any other in Africa. This is was what Africa was becoming. Though I was hundreds of miles off of the mainland, lost on a dot in the Indian Ocean, I was in an African country that was seen as the model of political and economic stability. But of course, nothing is the way it ever appears on paper.

As we proceeded to drive toward Thibault's apartment in the area known as Beau Bassin, we passed through the upscale town of Rose Hill. Yash pointed out that there were some great restaurants and very good shopping in the area, if I was interested in spending an afternoon there. "There is a particular kind of shopping to your left," joked Thibault. We began to chuckle at the sight of prostitutes to the left of Yash's car. Of course the "working women" were not amused. Had they only known of the range of emotions that triggered my hysterical laughter, I'm sure they still would not have been amused.

"WE COULDN'T HAVE WHAT WE WANTED TO HEAR..."

The music on the island is a reflection of the diversity in the country today. Because of the country's population, 1.3 million, the metal community is quite small and the genre remains unpopular in the mainstream dialogue. The roots of the country's rock and metal scene began growing, like many other places, during the 1970s, when bands like Led Zeppelin, Deep Purple and The Who were heard, albeit seldom, on the airwaves of Mauritian State TV and radio. Local bands like Blue Star and Speed Limit were frequently playing songs from these artists in bars and clubs during this time. With just a handful of acts performing rock and metal, it is a wonder that the music was able to find an audience. But how did the early rockers discover the music?

Anwar Elahee of Mauritius' first rock band, Strength, said his love of this music was influenced by what was going on in Europe. "On local radio, we couldn't have what we wanted to hear. We had mostly French pop music." He shared that he knew of this music already, but was having difficulty finding new music to listen to until his brother moved abroad to study in the United Kingdom. "My brother was sending us all video tapes, and when you received a video tape, it became an event. Friends would come over" to watch them, he explained. Former Strength bandmate Eric Desvaux added, "Some of the most popular songs could be heard on the radio, like 'Smoke On The Water,' but those songs were seldom heard." Jax of the defunct band Paranoid described this music as an accidental discovery. "It is funny because I used to listen to Boney M. at the time. But then I saw on Reunion TV [from the nearby island] a program on hard rock [sic] and that was it. I think it was '76. That was at the time of Deep Purple and Blue Öyster Cult," he remembered in his heavily French-accented English. "Even on Mauritius TV, we used to have a concert done by BBC. [I heard] Pat Travers, UFO and from Reunion television you had [sic] program every two weeks," where Jax was introduced to AC/DC and Molly Hatchet. For Jax, this music provided a "freedom," one that he to shared with others.

"It was Jax who introduced me to hard rock," explained Thibault. "First album I heard was *Made In Japan* by Deep Purple. My parents were listening to classical music and French songs, and when I heard Deep Purple I heard classical influences," he said, describing the intricacies of guitarist Ritchie Blackmore's playing and keyboardist Jon Lord's technique. "Then it was Trust [a French band], Van Halen and Iron Maiden. It wasn't on the radio, and we didn't have MTV. We only had one channel at the time. The only way to know about metal was [word of mouth] or to buy magazines from France called *Rock And Folk* and *Best.* They had articles on metal bands in both. It was the only way to learn about new bands."

With the growth and development of the tourism industry, rock quickly fell out of favor to disco and dance pop as radio followed suit, though there was a metal program on public radio during the early '90s called *Pierre, Rock, Stone & Cie.* "I was one of the metal fans who gave the DJs the cassettes of the bands that got airplay, from Kreator to Sepultura, and all the thrash bands of the era," explained Thibault. Blue Star and Speed Limit continued playing throughout the '80s, yet it was Thibault's group Feedback, a progressive metal band, that gained massive popularity in the late '80s through the early '90s until, as Thibault said, "metal suddenly became uncool" because of the grunge explosion. Thibault was a little embarrassed telling me about the success of his band, which, as related by countless others, was a big deal in Mauritius.

In his speech, mannerism and overall demeanor, Thibault always kept his humility. The French-born, Mauritian-raised musician earns his living as an editor at one of the national newspapers in the country, but keeps his hands in music regularly. As a guitarist, his talent is second to none, shredding along to his favorite records or giving improvisational performances that froze listeners in awe. He was always dedicating precious time from his busy schedule to rehearse. I have heard thousands of guitar players, yet it is one in a thousand that possess the talent that Thibault does. Every night, my ears would adjust to stunning licks and flawless playing. Along with tutorials on guitar sounds, recording technique and practice methods, his insatiable appetite for musical acumen was never kept to himself. I would see local musicians reaching out to him often, asking for advice and help on recording as well as guitar lessons – all done complimentary. He allowed me to stay with him for the duration of my trip. His third-floor apartment with a wrap-around ocean view gave me a glimpse of just how much he meant to musicians in Mauritius. They always volunteered to come to the Beau Bassin neighborhood to meet me and, to perhaps – hopefully – catch a few minutes with Thibault as well.

"He was playing for another band at that time. He went to France for his military service, and when he was back, he decided to have a group. And that is when Feedback started," shared the band's drummer, Eric, who had previously played in Strength. Having moved to France in 1985 for his military conscription, Thibault returned to Mauritius in 1987 with a new outlook on music. "I used to play with some musicians in 1985. The band was called Rockers. I came back earlier than expected. They were playing things like The Police, but when I joined the band we were playing things like Van Halen and Thin Lizzy," remembered Thibault. "It was really, really good. In fact, we had our first gig together on July 3, 1987, at the Palladium, a discothèque. It was quite nice. Our first gig was a success, and there wasn't lots [sic] of bands then. And, I think the public – the people – were more receptive than they are today," he recounted in his reedy voice. Feedback (and former Speed Limit) vocalist, Bernard, shared, "there were people who were interested in rock music, but we don't have any band playing rock, or even a professional band playing in Mauritius. But I think we were successful because we fit that niche at the time. To have this heavy sound and playing well, I think that helps."

The bands that predated Feedback were few. Notably, Paranoid and Strength, which featured Feedback's future drummer, Eric. "We were all at school and decided to form a band, but it was just for fun." Eric sat quietly in Thibault's living room on a breezy morning, almost as if he was annoyed to sit with me. But, no sooner did he begin to tell me about Strength, that his mood shifted. Sitting up, lifting the baseball cap that covered his forehead a bit more, he leaned forward smiling: "But the response was what [sic] we decided to continue and write a few of our own songs. That was in '79. I don't think that [Strength] was the first rock band in Mauritius, but in the '80s it was the most popular rock band in Mauritius." Guitarist Anwar recalled with a beaming smile, "I think we were the first rock and roll band in Mauritius! This was different from what was going on in Mauritius. It was some kind of music that other people were not playing in Mauritius; we were making people discover a new kind of music. We had our own sound, influenced by The Police. That was '79-'82." What Eric and Anwar described was a country ready to discover something exciting, a new energy. "In those days, we had all this pop music from France, but we wanted to be above the crowd, to do something different. Rock music was so appealing to us. Not the easiest road to go. We were passionate about this kind of music, especially live music. I think we managed to do that in these days," stated Anwar. "We felt [at the time] we were the rock pioneers of Mauritius," he added.

Paranoid was another band active during the early 1980s in Mauritius. Sitting with former bassist Jax, he told me of the band's role early on in the developing heavy metal scene. "There was a friend in another school that was playing this, and he needed a bass player. So, he taught me a bit of bass things, and I started like that. He had a concert to perform in his school, and he knew me and I was interested in this music, and that is how I started." Though Jax was born and raised in Mauritius, his English had a heavy French accent as a result of having attended a French school on the island, much like Thibault's. But he would explain everything in detail even if he had to pause searching for the right word. "For the first year, we were learning other bands' stuff. And then we moved to compositions." Remembering that period he paused again, considering. "I don't remember. There was X Factor, a band called Hippo Camp. I think they were the first band to sing in Creole in Mauritius." These new bands faced interested and curious audiences. "When any band was playing, it wasn't in front of metal fans. But every time it was people who didn't listen to rock. But they liked this kind of music."

Fans eventually took to the music years later. It has been said in Mauritius that rock and metal hit a new level on a magical weekend in September 1990, when Feedback sold out the nation's largest theater two nights in a row. It was a moment that is still spoken about by those who were there, and discussed by those who were not. Thibault kept a lot of memories stored away in his apartment, but after having discussed this concert with him, he reached deep into his photo albums and shared an afternoon's worth of photos and countless newspaper articles the band had accumulated over the years. "When we played at the Plaza in 1990, we were building a following. We were recording demos of our songs on a cassette player/four track, and it was [sic] played on the radio. So when we played the songs in concert, people knew the lyrics." Flipping through photo albums, Thibault was silent, allowing the memories to flow through his mind with the occasional smile cracking through. I, too, sat silently, taking it all in. "In 1990, we were the only one playing metal," he reminded me. "Our peak [was] two sold out concerts at Plaza, the place for the biggest concerts. The articles from the press after the concerts were amazing," explained Eric.

With exclamations in the press such as *"You don't have to go abroad to see such a concert,"* it was easy to see why the members of Feedback would beam when discussing these late September evenings from 1990. When I asked Bernard what he remembered most from this night, he looked directly into my eyes. "What do I remember most about that? The fun!" Having 2,000 people sing your songs back to you was an unforgettable moment, one that was not lost on the members of the band, who remain close friends to this day. "We had people who were not interested in rock music coming to our concerts; I think that is one of the things we are most proud of. We opened the door for the next generation, and we are proud of that. We are the forefathers of Mauritius rock!" Bernard exclaimed proudly. Not long after the event, Feedback would become the first Mauritian heavy metal band to record an album. In a short period of time, Mauritians were developing an appetite for the genre.

UNITED THROUGH METAL

Once the '90s came, heavy metal found itself in the position of once again falling by the wayside of pop music. Feedback's success was temporary, as radio saturated the island with the pop fare of the West. The 1990s were also a crucial point for Mauritius. The economy was beginning to see growth, yet the mistrust in the government was high, as many recent high school graduates were looking elsewhere for college education because the country lacked the resources to provide for higher education. Those who stayed remained uncertain. The music they pursued was perhaps a strong reflection of uncertainty and despair, offering an expression of optimism moving forward. One specific place on the island became the center of the Mauritian rock and metal world – a place where a new expression came to life, and new bonds were formed.

Located in the town of Rose Hill, Smash Records was a record store and meeting point for local enthusiasts and budding musicians. Jean-Michel Ringadoo, a former member of Paranoid and local metal enthusiast, explained that though there were other record stores such as Power Music Shop, "You would go to Smash. There you would see people who share the same taste because this is the only place to buy [metal] music." The owner, Tony, was a passionate metal fan who encouraged tape trading, even inside his business. His business model was not really to import records for commercial use, but to sell cassette copies of records. "They recorded it on tape and sold it to us. The first death metal I listened to is Morbid Angel. [Tony] was the one make me discover [*sic*] this type of music," recalled Jean-Michel. Yash clarified, answering my confused glances, "Yes! He would sell them on copied tapes." As I understood exactly now what was going on, he shared the primary reason why Smash Records stuck to copies of records on recordable cassettes: "CDs hadn't reached Mauritius yet, as crazy as it sounds. No Discman, only Walkman. If you had a CD player in the late '90s, early 2000s, it was a big deal!"

Smash Records was also a place to buy rock and metal magazines imported from overseas, and fans were bringing issues they had read to pass on to a new set of eyes. The Mauritian economy had yet to reach full stride – magazines and cassette tapes were rather expensive, as were import duties – but the passion for the music was full on. Explaining more about the store, Jean-Michel shared that blank tapes cost 40 Rupees during the 1990s. "I'm talking '95-'96. You can do lots with 10 Rupees,[49] but you saved until you [had] 40, the least you can pay if you did it on a TDK or a Maxell." But as Jean-Michel told me, it was worth it. "He [Tony] heard the first LP of Morbid Angel, he bring it [*sic*] and wow, it was good! And then he started to bring more. He brought Kreator, he brought Obituary, and every time he brought one, we were buying blank tapes."

Throughout my interviews, one question I would ask everyone was how they personally discovered this music. For many in their late 20s and beyond, they pointed to this small stand in Rose Hill. Guitarist of the island's only death metal band, Cryptic Carnage, Yashil was one of those. "There was a metal shop, Smash Records at that time. They were selling metal albums and rock stuff, and that's how we came across this kind of music." "This guy, Tony, influenced us a lot. This is how I got into a lot of music," commented drummer Feizal Ghanty of the disbanded progressive act Humanoid. "We are talking, I went there from '91 to '94 then I went abroad to study,

---

49   According to the United States Department of Treasury, $1.00 U.S. equaled 18 Mauritian Rupees on December 31,1995. At the time of my visit, $1.00 equaled 35 Mauritian Rupees.

but he was still there. I remember when the *Black*[50] album was released. There was a hundred *Black* albums sold in two days," recalled Vedivyasar, Feizal's former Humanoid bandmate. Vedivyasar radiated with excitement recalling his memories of Smash Records. "After school I used to spend two hours there. I had a private tutor in the area, so I had to take a bus from Port Louis to Rose Hill," he said, about a 40 minute ride. "Sometimes I would just skip tutoring just to listen to music, for the love of metal." He would even tell me that he skipped school entirely the day the *Black* album arrived in Mauritius just to take it in with everyone else, as the record played on a constant repeat to everyone's amazement. His parents never knew!

Smash Records was a networking paradise, a way in which locals with a burning passion for this music, perhaps misunderstood in their schools and families, would come together and form bonds with others who felt ostracized. "Thanks to Tony, he was living on that. It was his living, and we respected him for that," shared Jean-Michel as his voice trembled with emotion. "He was like a guru bringing music to us." Local musician Hansley would spend most Saturdays there during his teenage years. A clerk for the Prime Minister's office now in his 30s, his affinity for this music was born in that tiny Rose Hill space. "It was like a meeting place for all the rockers here. I met several members of bands there for the first time. He [Tony] promoted rock and metal, sold concert tickets and some originals, like box sets and special editions, but I think all the rockers my age

---

50   The 1991 self-titled release from Metallica, called the *Black* album by fans because of its all black cover.

bought their cassettes there." "One thing I discovered, the thing I loved about metal, is that I met loads of people, and everyone was so friendly," shared Feizal.

I was curious, so I asked Feizal if I could meet Tony. Everyone assembled in the room quieted. Dropping his head for a second, then raising it again with a look of reminiscence, Feizal whispered in a somber and quiet voice, "Tony died in 2011." Through the stream of Internet downloading and digital music sales, Tony was still able to maintain his business of selling original and copied records until 2010, if anything for the connections and friendships the store brought. Metal fans were able to connect, form lasting friendships, bond over their frustrations, connect their energy and start bands of their own – the lasting legacy of not only Smash Records, but also its late owner, Tony.

"IT'S JUST NOISE TO THEM..."

They came earlier than expected, which was a wonderful surprise. Hansley and his bandmate Devin had come to drive me to their band's rehearsal space. Hansley was just out of work from his job at the Prime Minster's office, and came wearing a shirt and tie with formal slacks. Thin, he had a curious smile, short hair and a distinct voice. Of African origin, he was more than willing to help me out, as much as I needed it. Like Yash, he called often and would stop by to check how things were going. He was typically adorned in his gauge piercings and a Dream

Theater T-shirt, with six-pack in hand – a stark contrast to his daytime office attire. Devin is, to me, the typical metal fan: extremely shy, articulate, reserved and very polite. His proper etiquette never gave in, nor did his charm. He spoke only when spoken to and was always well spoken. The three of us quickly bonded.

"It's just noise to them," laughed Hansley, while turning up the music in the car loud enough to be heard by everyone nearby. Not terribly loud, but enough to get curious looks in our direction. I wondered if the perception of metal here was similar to that in other African corners. Mauritius was different. It reminded me so much of South Africa, minus the poverty, but, of course, South Africa has a conservative movement that is potent in terms of its determination to convince the public that heavy metal is a destructive art form. But how could this happen here? Mauritius was incredibly loose, as relaxing as the breeze that calmed everything down. Or, at least that is what I thought. Devin and Hansley are members of a young band, Breed Apart, a band making its way into the small rock and metal community. The active bands at the time of my trip were few; rock and metal groups Unmind, Cryptic Carnage, Circle Red, Crave, Divoltere, Crossbreed Supersoul, Heretics, Amakartus and Shred The Glory were the current bunch that encompassed the entirety of the scene I encountered. That was it.

"In the parliament, they want [sic] to make a law to stop heavy metal here, I think two years back [2012]. Just because of Marilyn Manson," explained Hansley. The American musician has found himself at the center of much criticism and controversy over his career, acting as a scapegoat in mainstream and conservative circles for what those outside the music's periphery see as what exemplifies this music and its culture. The two were driving me to the home of their band's drummer, Steve Pumbien, for an introduction and a rehearsal. Riding down the main road that connects Rose Hill to Beau Bassin, which would take you right into the skyline of Port Louis if you continued, we rolled the windows down and let the sunset get some music into its soul. With nothing but the ocean appearing in the windshield as the hill crested, we were playing an album from the British band Carcass when I turned down the music for a second as I paused to confirm that I heard what was spoken correctly. "The government wanted to ban heavy metal?"

We arrived at Steve's bucolic family home, which also doubled as the band's rehearsal space. A valley, split by a stream that bled into the Indian Ocean, provided a tranquil setting, otherwise interrupted by the sound of crunch, distortion and drum sets taking a heavy abuse. But for this moment, the sound of the birds flying around and the distant stream took me in. Steve possessed the looseness of and charm of Hansley and the cunning of Devin. Steve, too, became someone who checked up on me frequently, just to make sure everything was going well in Mauritius. With the wonderful mountain known to locals as *Le Pouce* standing tall behind their shoulders, the band and I continued the discussion that we began in the car. They explained that after a recent incident where two drunken teenagers (in black T-shirts) took photos of themselves at a graveyard[51] in the town of Saint Jean, local rock and metal took a punch in the face. The two youths pointed middle fingers at the camera, posing in front of headstones, even laying down on one in mockery and sitting on others while flashing the universal symbol of heavy metal, the "goat." Society and the government felt the need to place the blame on heavy metal. "I am a teacher in high school, and when I tell them I play metal they think Marilyn Manson. That is their perception. We have to change them. We have to tell [them] heavy metal is not Satanic," shared Devin, who teaches tourism business classes. The actions of these two drunken teens set the rock and metal culture back, furthered the stereotype held by many and shed a negative light on the culture of the metal fan for others. Crushed, rock and metal bands saw fewer live performances and radio plays as well as an erosion of their pride.

The multicultural facets of Mauritian life and upbringing, which many hold close, came into the forefront. Most of the musicians interviewed were of Hindu cultural descent, like the two young men in the photos. The two teenagers in the graveyard not only struck a nerve in a

---

51   "Mauritius: The two Gothic teens who had desecrated graves arrested this morning." Indian Ocean Times. Thursday October 31, 2013. http://en.indian-ocean-times.com/Mauritius-The-two-Gothic-teens-who-had-desecrated-graves-arrested-this-morning_a2440. html SEE ALSO: Satanism In Saint Jean. Le Mauricien October 31, 2013. Opinion piece. http://www.lemauricien.com/article/satanism-saint-jean;   also   http://www.defimedia.info/live-news/item/41607-profanation-de-tombes-les-quatre-jeunes-liberes-sous-caution. html;   http://www.defimedia.info/dimanche-hebdo/dh-actualites/item/41462-le-profanateur-de-tombes-gothique-se-cache-de-la-police-v-b-je-vous-demande-pardon.html

country where ancestral culture remains close, but they also upset the otherwise passive rock and metal fan base, changing the discourse in the metal community.

BITS AND PIECES OF THE WORLD

"It is a multicultural country, so it is a big deal when you don't respect a religion here. If you don't respect any religion, other people are going to react, especially when you are from a different religion, you are ruining the image of another religion. That is a really big deal," said Akshay Bundhoo, guitarist of local metal band Shred The Glory. He continued by arguing that this music is poorly labeled. "I mean, you can say it is practically not allowed to play such songs on the radio. The label will destroy everything. This kind of music won't go far." We sat up late, likely until around 3 or 4 in the morning, having a few words with music entertaining in the background outside of an off-license liquor store on a pitch-black street with only the faintness of a street lamp illuminating the distance. He pointed down to the radio in his car, "They don't play our songs on the radio here. It is killing us. We are struggling. We are always struggling and we will never stop struggling." From the defeat in his voice, I felt the stigma of this music and its fan base had seemingly followed me from Madagascar. Though the hooded sweatshirt that got me cornered in that small Madagascar café was unnecessary in the tropical heat of this paradise, the glances drawn by the T-shirts with unreadable band logos and "unpleasant" imagery were still common. "There were some guys that went into the cemetery and did something to the tombs, and that's why it gets that perception," explained Doyo from the '90s thrash metal band Scar. "The government didn't need that to blame people because they listen to metal, it's still here," followed Doyo's former bandmate, Anthony, who explained that most of the perceptions of Satanism lay in the cultures that many are raised with.

"We are influenced by many cultures. We are not Westernized; we are just a little bits and pieces from around the world. It's hard to get into heavy metal here, hard for people to accept it," shared Darshan of the extreme metal band Amakartus. "Everyone has a cultural background, but it's Mauritian first," he boasted. Mauritian music was something that I now wanted to learn more about. Mainland Africa is synonymous with its traditional music, though much of that traditional music is drifting from Africans as their worlds get connected to the rest of the West. In Madagascar, Malagasy culture has had a solid evolution; its culture and norms have come from the generations that are deeply rooted on the island, most of which went through periods of isolation. However, Mauritius did not have that history of a people rooted into its land evolving into a unique identity and establishing norms and cultural traditions as deep as Madagascar's. The Dutch who originally settled had left, the Portuguese never stayed and the Europeans for the most part returned to their mainland. Indians who were brought to the island as indentured servants held their cultures close. Africans who were brought as slaves were only able to retain an identity and culture in modicum, as was the case wherever enslaved black Africans were exported. The result was an identity and a sound expressed in the language that became the tongue of the island slaves.

Sega is the music of the island. Born from the slaves of East African shores, the style of music has become synonymous with country. "The slave beat," as Hansley described, "6/8 beat with syncopated patterns, high hat and clean guitars." "Sega is a certain type of beat, like a skip beat almost. When people try to integrate it, it doesn't sound that good. Sega sounds good on its own, metal sounds good on its own," but the mix between the two would be difficult, explained Armand Gachet of the popular fusion rock band Crossbreed Supersoul. A life-long metal fan, the South African-raised Armand has tried countless times to fuse rock and Sega, with mixed results, much like a few others. Sung in the local Creole, Sega incorporates that polyrhythmic feel that I often heard in mainland southern African countries and employs local instruments such as the *ravanne,* a goatskin tambourine; the *moutia,* a hand drum; and the triangle. Other instruments such as the electric guitar, keyboards and the modern drum set are also very much a part of Sega's sound.

Lyrically, the music focuses on the lives of slaves on the island instead of a life once lost on the mainland, as well as social issues and injustices. The music was heavily frowned upon on the island, much like rock and metal are today. Musicians used to play this music in rural areas, away from populated areas, with accompanying all-night dances – based on Sega rhythms – and performances to share in their frustrations of Mauritian life as a marginalized population. Though Sega has been embraced by the population and recognized as a local music, it has also seen an evolution and infusions with other popular genres such as reggae, often called "Seggae," and Bhojpuri[52] fusions.

"If you don't sing Sega, Bhojpuri or reggae, you are out of the game," noted Jean-Michel. His deep voice carried for miles, as it should being that he also performs as an opera singer – "the nation's only confirmed tenor," he boasted under a Sunday afternoon sky. "It is our local music. I appreciate it, but there is not lots [sic] of work in that. It is not technical. We have to engage Sega. It has a meaning. You have lots of poor people in Mauritius, and there were lots of people singing it, they were suffering," he said. "And some were singing about political parties, but they were genuine. And politicians at that time, they were doing genuine things. Now they are only filling their pockets." Much like rock and metal, the music is not for stimulating dance floors as much as it serves to unite people under its themes. Lyrically, traditional Sega themes have a lot in common with rock and metal. But what about musically? Could a fusion work?

"We tried before, to play Sega and rock," but as Yashil explained, it didn't go as planned. "I think you can, maybe, if you are a progressive band, you can do it," posited Feizal. "If you are a heavy metal band, incorporating that stuff like Sega, you can practice that fusion," added Vedivyasar. Joining Vedivyasar and Feizal was Bernard of Feedback,

---

52   Bhojpuri is a language that is spoken in northern India and still has a small base in Mauritius.

who interrupted the two and concurred. "Mauritius is a multicultural island. It is a part of legacy that we embrace all this music." I shared Bernard's comment with Thibault, who wrote the songs that Feedback had generated into the soul of the country's rockers, and he snickered a bit with the greatest respect for one his best friends, saying that would be "a gimmick, really. It's two different worlds."

"We don't have that need to incorporate that music with ours," commented Jean-Paul from the hard rock band Skeptical, adding, "we don't deny it. It's a style of music unlike any other style, and it's cool to listen to all the Sega songs of the '80s, but I don't think we will use elements of that." Jean-Paul reiterated that incorporating this music with rock or metal would most likely not do anything to bring in new fans, as others throughout Africa have expressed. Every type of music, except for the occasional pop songs from the West that seep into their island life, is viewed with skepticism. "If you are a Hindu, you are going to listen to local music, Sega music, but you are going to have a stronger background in your culture," explained Akshay. According to Akshay, Hindi music and culture was very much a part of his upbringing, which once included his mother paying him 1,000 Rupees not to listen to metal. A scared mother rejoiced when her son threw out those early metal album he owned. But of course, he used the money to buy new metal records!

One band I was told to meet during my visit was Divoltere. The members are young, ambitious and outspoken, with a confidence they shared when they came to visit me at Thibault's place one evening. With the sight of the Indian Ocean over their shoulders, cold beers in their hands and an attitude that demanded attention, the members were ready to sound off. The band's sound was highly praised on the island. Genuine and unique, even non-rock and metal fans knew their music: a distinguished sound that combined the musical traditional elements of Sega with the brutality of heavy metal and the lyrical honesty of both. "I don't like to describe it, because it changes a lot. I would call it metal because it envelops the whole full-on power and noise from the past to the crowd, the energy I like to see in metal," said Rambo, the band's leader and vocalist. His handsome, catalogue-model looks, light, almost olive skin, long dark hair, and green eyes stood firm, clutching a beer. "Sega was invented by the slaves here because of repression. Everything. The beatings. The rapes. It was a gathering of people just getting the whole shitty part of life out of their system. Kind of very tribal." Asked about his motivation, Rambo stares at me briefly, holding his drink, exposed arms taking on the evening breeze. "The purest form of music is what you are feeling at that time. It has nothing to do with your roots. I wouldn't say I'm proud to be Mauritian. I don't like the idea of being proud of something you haven't chosen. I'm proud of myself, proud of being in my band, but proud of being Mauritian, I don't know." I was taken aback a bit by his comment, but pressed on, asking what he meant specifically. "We talk about the police, the government, the way they push it in people. The art of pushing it in people is enormous here, and everyone seems to be OK with it. It is never going to change unless someone does something radical, and no one does something [*sic*]. It is called a democratic country, but it's not really."

OUT OF THE TEXTBOOKS AND INTO THE FIRE

What Rambo alluded to during our interview was a repetitive theme throughout my trip to Mauritius. My work in Washington, D.C., as a pedantic intern and studies as a graduate student told me that Mauritius was unique among other African states. Mauritius was the leader in Africa on its economic and democracy ratings, far above any other country economically, and in line with Cape Verde and Botswana in political stability. Poverty was nowhere to be seen in Mauritius, though there were a few homeless around. One homeless man particularly took a liking to me in the Beau Bassin area, asking me to buy him a "Coca" every day, assuming he meant Coca-Cola. He would shadow my every move until he realized that I was not interested in his requests, and, after about four days or so, he realized that I did not speak Creole. Every day I would wake up and grab a coffee just two blocks away and run errands. Visiting the post office, bank, grocery store or getting lunch in the neighborhood became a purpose for my friend to harmlessly follow me around. I was told that there was poverty in certain regions of the country, but it was seldom seen. "It looks better on the postcards," stated Vedivyasar, who grew up in abject poverty in a rural town on the island. Though he admits that things have changed for the better since his childhood, with more opportunities around, tourists would be hard pressed to see this poverty. It stays away from the pristine coastlines, sandy beaches and high-end tourist resorts. The trip to Mauritius also highlighted one thing: all the things I have learned traveling to the countries were different than a document or a textbook could prepare me for.

Politics are a different story. Highly ranked stable nation Tunisia saw a collapse play out on the global stage with the rise of the Arab Spring. The same political party had controlled Botswana since independence, very much like Mauritius. I landed in Mauritius just one day after the prime minister had dissolved parliament, demanding new elections – a move that upset everyone I met, but provided me with a great insight into the chicanery that occurs in this country. "We have two faces, one of which is the tourism industry where they show you everything is perfect, then you come here and talk to people like us and you know what is really happening," said Eddie of Amakartus, as he and everyone in the room began to chuckle. "That is fine, talking about ourselves as the model of African countries, but what about comparing us to Singapore," added local musician Hiresh Etwaroo, who accompanied me to my interview with Amakartus. Devin, of Breed Apart, added, "If you compare us with African countries, then yes. If you compare us with European countries, then no," we are not politically stable.

Like Botswana, Mauritius has been under the control of one party since independence in 1968. All of the nation's prime ministers have been Hindu, with the notable exception of Paul Berenger, who ruled from 2003 to 2005 and whose political party became the lone exception in the nation's history of political rule. Though the country has three main political parties, it is apparent that the minority, non-Hindu population is poorly represented in government. With elections approaching, I would watch from outdoor cafes as campaign posters were hung and politicians began to make their rounds. Every single day in Mauritius, I was asked if I had been approached to cast a vote for someone, and if I was, what was I being bribed with? A watch? Money? A job? I was stunned by what I was hearing. This is Mauritius, the leader in the Mo Ibrahim[53] Index of African Governance and the nation that ranks 24th in the world in democracy, according to the Economist Intelligence Unit, making it the only African nation with full democracy status. But Bribes were what won elections in Mauritius, apparently.

"We don't have rogue elections," laughed Bernard. "I don't know if for [sic] the next 10 years our democracy will remain." The room erupted with laughter, though I knew the musicians and friends present were not laughing in mockery. The energy insisted nervousness. "You can say

---

53   Born in Sudan, Mo Ibrahim is the wealthiest African alive. A billionaire, he earned his money in telecommunications and later established his eponymous foundation, which awards African leaders initially with $5 million, and subsequent annual payments of $200,000 for leaders for transferring power democratically, providing security, health, economic development and education for their constituents. Though, to date, only former presidents of Mozambique, Botswana and Cape Verde have been recipients of the prize, said to be the largest in the world, exceeding the $1.3 million awarded to recipients of Nobel Prizes.

it is safe here, no one is killing each other on the streets, no riots, but now…with the elections," pondered Eddie, sharing that the recent election process was exposing the nerves in the hearts of the Mauritian people. One musician I met, who chose to keep himself anonymous due to his profession, stated that Mauritius was the "most corrupted country in Africa," insisting that vote buying was completely legitimate in Mauritius, and was not a rumor or myth.

One thing I found peculiar was that my rides around town were conducted with trepidation. Those who picked me up for dinner, rehearsals or drinks did so with hesitations. One specific comment from a musician early during my stay registered after a few trips around the area when I would meet people for dinner or for an interview: "Keep 500 Rupees with you, and give it to whoever stops you," he stated, referring to the local police officers' tendency to set up "checkpoints." "Do you have your passport?" I was asked daily by whomever was driving, which was typically followed by, "OK, I'll avoid the main roads, but just in case." Yash, who collected me often, explained that police checkpoints were around the main roads in larger towns. He shared the standard procedure of officers checking sobriety, as well as asking for IDs from all passengers. In my case, carrying a U.S. passport was exactly what they were looking for: an opportunity to exploit. He confided that he knew this from experience, and it was verified by every single person I asked – even to the point of hearing the testimonies myself every time I stepped into someone's car, to the effect of, "Since you are in the car, we are avoiding the main roads. I don't feel like paying a bribe tonight." Once local police realized they had foreigners they could exploit right in front of them, sensibility was out of the question.

"Politically stable? I don't think so. No! No! No!" commented Dario of the band Crave. "Many people will tell you the same things. Our lives are difficult," he added. Most of the frustrations I heard I believed to be an extension of economic frustrations. Most were unsatisfied with the low wages and future prospects. "Our unemployment is on the rise, but you can say it is safe here: no one killing on the streets, no riots. That is good!" commented Darshan. He shared that so many people on the island feel that finding work is impossible. Just about everyone I spoke to was working outside of their area of training and had ambitions of relocating to another country. Large Mauritian communities fill cities in France as well as the United Kingdom, all having emigrated for work opportunities. Paying for work is also something I was told occurred frequently, with jobs going to the highest bidder instead of being filled by those with the best qualifications.

But the numbers were still high; Mauritius is one of the good stories from Africa. Unemployment is low, investment and growth is high, as is literacy (in multiple languages) and the nation is still one of Africa's least-corrupt countries. And, most importantly, many remained. As Jean-Paul from Skeptical reminded me on the way out of the living room where we had been talking, "our economy is working. I don't know for how long, but it's working. Small and stable, it's not so bad. Most people have jobs. Mauritius is quite a nice place. A peaceful country, and, we have the beach," he laughed. For what frustrations remained, this current stock of musicians, young and old, has an outlet for their energy.

"WE HAVE A BAD FUTURE, I THINK."

"Rock and metal just allows you to release something that is inside of you," explained Armand Gachet. "It is a way of transferring your inner feelings into a musical expression. Metal is the musical form for channeling inner feelings, for everything, in fact," said Vedivyasar, his face gleaming. The honesty and sincerity of the music has connected with so many around the world, a spirit that is strongly carried by many in Mauritius. "It has been such a powerful tool for me, because I was someone really angry. We don't like to do bad things, so this is the best thing to do. It just connects to me, to us. Heavy metal is our god. You know it is the only thing that is constant there, and there is nothing that will take it from you," elated Rambo. "This music is so well cultured," commented Ravish of Shred The Glory, adding, "The techniques, the energy, the vibes you get are always positive. Even when it is aggressive, you feel the music." Bandmate Akshay nodded his head also, stating that "metal is a different energy. This music talks to me. It is the power that it delivers. It's the way you can do what you can do with metal." "The energy! This music is not afraid. We don't have to hide behind curtains to say what we have to say. Just say it, growl it or shout it. We let out what we have to say," stated the proud Darshan. Proud of admitting to the whole world he was a metal fan, he brushed aside his reservations about meeting, realizing that this music had the same impact on him as it did on so many around the world. As a heavy metal fan, Darshan knows he never walks alone. Though there was still something holding him back. Like so many youth in the country, they were hesitant to imagine a future where they could do what they aspired to do, not what they had to do to survive.

Pessimism in Mauritius was the prevalent mood as I made my way throughout the country. A handful of rock and metal acts dot the country of 1.3 million, reaching what was the peak for this music during one night in September 1990. Mauritians "are too simplistic. The rock community, compared to the rest of the population, is nothing. When people talk to me about the future of rock music here, it's like, 'whatever'. It is not going to go very far. Most of them move from Mauritius. If you are a musician in general, even local music, I wouldn't make that my life. I would much rather move," noted Anthony Grant, a hard rock musician in his early 20s. The young, long-haired vocalist had recently formed a band, Circle Red. He kept speaking about how much he wanted to move out of Mauritius. He felt trapped. Wearing all black, with a sport coat for irony, and overall Goth appearance, it was as if he had given up on his country.

"We have a very bad future, I think," commented Dario. "Unfortunately, there are some very good musicians that are in the wrong place. I always say I was born in the wrong country. We are not improving at all," he added. I was curious if his comments were just from a musician's perspective about having a bad future. He responded with figures from the economy and job growth. He, too, was feeling constrained. Was there a small island melancholy? Was the isolation of living in a country that had to be found on a map using a magnifying glass fueling cynicism? Perhaps. But, the lack of progress of the country's rock and metal music was a clear indication that many felt they would only be able to share this music with themselves.

"It's not going to work here. Not here, not now. It's not the time, it's not the moment," posited Rambo. "You will still have the young guys growing up having the metal culture, but the way the society is, we are the bad guys," lamented Jean-Michel Ringadoo. Also, the resources available to musicians just did not seem that apparent. Instruments were still imported at ridiculous costs; club owners and promoters did not want to take a chance on booking metal, nor did anyone else for that matter. Rock and metal bands pulled together in the country for concerts and promotions unlike anywhere I had seen in Africa. The Rock Society Mauritius, founded by Yash, did everything it could to promote upcoming events and music from local bands. Rock Mauritius Radio, an online music channel founded by an American ex-patriot living on the island, was also promoting this music, hoping to expand the audience. But, the lack of an audience, venues, affordable instruments and recording facilities took its toll on musicians. Devoid of the poverty and obscene corruption of other African corners, Mauritians suffered from what could only be described as "island melancholy."

"Definitely, it's a challenge. In fact, I don't think we would continue doing what we do if we said to ourselves that, 'OK, we live on a small island, and there is no place for rock here'. I think we play for passion, for progress," shared Jean-Paul. But could musicians in Mauritius succeed and create a reputation outside of their island? "Probably," relayed Thibault, but "many musicians from here don't realize what is needed to be successful. One of the problems here is you don't get bands from other countries coming to play here. Most of the musicians don't see what level is really needed. We don't have enough self-criticism. I've seen enough bands playing here that aren't tight or not playing well. The musicianship level needs to be higher than what it is." It was fantastic to get his stirringly honest opinion on the matter, being that he carries a clout on the island that is well respected. "We know there is no future for it here, but we do it because we like it. We still have hope that we will sell albums outside, or we go to play to Reunion or other countries. Today, we don't have these ambitions; we do it because we like it. We have a gig and that's it, we can't do anymore. It's hard to sustain ambitions with the lack of opportunities we have here," he continued. But, as he hopes, it is just a matter of time before a band from Mauritius is able to make their mark.

"Maybe it's just because of life or whatever, everyone is self-centered in some way, maybe that's the culture. Everyone has their own personal reasons, but we can't keep the bands growing," pondered Steve Pumbien. Unsure of what the future of Mauritian rock and metal held, he sat silently for a while, not sure what else to say. We were at the wonderful waterfront marketplace in downtown Port Louis. High-end retail stores bumped against restaurants and bars. Locals walking about, with mariners from every corner of the world unloading the stress of being trapped on ocean-faring vessels for months at a time – one beer at a time. Elbows against the railing, staring out at the empty sea – city skyline to our backs – the young, honest and confident Steve broke his silence to ask if I enjoyed my stay in Mauritius, while staring at the skyline's lights reflecting off the still harbor. I was departing the country the next day and as a measure of his gratitude, he wanted to show me his hometown's charm, and, of course, to make sure I was eating well. A few musicians had come to meet up one last time – no voice recorder in their face, no questions, just a night out. We drove around Port Louis, took scenic photos, shared some great stories, laughed, and, of course, listened to metal.

Darshan had come by again to Thibault's apartment the day before to pick me up and share his favorite vista on the side of a mountain with his Amakartus bandmates, and to present me with a few gifts: a traditional instrument, a bottle of Mauritian rum, and a card thanking me for my visit. Handshakes and photos have been a part of every trip, but the gifts, CDs and T-shirts were always humbling. I only wanted their stories; instead I got their friendships. Those at the waterfront that night wanted to thank me, too, much like Darshan did the previous day. I was graced by their generosity. Their country, their cultures and, of course, their beaches were something I was happy to experience for myself. Though these particular metal fans were isolated, they were not alone. Rock and heavy metal music was an extension of passion, life and the continued understanding that no matter where you find yourself as a metal fan, you are always in great company.

I stared out to a pitch-black sea with Steve, backlit by the night sky now, as the downtown lights were shutting down, knowing that my map will always have Mauritius a little larger than most. I woke up the next day and headed for the airport, once again accompanied by Yash. I smiled, and went about everything without frowning once. An unexpected memory happened in Mauritius, and an unexpected trip to a new place popped up. I was off once again. This time it was Reunion Island.

REUNION ISLAND

Adjusting my eyes out of the window from the half-filled plane, one of the most majestic sights I have ever seen came into view. An ominous mountain range, full of sharp, jagged, slicing calderas and defiant peaks stared right back at me. The contrast of the green laying firmly on the mountains and postcard-blue water left me breathless. A small city and roadways also materialized, but my eyes were not leaving the mountains quite yet. I was oblivious. I never "prepared" for landing, I never fastened my seatbelt, I never turned off my portable music device, nor did I even notice we had landed. Reunion Island was a place I had only dreamed about and a place that I was convinced was not real – mostly because of how quiet the islanders were in their arts and politics. Even now, having been there, I still feel that the blur that was my time spent on the island was just that: a dream.

At just 39 miles long and 28 miles wide, Reunion Island was a place I had not really known much about. I heard so much from Mauritians about Reunion's music scene, and great arts scene in general, that I decided to book a trip over. An even smaller dot on the map between Mauritius and Madagascar, Reunion was just a little more than a hundred miles away and a short flight from Mauritius: just 25 minutes of crystal blue water to fill my eyes with. But was this Africa? This was a part of the geographic map of Africa, but politically this was France's overseas department. After I was able to collect myself and walk off the plane, the sign above Passport Control read, "YOU ARE NOW ENTERING THE EUROPEAN UNION." Well, legally, I suppose I was. But in just a few minutes, I was in a place that resembled nothing of the sort.

The scenic airport – mountain range on one side and ocean blue on the other – was soon behind me as I boarded a local bus,[54] heading south from the capital city of Saint-Denis on a highway that has no rival. Being that there was no population in the middle of the island except for a small number of those choosing life off the grid, I was taken aback once again by the highway that threaded the space between the ocean and the mountain range. Once out of Saint-Denis, a massive rock wall, about 200 feet high, sent a frightening shiver through me as I glanced up

---

54   The bus used to take passengers between cities on the island was nothing more than a city bus.

at this and noticed the fencing in place to catch whatever the earth felt like throwing down. Just four lanes of road separated this shiver from the hard crashes of the Indian Ocean, which punished the small wall protecting drivers from the sea's intentions. While the road rose a bit, and moved slightly away from the coast, the ocean stayed in view the whole time.

THE GODFATHER

Sitting in the terminal quietly – his elbows resting on his knees, hands crossed, head down, he lifted his salt and pepper head as to only be disappointed each time a person walked past. Finally, he did a double take – this time while standing up and smiling. The tall, thin man knew who I was, but still asked, "Edward?" "Yes," I responded, "Nice to meet you!" He insisted that I call him Blanc-Blanc, or Blanc for short. "White-White?" I asked; he laughed. His smile was large, and his stride showed confidence. He moved as only a man of stature could: never unsure, always cool-headed. Blanc was eager to show me around his adopted hometown, and country, for lack of a better term. Born in France and raised in the South American territory of French Guiana, Blanc not only manages a great performance theater in the city of Le Tampon, serving as a major player in promoting all types of music throughout the island, but he also fronts Reunion's legendary Nazca. The progressive rock band has released a record to much acclaim and has amassed a great deal of clout and respect locally. The "Godfather" of Reunion hard rock/metal, as so many referred to Blanc, had a moxie paralleled by what Thibault had in Mauritius, with so many eager to converse with the man "in the know."

I was curious about Reunion's rock and metal scene, one that I had observed as being extremely vibrant. Though not officially an African country, Reunion sat in the continent's greater expanse, and, after speaking with so many, the islanders identified more with an aspect of their roots that very much had everything to do with Africa, and less with Europe. The island was claimed by France in 1642, first as a penal colony, and later as a slave colony. Though Portuguese explorers had mapped the island a hundred years before, no permanent population settled until the French used Ile Bourbon, as it was once called, as a trading port for the French East India Company in 1665. Much like Mauritius, the island is extremely diverse. Slaves from Africa and Madagascar have a visible mark on the population, as does the heavy French influence. Arab, Chinese and Indian heritage also paints the island's 800,000 or so residents. And like Mauritius, though French is the official language, a local Creole is the preferred tongue. Though, I do not know how to swear in Reunionaise Creole.

Less than an hour after meeting Blanc, I was sitting in a well-equipped recording studio with the island's metal monsters, Warfield. The band was recording a new album, but was more than happy to stop and introduce themselves. Part of what brought me to them was the praise they were receiving from their contemporaries in Mauritius, who became fans of the band after a performance there in 2013. I was told that they were unique by so many, including Blanc and Thibault, who played me a video of the band performing something I had never heard or seen: an African metal band performing local music with a traditional band.

The music is called Maloya. Similar to Sega, the music has slave origins and also features a 6/8 beat, yet varies in instrumentation and presentation; Maloya does not feature the dancing Sega does. Instruments such as the *kayamba,* a rattle made of sugar cane tubes; *rouler,* a large barrel drum played by hand; and the *piker,* an idiophone made from bamboo, are all present in Maloya music. Also, like Sega, Maloya lyrics convey hardships and discontent, as themes almost exclusively address politics, poverty and, of course, slavery. "Music from slaves, real roots music," described local veteran musician Mangloo. "It's really music of the soul. I feel it is like rock music. It's a more spiritual music. You can find the same energy in the Maloya. It's raw, really raw. It works really well for that reason," he said of the musical infusion.

Mangloo is a confident man. He has performed for over 30 years and was more than happy to sit with me, though he confided that metal was not something he understood as well as rock and roll. Yet, he had grown quite proud of the reputation being developed by a few metal acts on the island, notably Warfield, who have not only taken to incorporating Maloya into their band's metal music, but have also performed and collaborated with noted Maloya act Lindigo.

THE PRODIGIES

"With this project," explained Warfield's drummer Guillaume Montauban, "Blanc put [us] in contact with the leader of Lindigo, who was interested with this heavy sound of hard rock and metal, and he knew that we were already inspired by Maloya, so it was very natural for us to work together." Though the members of Lindigo initially rejected the idea, Warfield pressed on. "This was an exception. And with this project, it's specific even because metalheads hear that it's still metal even if you can hear a *kayamba* or *rouler*. For people who are not metal and for general people, when they listen to Warfield and Lindigo, it's metal for them. Even if it's mixed, the project, the music it's very," Guillaume paused for a second. "I think it's quite possible to say that this kind of music, it's not metal, but it's a very a big part of us. The Maloya is not the way to play music; it is in the spirits of the songs, a way of expressing yourself. Metal is the music I really like, but Maloya, it's in my blood," expressed Guillaume, who was joined by his brother and guitarist Alexander, who nodded his head up and down. Guillaume hid his shyness behind surfer model looks: sunburnt skin, blue eyes and rugged long hair. He confessed his English was not that great, but was more than willing to try, so long as I spoke slowly. In contrast, Alexander was the toughest looking man I had ever come across. Extremely ominous, large, well built, his eyes imposed fear, yet his body language did anything but. Though Alexander barely said a word, it was a nice relief to see him smile from time to time. None of the other members spoke English, but were more than happy to try. The Montaubans are descendants of some of the earliest settlers on the island, with a palpable slave bloodline as well, which is what led Guillaume to proudly proclaim this music was in his blood. "It has become natural to include this kind of rhythm in our music. We are proud of our culture, and that is why we play." The members of the band explained that it was not something that happened overnight, but gradually since the band's inception in 2005. Forming as an extreme metal band and evolving into what Alexander describes as "metaloya" took the better part of 10 years.

Though Warfield are unique in their approach, other bands on the island have not shied away from the influence of Maloya. Ludovic Maillot fronts the Le Tampon-based Rebirth, a thrash metal band whose semblance onstage conjures the history of the island. "I am inspired by the imagery and this period [slavery] of Reunion for my lyrics. I'm inspired by the traditional things from Africa, but it's hard to color all the songs with Maloya rhythm unless you want to take another musician. It's hard to find musician," stated the reserved vocalist. Sitting under a starlit sky, we were surrounded by musicians from other bands who could not overstate how important Warfield was to the island, as well as how much their infusion of Maloya was influencing others. "I have been influenced by them for two years," affirmed Rudy of the band Nightmare For The Child. "I want to push forward this laboratory that is music to try different local things in music. The metal spirit is here." "But it is more interesting to try every sound we can find in Reunion," interjected his bandmate Nicquez. Yann Cadet, a local metal guitarist of the band Vacuum Road, also explained the pride that came from Maloya music was the result of the celebration of being from Reunion Island: "We are French, but our story is for us [sic]. It defines our history; we don't have the same history of France. We like to dance different," he exclaimed. "It's our story, our roots. It's the music to show the difficulties of life. It was the forbidden music," added Eric, vocalist of the thrash metal/roots band, Black Babouk.

"You have to know that 30 years ago you couldn't play Maloya. You had a white government; you had black people playing this music," explained Mangloo. Blanc, sitting next to him, nodded his head and helped explain that the music's history was so controversial that Maloya was banned, not just frowned upon. "It's against establishment," exclaimed Blanc. He added, "35 years ago if you played Maloya, you went to jail. You had to play music in sugar cane fields. The music was protest, and the music was the tool. The music was forbidden for that." In recent memory for a certain generation, Warfield would have been public enemy number one as Blanc described, solely for incorporating Maloya.

The banning occurred as a result of the perception of communist teachings from the Creole language lyrics. Lyrics of protests, injustice, racism, economic inequality as well as the island's slave history were taboo. "There was a political message against the French government from the people of Reunion. It was a conflict by the people from the slaves and the white people from France. This was the ending of colonialism," explained Blanc, who remembers this period well and is ecstatic that members of current rock and metal acts are actively involved with keeping Maloya's spirit fresh through a new interpretation. "This is very interesting for the future, these bands are trying to put their influences of Reunion in their music. They listened to rock and roll music when they were young, but now they add the local rhythm and instruments," he stated as he smiled proudly. By the 1980s, Maloya was free.

THE LEGEND

Blanc had seen rock and heavy metal music grow significantly over the past decade or so, and it was not always popular in Reunion. Rock arrived in Reunion around the same time the electric guitar arrived on the island in the 1950s. The very first rock groups formed during the late '50s and early '60s, much like in the West. Groups such as Playboys, Les Superjets, Les Djems, Les Rhythmers and Pop's Experience were the very first to grab the spirit of rock and roll on the island. Though the acts were playing cover songs, audiences were excited at this new sound and energy carrying them across dance floors. After a few years, acts began performing original music. Bands such as Test, Carousel and Fun In The Sun came around the late 1970s and early '80s. "You know we had friends, and you talk to them and they had the same records, the same people, the same artists, so why not play these things together," explained Jean-Michel Pouzet of Fun In The Sun. "We were about three bands, and it was very easy for us to play everywhere," The Mauritian-bred musician recalled those early years with fondness on the balcony of his home overlooking the ocean. Wise and respected, his fondness for the music was apparent, as was the pride he had in explaining those early years to me. Most of the musicians from that period have moved on, disconnecting their cables from their amps entirely, yet Jean-Michel remained active and connected, earning a living as a music teacher. Recalling that period, he continued, "at this time they [fans] were very hesitant, I think. We didn't play covers. We played our original songs, and it was very hard to force them to listen to these songs. Without being pretentious, I think we opened the road. We were the first pioneers. When they were young, they came to see us play," he pointed to Blanc sitting next to him. "They saw on us on stages, guitars and effects. So many young bands, they started because of us." Blanc nodded his head back and forth and smiled, affirming, "I wanted to make music because of them!"

It was not long after he was inspired that Blanc formed his first band, Overkill,[55] in 1983. "I made music because of Test and Fun In The Sun. I saw it on stage and being loud saying, 'This guy loves what he's doing'. This is the miracle of stage. It's like going home." Sifting through old photographs and newspaper cuts from those early days, Blanc laughed

---

55   Halfway across the world in New York, a band of the same name was performing and recording, unbeknownst to the Reunion Island band members. The U.S. Overkill is widely considered one of the best bands in thrash metal and has amassed a great fan base worldwide, including Reunion Island.

out loud, perhaps in a sign of embarrassment, putting the photos in front of me. "A lot of people remember this band because we were on stage with a lot of visuals. You see this look we had? It was heavy metal. I was 19," he exclaimed while glancing at his photo that graced the front page of a newspaper: hair grown out, makeup on his face, tight black jeans, white high tops, and a ripped sleeveless shirt. He sat quietly for a minute in reminiscence. While there were plenty of other acts, few were able grab the attention that Jean-Michel and Blanc did with their groups.

During this time, Blanc also had the opportunity to spread this new love of metal to others by way of the airwaves. At the time, radio was slow to promote this music, so Blanc took the initiative with two friends. "I did a metal show in the '80s, before we had the band, called Overkill regarding [sic] the Motörhead song, and we also named the band after that. Maybe two, three hours on Saturday. It was nice. The name of the radio was Azote 102." Along with future Overkill bandmates, Kismet Patel and Pilou, they played everything they could get their hands on during the time of free radio in France, 1981. I recalled a conversation in Mauritius with Thibault about hearing metal on Reunion radio in the early '80s when he would visit his grandmother, who was living on the island. "When I was going to Reunion, one thing that strike [sic] me is they have three radio stations, and one of these radio stations was playing metal music, and it was Blanc-Blanc. I brought my radio cassette and I was recording the show. I discovered a lot of bands. I discovered Accept first on his show, and a song from Dio, 'Holy Diver'. I didn't realize it at the time, but I was about to meet Blanc-Blanc four or five years later when he would come to Mauritius as a sound engineer." Blanc smiled and recalled the moment that Thibault approached him and recognized his voice. The two of them became close friends and even perform together from time to time when Thibault joins Nazca, a band that has become well revered on the island by rock and metal fans, for the occasional performance.

Rock and metal continued to grow through the '90s and '00s and remains a very close-knit community within Reunion Island. Countless rock and metal bands have formed since the 1980s, with a strong tradition continuing today. Reunion boasts several music festivals throughout the year, including a metal festival in October. The island's size in this case does not feel like the inhibiting force that many in Mauritius attributed to pessimism in the scene. Like those in Mauritius, many felt comfortable with life in Reunion. Scenic, every ride around town always had the driver, whomever it was, pointing out the surrounding landscape, contemplating why anyone would ever want to live anywhere else.

There were many who feel that rock will continue to expand on the island, notably Jean-Michel, who helped put rock on the creative map for the island. He explained to me that musicians typically hold their guitars close, but on Reunion they hold theirs closer. Perhaps it has something to do with the island's musical history and the period when rockers were surreptitiously defending their peers performing the "forbidden music" of Maloya. But the heart of the musicians kept pulsing for a chance to be heard elsewhere throughout their region, their continent and this world.

Part of the absence of pessimism comes directly from the overwhelming funding that Reunion Islanders have for the arts from the French government. Given Blanc's status as a director of a theater and organizer of the island's annual jazz festival, he gave a valuable insight in how much the arts were looked after, even taking me to the Office of Arts and Culture on the island. He explained how lucky they were to have this luxury. The French, throughout their history, have held the arts and culture to high esteem, which includes rock and heavy metal music. At the time of my trip, Nazca were booked to perform in India and needed help buying airline tickets, so Blanc went to collect forms to apply for airfare support. He even once took advantage of extra funding to book Brazilian heavy metal giants Sepultura in 2010 to play a free concert. Things are different here, to say the least. Nonsensical claims of Satanism and evil-doing by the rock and metal community are absent. The Montauban brothers told a comical story of a concertgoer asking their grandmother how she felt having raised two grandchildren who played the Devil's music. Through Guillaume, she responded facetiously, "Oh really? I didn't know Satan had his own music!" That incident was the only time the matter was even brought up during my trip to the island, and the story still amuses many. Fact is, heavy metal has a different life and reputation on the island for two reasons: the strong liberal European influence that still permeates the island,

and the inclusion and respect for the island's true musical history, Maloya, from the heavy metal community.

THE DEPARTURE

My visit to Reunion Island highlighted a wonderful culmination of Africa's Indian Ocean islands. Passing by is never something a traveler does. After a certain amount of time, a piece of you is left. Whether you meet just one person or a whole village from that new place, you have created a memory in a new frontier. As always, places leave a mark in memory and heart forever. Mauritius and Reunion reminded me of what I set out to do, and oftentimes left me speechless. These three islands also showed me just how diverse Africa really is: from Madagascar, one of the poorest nations in the world, to Mauritius and Reunion Island, a little piece of Europe's industrialized economy floating between the two islands. This specific trip had also showed me just how powerful rock and metal music can be: how a genre without commercial appeal transformed itself into something so inclusive. Blanc insisted on driving me to the airport in his oversized work van so I could get a view of the volcano side of the island – an active volcano that sometimes wreaks havoc on Reunion Islanders. Numerous instances have tested their grit: riots over living conditions and employment levels, the chikungunya disease epidemic in 2005-2006 and volcanic eruptions that have stopped the island's motion. Reunion Island was a test for me on certain levels, too, and as I kept climbing the scenic mountain highway, enclosed by the same stunning greenery I saw from the airplane window, I just kept thinking of how I needed this journey to continue.

Blanc shared how grateful he was that I had come to visit, even if for a week. He had been following my travels and articles on the Internet and was excited about the opportunity to be able to introduce me to the island's rock and metal musicians. This music, he reminded me, was not "for people without brains," hoping the local musicians were gracious and articulate enough. I laughed and thanked him for his generosity and hospitality. Reunion Islanders were beyond gracious. And again, I was blessed with friendship in a place that I never even knew had a population until I began to hear from metal bands on the island. On extremely short notice, they took me in, accommodated sleeping arrangements, invited me into their homes, made sure I had transportation and of course, made sure I was fed.

As the boarding pass was returned to my hand, I turned to Blanc saying, "*nartrouv*," the local word for "thank you." He laughed, bowing in his gracious manner, smiling and thanking me once again. If he only knew just how grateful I was at that moment. I turned and walked toward my boarding gate. My eyes, my body were exhausted. Yet once again, I was ready for what was in front of me.

With Reunion Island's At First We Scream. That is Blanc in the middle.

Breed Apart rehearsing. They could be heard for quite a distance!

Mauritian badasses, Divoltere.

*With Darshan (L) and Eddie of Mauritius extreme
metal band, Amakartus. Two of the nicest guys you could
ever meet.*

With Bernard of Feedback. Notice a shy Thibualt in the right of the photograph.

With members Warfield, Nightmare For The Child, and Rebirth in Le Tampon, Reunion Island.

(L to R) With Yashil, Steeven Pumbien, Hansley, and Yashil's Cryptic Carnage bandmate, Ivan in front of downtown Port Louis, Mauritius.

ZIMBABWE

6

ZIMBABWE

Reigniting Africa's Broken Heart

"Last call for passenger Edward Banchs, flying to Luanda. Last call for passenger Banchs, flying to Luanda. Please report to the boarding gate now." That is what I imagined the airport agents repeated over the intercom. An empty seat in an airplane heading to the capital city of the country I was to be flying to, as one lucky passenger got to spread out just a bit more because of the space I would not occupy. The months of worrying as to whether I could secure the proper travel documents to one of Africa's largest mysteries, Angola, passed by while I tussled between embassy phone calls and letters. I now had a resolution – I could not secure them. Instead, I found myself scrolling through my iPod and a book waiting quietly for a flight to another African capital, one that had made the news for all the wrong reasons over the past years.

The sun set ever so slowly over the brown and dusty landscape as the twinkle of the city lights came to view. Harare is difficult to describe; it is a contrasting network of well-built neighborhoods and a beautiful skyscraper-filled city center that takes your breath away, as much as it is the symbol of this continent's despair. On paper, Zimbabwe is the second poorest country in the world: ruled by an oppressive leader whose nefarious ways put him in the same despot class as North Korea's Kim Jong-un. The country had been devastated by troubled stories of genocide, mass murders, the world's worst economy since the Second World War, as well as complete disregard of social and political rights.

This was now my second trip to Zimbabwe. I previously visited in 2007 and fell in love instantly. I had fallen for a country with the second worst inflation in the history of humanity, as well as a severe food shortage that left supermarket shelves empty. Hungry and broke, millions fled to neighboring countries, while the country dwindled away into further despair. Why would I ever want to go back?

I came to a country with just five active rock and metal bands in the hopes of understanding how the musicians live and to what adversities face them. I found a close-knit group of musicians working together to build a healthy and sustainable music culture. Though there are plenty of trepidations, and even fear, the members of the bands push forward with the same goal: to validate their efforts. This trip became more about life as a Zimbabwean than life as rocker in Zimbabwe. One aspect that also became very clear to me early on in my trip: Zimbabwe is one of the most difficult, if not the most difficult, country in Africa to exist as a musician.

ZIM-BOB'S-WAY

It was dark and quiet as he approached. The lights outside the airport were barely lit, as a gentle breeze made most of the noise heard for miles. The snapping of the flag and the clanging of the halyard of the nearby flagpole kept me distracted for about half an hour just before I heard, "There he is!" over my right shoulder. Turning my head slowly, I watched him lumber my way in his long shorts and oddly out-of-place hiking boots. "Hey, I'm Chris," he said. The founder of the country's most popular heavy metal band, Dividing The Element, put his hand out, with an effervescent smile. "Nice to finally meet you," I replied, as we locked hands. He was more than happy to take me in on short notice; it was that morning that I called him to inform him I was flying into Zimbabwe. Having flown back into Johannesburg for a night with the intention of departing for Angola the following morning, instead I found myself at the airport calling Chris to tell him I had just booked a trip to Harare. I knew of Dividing The Element, and Chris and I had traded stories about Zimbabwe and metal over a few late-night Internet chats, but to be there was a quiet relief to the stress that was tested in the hopes of an Angolan visa.

Chris is a one-of-a-kind personality. He was always pacing. Back and forth, side to side. It always appeared as if he was looking for something. The frantic nature of his pacing was complemented by his unrelenting worrying. He always seemed to be worried about something, though what remained a mystery. His beard was long and covered most of his freckled face, his ginger hair longer – hiding his pencil-thin glasses. He forgot things constantly, even the most trivial. He seemed confused by where he was going half the time, even though he had lived in Harare his whole life. The money in his pocket was never organized – always balled up. And, he always asked twice about what everyone was talking about. His mind seemed to wander quite often. Well, at least it always seemed that way. Also, he had a manner about him that was constantly seeking approval. He is the type of person who is afraid to disappoint whomever he was trying to please, and his emotions were never far away as every reaction was genuine and sincere – a trait that is peculiar and charming at the same time.

Hastily, Chris marched me over to his car while he fumbled his keys between his hands and his pockets. He needed to be somewhere in town and apologized for his tardiness. Throwing my suitcase into the trunk, we began the drive into Harare. The drive was slow. The streets were dark – there was no electricity. Potholes rocked us back and forth and had us weaving left to right, around the imagined and unseen, as we kept up our conversation. Zimbabwe's roads are atrocious. Except for a few – those leading to and from government offices, high-end residences, and any other destination favored by the country's president, known locally as "Uncle Bob" – roads here remained without proper maintenance.

"So things are still 'Zim-Bob's-Way'?" I joked. Chris laughed with a hint of tragedy, saying, "Things still have not changed." I was excited to see the differences with my own eyes, but, of course, was nervous, too. Zimbabwe is sadly "one of those countries" – the type of place that satisfies the imagination of African cynics and "told you sos." The world silently watched this country collapse. Few knew about this country and its leader, even fewer understood Zimbabweans.

My reason for returning to this country was not just my curiosity of metal; it was because Zimbabwe is my favorite African country. I did my dissertation work on the country and easily know more about this country than any other in Africa. Hell, most Zimbabweans even think I'm from there. There really is no place like this on earth for me, nor is there anyone like Zimbabweans – the most endearing and caring people I have ever encountered.

But I had patiently waited for metal to flourish. I knew it would, but things were still not well enough for the genre to evolve like it was in neighboring countries. During a trip to Victoria Falls in Zimbabwe's north in 2007, I bonded over my love of the American band Machine Head with a local metal fan. We both spoke about metal, and how much we would enjoy seeing metal flourish in this country. In some ways, *Heavy Metal Africa* was born from that trip. I relayed this story to Chris over the drive to his house, and he, too, was excited that this music had begun to take root in the nation. However, there is always a bit more behind the veil, and Zimbabwe came with a set of problems that musicians in Africa seldom encountered. It was clear from the outset that this story was going to be less about music, and more of hope and optimism instead.

Chris' family's home is situated in one of the many quiet and picturesque suburbs of Harare, Greendale. Wide tree-lined roads mark the paths of one of the most beautiful cities I have ever been through. Walls gave the homes some privacy, but were still able to be seen through driveway gates. Massive, mostly single story homes built in the in 1960s with spacious yards came to view for split seconds as we drove by. These bucolic homes are a reminder of how the people in this country used to live – a life limited to just a few now.

Chris was elated when we pulled into his home and found the lights on. Electricity, or "ZESA" (Zimbabwe Electricity Supply Authority) as it is known colloquially, ran for just a few hours a day. In his home, it ran about four to five hours from about eight p.m. to midnight/one in the morning. Some had their power come on while they were at work, others while they slept. I considered this a brush of luck in a country that is under the constant hum of generators. It gave us time to charge our computers and cell phones, and fire up the stove for a proper home cooked dinner at the same time every night. Chris and his family admired my quick adaptation to the local situation. They were embarrassed, but I reassured them I felt right at home.

A gas stove outside their house was sufficient for breakfast and coffee in the morning. Lunch was a luxury, and dinner was accommodated however we were able to do so. Chris' father – wizened, continually frustrated, but calm – always led the conversations. On my first night, he shared a classic joke that has become a synonymous greeting for newcomers. "What did Zimbabweans use before candles?" he asked. I waited, knowing the punch line as I have heard this one before, but it never gets old. "What?" I responded naïvely. "Electricity!"

We were eating dinner in the dark every night with the exception of candles and moonlight, but it was a way of observing a local family live through a struggle in a unique way. However, engaging with Chris and his family over dinner, sharing stories, jokes and anecdotes, it was easy to forget we were in the dark.

The day after I arrived, I was able to see their house and the surrounding property. I had to laugh at what I was seeing. A large brown yard housed the dusty collection of old European car frames stored around Chris' family's home. Quietly marking a time gone by, Volvos, Mercedes and Volkswagen Karmann Ghia frames sat silently collecting dust – car enthusiasts would salivate at the sight. I started to laugh. Not meaning to mock the collection, I could not help but notice the subtle irony of, once again, finding myself surrounded by abandoned cars: in Botswana with Wrust, in Kenya with Parking Lot Grass, and now here, in Zimbabwe. Chris noticed my chuckle but did not bother to ask why I was smiling. For Chris and his father, these old and unusable car frames were just gathering cobwebs and rust; no one was interested in buying them. Chris walked past them, describing their ambitions to see those cars move again, but the reality of such a task in this corner of the world seemed distant.

Just feet behind his house sat the garage. He opened the door to reveal the emptied out space his band uses to rehearse. Drum set, guitar amplifiers, and microphones came to view in the vagueness of the moonlight. He excused himself for a few minutes so he could tend to the generator, behind the garage. A few minutes after verbally questioning aloud what plug went where and clumsily starting the generator, the garage lights turned on to reveal empty beer cans scattered about, as well as a few band posters.

Smiling as he re-entered, we sat for hours sharing music, trading stories and adding to the collection of empty cans. He played me some of his band's music, all of which is performed in Chris' second language, Shona. The song he played was called "Upenyu," which means "Life." It was a message, he explained, for all Zimbabweans to remember what matters most – even through hardship. Though many in the country speak multiple languages, for outsiders, the sight of a Zimbabwean of European descent speaking local languages is perhaps unexpected. Truthfully, this is not uncommon. Chris learned the language of his neighbors, schoolmates and friends a long time ago, and was always communicating in Shona. It was a perfect complement to the heavy metal I was hearing, as the rhythmic nature of the language blended efficaciously to the punishing, localized bounce of the music. "You want to get a metal scene in Zimbabwe, do it in a local language," he said, as his back turned away briefly to fetch two beer cans. "How are you going to do that locally without speaking Shona? Most of the white people aren't metalheads anyway," he shared in a matter of fact tone, sitting down next to me holding up his can for a toast.

Chris' Dividing The Element members – Archie, Matt, and Newbz – joined him the following day for a short rehearsal. They were excited to gather and share their stories with me. The band was two weeks removed from their first concert. They boasted that it was the very first heavy metal concert in Zimbabwe, which to an extent was true. "It's a very high energy, and people saw that energy," explained Chris. His cousin, Derek, who fronts the band Evicted and sat just feet away, shared, "When Dividing The Element did their gig, a lot of people had never been to a heavy metal or hard show in their lives."

For music fans, metal or not, this was the beginning of a new day in Zimbabwe's music scene; a generation that had grown up in a country on the way down was working to bring positive attention to a country in desperate need. Even those not particularly fond of extreme music were happy to see this event taking place because it marked a positive step forward within the local arts community.

Things had changed drastically in this country over the past 20 years.

Every single person you meet who is old enough describes their country under different circumstances, an era of enjoyment and bliss. That era was when Zimbabwe had the best quality of life on the continent, the best education in Africa, the largest middle class in the whole world, the lowest unemployment and was the largest food-producing nation in a continent riddled with hunger: Africa's breadbasket, as it was once known. Zimbabwe was not only Africa's leader, but it was also a nation on par with many of its European counterparts. Zimbabwe was paradise. What many have described to me as the greatest time in the greatest place on earth must have been the 1980s of Zimbabwe. Life was a breeze – pleasant, peaceful and prosperous. Life in this place at this time was perfect.

The country once known as Southern Rhodesia found itself in turmoil and war during the 1970s. Under the rule of Ian Smith, Southern Rhodesia was fighting two battles – one amongst its rebel movements and one among its colonizer – when Smith declared independence from the British in an act known as the Unilateral Declaration of Independence (UDI) in 1965. With the UDI came economic sanctions, the first of their kind anywhere in the world. War also hit the colony as the wave of independence that swept across the continent passed right over Rhodesia, and many in the country felt it was their time to move on from minority rule. Eventually a truce was reached in 1979, as fighting sides ended their battles. Independence was declared in April 1980.

The opposition movement, Zimbabwe African National Union (ZANU), was led by an erudite product of Jesuit schooling named Robert Gabriel Mugabe. Having spent time in and out of prisons as a political prisoner, in

1975 Mugabe made his way to Mozambique, where ZANU took up arms against the Smith-led Rhodesia in what is referred to as the Rhodesian Bush War. That war ended in 1979 after a formal ceasefire in December. Mugabe stood defiantly against Smith and his minority rule and emerged as a liberation hero for his country and a continent. In April 1980, he was elected Zimbabwe's first prime minister.

Mugabe took complete control of the government as president in 1987 and presided over a one party state. Every aspect of life was affected, including music. Mugabe is a dictator as terrible as the world has seen. Zimbabweans now live in fear as a direct result of the country's leadership. Chris and his family understand this very well as they asked me kindly not to use their surnames. Some of the musicians you are about to meet have also adopted pseudonyms for their protection.

AND THEY STARTED TO SING

Navigating our way into a quiet home in a neighborhood not far from Chris', he and I discovered a pleasant smell coming from the kitchen as the quiet gentlemen was cooking lunch on his gas grill. He had not had electricity for two days, but was unfazed. The sun was out, the weather was pleasant and good spirits filled the house. Ike Mhlanga is the sort of person who could make any room feel the way his living room did that day. With an ever-present smile and jovial demeanor, he carried his manners well, much like the two grown children that he proudly raised on his own. An ageless soul, Ike is one of the very few left in the country able to speak to me about the rock community in the country before independence.

Ike had joined the already established rock group, The Vandals, in Harare (then known as Salisbury) in 1975. Formed in 1966, the group performed during a time of discovery in Rhodesia. "When you grow up listening to a particular type of music, it's difficult to say what really appealed to you. But I think the lyrics, we could identify with the lyrics. It started with The Beatles in the '60s. There was a difference between white music and our music. The music in those days, the lyrics were more poetic. They meant something. You could identify with certain things that were in the lyrics that people wrote those days. It was more poetry that people wrote those days. If you listen to Bob Dylan, you understand what I mean. The lyrics that he wrote about the war in Vietnam, it was things that was happening then, which affected all of us," Ike explained. There was a natural shift in what was transpiring between the streets, the world and creative minds. Like many in the West, Zimbabweans also wanted more expression, and rock and roll was their outlet.

Ike described himself as a hippy. Rhodesia in the late '60s and early '70s very much resembled a Western country. With the increasing protests against the United States' involvement in the Vietnam War, many of the anthems that stood defiant found their way to Rhodesian radio stations and embedded themselves deep into the souls of those who absorbed them. Many could relate, as Zimbabwe was also in the throes of war. "Here in Harare there was Dr. Footswitch,

Sound Effects and the biggest band was John Iyate and The Sparks," he recalled. Continuing, he explained that this music also spread beyond the capital. "There was Musi-O-Tunya from Victoria Falls and coming from Bulawayo there was Eye Of Liberty, Wells Fargo, Pebbles Zinc Stone and The Otis Waygood Blues Band." Bands in the country enjoyed the benefits of audiences who were excited about this new sound making its rounds throughout live music venues. Several of these acts were also able to produce records and garner radio play, exposing them to an even larger audience. Though, as Ike explained, there was still some apprehension by those outside the periphery of this music's fandom.

"What actually happened, was during the war [Rhodesian War], the guerilla fighters during that time were trying to concentrate the black majority to their rise, so essentially everything that was white was evil. The majority of the people were black people, they were the ones who were playing rock music. The audience was a mixed audience. They planted into the black majority that the music wasn't good for you. You shouldn't listen to that. When you listen to Black Sabbath it was the devil's music. The way it got interpreted in this country was sort of blasphemous music. It sort of marked the end of rock and roll. Basically, that is what happened in this country; the politics began to dictate the pace of what was happening. If you wanted to go into a place to play rock and roll music, the chances were you got pelted with bottles and things like that."

The "white devil," as was described by a few off the record, was how this music was perceived. The white governments of South Africa and Southern Rhodesia had ostracized and controlled the airplay and supply of rock music in their countries, and now the revolutionary forces of the independent Zimbabwe had also taken liberty in brushing this music aside by patronizing its fandom. It is any wonder how this music persevered and pushed forward.

The white government of Rhodesia in the late 1970s had gone through the sanctions, much like their neighbors in South Africa. With Ian Smith's Unilateral Declaration of Independence surging right ahead, the difficulty of getting this music at their disposal was real, as record distributions were essentially shut off. However, there was still a way in which records were being acquired.

"It was based in Rhodesia, and they had a plant in Northern Rhodesia [Zambia]. They were pressing records from the '50s through the '70s. And they brought the plant from Zambia to Harare. It sort of became the Zimbabwe Music Corporation [ZMC]," explained Gordon, a Harare-based record dealer. He graciously invited me into his home to show me his meticulously kept record collection, the largest in the country and most likely the continent. He sells records from Harare to collectors all over the world seeking Rhodesian-printed albums. With his collection in the tens of thousands, he showed me everything from the esoteric to the mundane.

"They would have produced records for the region. I know that some of them were exported to South Africa. I have only ever found one pirate. All of these would have been licensed," he described casually, reclining on his sofa sipping a cup of hot tea, while his television was tuned to the international news on a very quiet volume.

Record companies sent masters to be pressed in Zimbabwe, which was done by Toolex Alpha machines that were sent to southern Africa from Sweden. Only about 2,000 copies of most records, from any genre, were pressed. While showing me his collection, Gordon pointed out that some of the records received artwork variations, but were still pressed to the quality of their original masters. This allowed Zimbabweans to access artists they had heard about or heard played on the radio, including acts such as Black Sabbath, Iron Maiden, AC/DC and the rare Metallica album. "I'm sure some of the bands wouldn't have known. Such a far-flung, obscure place in the world to think you are selling records [sic], because the Zimbabwe pressings were done in such few numbers. Some really obscure stuff was pressed here," he laughed. "Manowar *Sign Of The Hammer*, a few Maiden records, a lot of Black Sabbath. *Dr. Feelgood* [from Mötley Crüe], *Metallica*[56] was made and released here," he shared.

Heavy metal fans were more than happy to get their hands on the few metal records that made it to the local presses, as they provided their escape. But as Gordon reminded me, those times were difficult for metal fans.

---

56   Referring to the eponymous release known as the *Black* album.

"Heavy metal wasn't popular here. There was a guy, Rob Mackenzie, going around the schools giving speeches about how 'Satanic' it was. He sort of put a lot of people off, so they were produced in such small amounts. So for that reason, some of the most valuable Iron Maiden records were produced in Zimbabwe," he recounted. "[Mackenzie] wrote a book called *Bands, Boppers, and Believers*. It was published locally, and he went on some crusade against heavy rock, heavy music. He went giving speeches in schools all around the country, even in the south. And, of course, we were like, 'That's the music we want now'. You're going to tell a 16-year-old boy that it's bad and it's wrong to listen to this, what are they going to do? They're going to listen to it!" Gordon now began to smile even more, taking a sip of tea, sharing that the irony in all of this was that Mackenzie provided his introduction to heavy metal. "I remember seeing the videos, and I would be impressed by the guitars and heavier side of music. When I went to school in Plumtree, the cassettes were handed around like contraband. Someone handed me a cassette and said this was 'Satanic' music. One side was *Number Of The Beast* by Iron Maiden and the B Side was *Back In Black* by AC/DC. I went home and listened to it, and after that, that was it!" he shared joyously, while pointing to his personal record collection from his favorite bands, Slayer and Napalm Death.

"The factory is sitting as it was left, in Southerton [a suburb of Harare]. It is sort of like a museum," Gordon explained with a slight hesitation, as the plant – a vital aspect of Africa's musical history – is being sold and moved to Germany. The pressing plant was a blessing for local artists as it not only allowed for locals to gain access to albums from international acts, but it also allowed for Zimbabwean artists to press their own records. Others artists from nearby countries also took advantage of this pressing plant, such as those in neighboring Zambia who produced and marketed their own music.

Albert Chimedza was extremely forthright – the sort of person whose confidence pushes them to interrupt someone mid-sentence in order to correct a misspoken fact or to agree with the speaker. Tall, slender, with a deep voice, Albert is as interesting as they come. He is the sort of the person who just seems to know everyone and has a great story to share about every single place you speak about. Sitting comfortably on the patio behind his house, he leaned back in a white collared shirt, top two buttons undone, barefoot, cigarette in his right hand, ice cold beer in the left. He wanted to make sure I understood something. "Zambia had real rock," he explained. "In the '70s, you could get a record within a week. They were playing, as it happened – not 20 years later like they did here. I grew up on rock. I mean Black Sabbath, Deep Purple, every kid like 15 or 16 grew up on that. The rock scene in Zambia was way, way better. It was proper rock music within Africa."

As a result of the UDI, Zimbabwe never had real rock, Albert felt, unlike his birth country of Zambia. Artists such as The Witch, Amanaz, The Peace, Paul Ngozi and The Ngozi Family and Musi-O-Tunya (the same group that once based themselves in Victoria Falls, Zimbabwe) were following directly in their influences of Western rock and roll, along with the traditional infusions in what was called ZamRock.

ZamRock has witnessed a resurgence among underground record collectors, even having received proper attention by an American record company that released a box set of the most treasured ZamRock records. Part of the reason this music exploded in Zambia was because of the rotation this music received on the airwaves, as well as the accessibility of rock in the shops. Arthur's point was to opine that little of this happened in Zimbabwe, a country he relocated to after independence and one in which he was surprised to find a lack of rock music. "When I went to the ZBC [Zimbabwe Broadcasting Corporation] in 1990, I went to the library and just about every rock record was banned. So the Stones were banned, The Beatles were banned. Floyd was non-existent, because they made trouble. Little Richard, Chuck Berry, all these people, they didn't have them. So there was a lot of pop music. Those were the kind of records that was considered rock here. Simon and Garfunkel: banned; Miles Davis: no one knew who he was; Hendrix: they knew the name, but not the music; Emerson Lake & Palmer, Traffic, Allman Brothers, Janis Joplin. I could go on!"

The music that was enjoyed in the country leading up to independence was a limited amount of rock. As was explained to me, "We were always up to date with rock and music generally, as there was a lot of 'sanction busting' going on, and someone always keeping us up to date and bringing it in. And, also having South Africa [nearby] helped," explained the parent of one of the musicians I spoke to (preferring anonymity), who remembers that time well. Heavy metal, however, was virtually non-existent. What was being played on the radio dominated the culture. After Bob Marley's Independence Day concert, reggae surged. Jazz was also dominating the airwaves. The newfound explosion of global culture marked the musical shifts within the country. When independence came, the "white" music was essentially stigmatized. During the 1980s, very, very few rock musicians performed.

AND THEY STARTED TO LISTEN

Rockers in Zimbabwe, after independence – even during the years of the strongest middle class in the world – fell silent. Musicians either fled or gave up. Rhodesians resettled in Western countries because of uncertainties and animosities. Little was left and the musicians of the pre-independence era were not around to guide the next generation. The bands that I came across that existed post-independence – a mere handful – were acts performing covers for pubs and country clubs.

The next collective of musicians had to re-build from the dust that sat collecting on the memories of what once was. It would be another 30 years before rockers came to perform and record original music.

"We grew up listening to this. My parents still have their Black Sabbath, Uriah Heep and Guns N' Roses records. Rhodesian radio used to play a lot of rock. When

I was 15, there used to be a guy, Simon Parkins, playing Korn on the radio. By 1998-99 he was the only guy playing that," explained Derek. Reminding me that heavy music was never completely off the radar in Zimbabwe, nor was this country completely isolated from the world around, many in this generation spoke of being connected to this music through their parents' interest, radio and a curious benefit of cable television.

Wes Niemandt of the UK-based Kamikaze Test Pilots, who grew up in Zimbabwe and formed his band here, recalled late night adventures with his brother and bandmate, Ryan. "Our introduction to proper metal came in the form of satellite television and MTV. Riki Rachtman had the 'HeadBanger's Ball' and we used to stay up until 2 or 3 in the morning recording various music videos and making our very own music channel, so to speak. That was our first taste of the heavy music like At The Gates, Cannibal Corpse and Pantera. We were very sheltered out there in the bush," Ryan shared, noting that he and his brother grew up in a rural mining town hours from any city. "Thank the gods for satellite television," he laughed. "I remember me and my brother plucking up the courage to ask my mom for six bucks [Zimbabwean dollars] to buy *Appetite For Destruction* [from Guns N' Roses] in Bulawayo. I ended up getting it after all the pokes and prods. I guess we expressed an interest in the music, and it kind of snowballed from there. Our aunt then bought us Iron Maiden's *No Prayer for the Dying*, and Guns N' Roses' *Use Your Illusion II*, bearing in mind that she had recently been on holiday to South Africa, and we had asked her for some music as a Christmas present."

Radio presentations were thin for rock and especially heavy metal. Television was limited to Western channels sneaking in and print media was even thinner, even though Zimbabwe has the benefit of South Africa and Botswana as prosperous neighbors. The sanctions imposed during the Mugabe era did not heavily affect the country until the mid-2000s. Yet, there was little benefit in political and cultural isolation. Accessing the music they were enjoying was difficult until the Internet era exploded.

The country hit a few major obstacles that not only challenged the lives of people living in the country, but also drove many to surrender their hope and leave Zimbabwe altogether. A looming crisis gravely affected everyone in the country and sent the country into a downward spiral unlike any the modern world has seen.

THIS LAND IS YOUR LAND, THIS LAND IS MY LAND

Life in Zimbabwe was flowing well until the late '90s. No one complained about difficulties. Until then, feelings of diminishing realities were not the norm. So what exactly happened? As difficult as the demise of a nation is to generalize, for me, and many others, the tipping point came via farm invasions. By the mid '90s, Mugabe began to lose political favor and could see his grip loosening over the country. One particular group wanted to ensure that if their demands were not met, they would see that Mugabe lost his power once and for all. Calling themselves the "war veterans," this disenfranchised group was led by a man named Chenjerai Hunzvi, a medical doctor (he took on the name "Hitler" during the independence struggle) who assumed the leadership of the Zimbabwean National Liberation War Veterans Association in 1997.

Shortly after Hunzvi began his post as the leader of the war veterans, the fortunes of the country turned for the worse. The loss of political clout for Mugabe, as well as the demands of land reciprocity for the war veterans, equaled an atrocious offering. The farmland sought was the crowning jewel of this country. One of the most successful farming countries in the history of the world, Zimbabwe fell into a horrendous state of disrepair once the land seizures began.

This controversy of land ownership in Africa was nothing new, as land rights were always questioned in nations with a strong colonial history and a permanent European population; many nations in Africa had also dealt with land distributions in more diplomatic ways after the turnovers from colonial to self-rule. Zimbabwe, too, managed to come to a compromise of sorts with the British government with an agreement known as the "willing seller, willing buyer" compromise and financial recompense. And, yes, understandably so, the issue needed to be resolved. However, in Zimbabwe, it was the blatant disregard of dignity that complicated every aspect of the matter. The war veterans did not care about the legal system, nor the compensations worked out in treaties and peace agreements. They wanted land. And they wanted everything as soon as possible.

All they asked from Mugabe was that he turn his head – and that he did. What followed was one of the worst economic collapses in the history of the world, and a human rights crisis.

The war veterans (many of whom were not even old enough to have fought in the war) began seizing working farms by notifying the owners of imminent seizures – by lethal force if they had to. Much of what occurred, and is still occurring, was done by force, at times with deadly results. At independence one third of the country's workforce was working on any number of the 15 million hectares[57] of commercial farmland. By 2000, over half of that land had been seized.[58] Between 2000 and 2009, according to a *Washington Post* article, over $12 billion in farming revenue had been lost.[59]

Mostly white farmers were subjected to watching their families murdered or were murdered themselves after having been given just minutes to leave the only places they had ever known as home. A few were lucky enough to escape. Some farmers were given "polite" notices – a two-week notice of sorts. Zimbabwe's Supreme Court ruled that the seizures were illegal, but neither the veterans, nor Mugabe, cared.

---

57   1 hectare = 2.471 acres
58   Scoones, Ian et al. *Zimbabwe's Land Reform Myths & Realities.* Weaver Press, 2010.
59   Sieff, Kevin. "Zimbabwe seized 'white farmers' land. Now some are being invited back." *Washington Post.* September 14, 2015.

But nothing could stop those who wanted the land. As Newbz lamented, "I don't think many people were paying attention." Even with photographs circulating around the world of murdered farmers and their families, humanity seemed to treat Zimbabwe as the world's car accident; curious, but careful to avoid eye contact, and eager to forget about what they saw.

Once the farm invasions happened, the nation's tranquility was shattered. Everyone was affected. Everyone in the country witnessed one of the worst economic collapses in the history of mankind. And everyone suffered from the demise of normalcy.

The farm seizures were not initially a part of my questions to musicians. The issue was brought up through their curiosity. During my interview with Dividing The Element and Evicted I was asked why I had an interest in Africa, which then led to the topic of land reform in the country, as I had done my master's thesis on the topic. I briefly shared some points of my research and previous trip to the country in 2007 during much of the heavy turmoil. After that, I thought I would leave the matter alone.

I noticed how two of Chris' bandmates, Matt and Newbz, shuffled uncomfortably in their seats when I brought up the topic of land seizures. Then everyone quieted. Matt, who had yet to speak, faintly said the word, "Mutare." A city in Zimbabwe's east, Mutare is where Matt grew up. "In 2003, they kind of showed up, and it progressively got worse. We had a week," he whispered. Matt and his family had their farm seized. "I suppose we were somewhat lucky. I was at school. I wasn't actually at the farm" when all was lost. I left him alone, and the looks on the faces of his bandmates just showed that this was a matter he was still upset about.

"I had an hour," shared the otherwise quiet Newbz. He sat and watched Matt utter the same words he just did to me quietly and mustered up the courage to speak himself. "When news first came out that several white farmers were being forced off their farms – some with the use of violence – I didn't really know what to make of it, as I was young and naive. It was unsettling, but word was it was just a bit of political stirring and so I thought it would not affect my family. However, as the idea of land redistribution and mass evictions gathered momentum it became inevitable that our turn would come. It did."

Newbz assembled the strength to speak about that time, which was not an easy topic to discuss. But with the confidence of his bandmates by his side, he spoke up. "It was pretty scary. A bunch of people rocked up. We didn't have a fence, so they just drove right up to the back door. Literally." He described the horror he felt of wondering if the motive of the angry mob – or "rent-a-crowd," as Newbz called them – who showed up to take his family's farm was to make a political statement or, worse, kill. The motives were to remove his family. "[We] packed up our shit. We were given an hour to pack and leave. My ancient Datsun was quickly filled with old photo albums, my drum kit and three dachshunds. The drums and dogs: put them in the car and came to town.

"My life had been turned upside down and I had to accept things would never be the same. Some of the historical injustices of the colonial past had finally been set straight. We were just living in the wrong place at the wrong time. Our little patch of paradise was gone, and I was bitter and upset at first. Not so much anymore. Life goes on. Over the centuries throughout the world, land and territories have changed hands countless times, and it's never fair and rarely without violence. [Zimbabwe's] was done in a disorganized and ruthless manner. We left unscathed, and I guess that could be considered lucky. I agree that the land reform drive was necessary, although 15 years too late."

Newbz told me that his family, as devastated as they were, still checked on their farm to determine first and foremost if anyone had been hurt. They subsequently returned to follow up on the land itself. "Everything calmed down, and we moved back about two months later and carried on for about two years, then got turned off again. It was a bit more peaceful the next time. People just showed up and started farming." I was confused, so I asked if he and his family still lived on the property. "Farm is empty now," he bemoaned. "Employees are still there, but no one is paying them." After a few seconds of silence, I asked, "Would you go back?" "No," he responded without hesitating.

Wes Niemandt remembers visiting a friend's house for a night of alcohol-induced shenanigans, when suddenly a group of men stormed into the house. Everyone was taken hostage, while Wes watched his friend get taunted with an axe pressed against his throat. Wes thought this would be the end of his friend's life. Instead, the attackers issued a stern warning about their home and their land. Shortly thereafter, Wes and his family, who were not farmers, departed for the United Kingdom. Wes politely declined to answer as to whether his friend still lives in Zimbabwe.

The problem, for many, was that whites owned a large percentage of the farms – third or forth generation Zimbabweans owning and profiting greatly from a land that controversially belonged to the generations before them. The problem was simple on paper, but reality showed that tragedy was not the solution.

Farms before the land seizures produced and exported a plentitude of crops: enough to not only feed the country well, but also to export food to their neighbors without worry. Employment skyrocketed as thousands were hired to run the everyday operations on large-scale commercial farms. The loyalty of the workers to their employers seemed to many on the outside as an example of classic colonialism: "white boss, black farmers." But reality was far different.

"It was a very serious, scary time, especially after 2001. My worst memory is coming home from high school to find ZANU-PF 'war veterans' [stated mockingly, as those who confronted them were not old enough to be veterans] on the farm," remembered Derek. "By the time we got there, they had separated the women to be raped and the men to be 'cleansed' politically. At that time, my dad was on a list to be protected by the actual 'war veterans' leader in the area, so with one phone call some [veterans] arrived and dealt with the others. This farm at its peak employed 1,500 workers, and they are the ones suffering more than the white farmers; they are the ones most affected. Yes, a few of us [white farmers] were beaten and even murdered, but nobody talks about the working class families that lost everything. I truly believe the government was pissed off with white farmers for supporting the MDC financially."

Derek's home was stripped to the bone. "Within months. Roofs, electrical fittings – all," he shared. People came to live on their property and were granted parcels by those who seized the land, yet left some to his family. "We have people living off our land. They settled. We have 12 beneficiaries. Out of those 12, we have three farming successfully," he explained. However, his family stayed. "Things were resolved," he exhaled with a glimmer of relief.

Derek sat collecting the last glimpses of that day's sun on his face, sunglasses taking me away from what his eyes were hiding. He told me that land reform was necessary in Zimbabwe; perhaps it would have been better done more diplomatically than violently. The otherwise cunning and lucid frontman (whose band name, he said, was carefully chosen) told me some other day in the future would be more appropriate for a glimpse into his farming life. But not now.

We agreed to change the subject.

IN THE LAND OF NOTHING

I often wondered how this group of musicians pulled through. More so than any other group of rock and metal fans/musicians I met, they had to endure difficulties unlike any in the continent. How did they survive the tumultuous years of terrible inflation and food shortages that occurred during the mid-2000s? Often in Zimbabwe and South Africa, you hear people making arrangements to meet up or to tend to complicated matters by "making a plan." A humble colloquialism equating to resolutions, I often caught myself saying, "We'll make a plan," when establishing meetings and interviews, leading most to reason that I was also a Zimbabwean or South African. The words came to flow so much that I began to understand exactly how they survived: Zimbabweans "made a plan."

This was not my first time in the country. I had previously visited a dear friend in Zimbabwe's second largest city, Bulawayo, during the peak of despair in 2007. Relaying a few anecdotes from that trip, most were curious how I, as a tourist, was able to pull through staying outside their tourism periphery. I suppose I made a plan, too: meal by meal, day by day, things worked themselves out. I recalled some memorable stories about my previous visit to the country, sharing anecdotes and conversations. Many appreciated that I, too, was able to relate to their lives – albeit briefly.

The 2007 version of Zimbabwe was unlivable. The global community was hammering the country down with vitriol directed at Mugabe, ceasing trade, forcing sanctions and collectively shaking their heads in disgust at his policies. Now the people of Zimbabwe were paying the ultimate price. What I remember most was the empty supermarket shelves. As I was recalling the sight of empty shelves, I remembered the chill through my body when I stood in those grocery stores. Utter disbelief.

Sanctions had taken many necessities away from them, especially when faced with the realizations that the land reform policies were failing quickly. There was literally no food. Items came in slowly and in modicum. What items came in arrived randomly and would sit on the shelves for a matter of hours, typically purchased in bulk by individuals. Any item, such as a bag of sugar, for example, would arrive without notice and be placed on the shelves alone (though still in its assigned spot). Once the item was discovered, those with the money to purchase the good would buy all that they could and let everyone know they had the sugar. Now they had something to barter with. Bread, eggs, produce and meats were so precious they became luxuries. Another item that become a valuable resource was gasoline.

Given a tour of Bulawayo by my friend, turning the corner of an empty thoroughfare I noticed a long line – as far as I could see – of cars. "They are queuing for petrol," he explained without me even asking. A gas station in the distance had been buried by a line of cars, patrons hoping to purchase government-issued gas. Only customers with legal, government-issued vouchers were allowed to purchase a small amount of gasoline. "How does one get vouchers?" I asked. "You have to know someone," my friend snickered. Everyone had the same story and details to share. "You have to know someone" to get gasoline. In fact, it seemed you had to know someone to get anything, including food.

Part of the reason things had spiraled to this point was because of the inflation that had been plaguing the currency in Zimbabwe over the past year. The inflation had become one for the books. It was devastating. My experience was confusing at first, but one I settled in to as I traveled throughout the country. My first lesson in hyperinflation came from a cup of coffee. If you walk into a coffee shop in the morning anywhere in the world and order a cup of house coffee, you will pay whatever the set amount is as posted. Walk into that same shop a few hours later and order the same drink, and you know the amount that coffee would cost you. In the 2007 Zimbabwe, this was not the case. The price of the cup of coffee would increase as the day went on. The price increase between the morning and afternoon was exasperating. Again, a few hours into the afternoon it increased even more. Walk into the same shop the following morning and you paid triple what you did the morning before. It was the second-worst inflation in history. The price of goods would double every 24 hours. This pattern continued for years, plaguing locals, and infuriating investors and business owners alike.

The Zimbabwean inflation became so bad that it became parody.[60] The local bank notes had to keep getting reprinted to add more zeroes. It got exhausting – and comical. In a bit of irony, the poorest people in the world became billionaires. The Zimbabwean dollar had devalued so much that the bills, once printed in 1, 5, 10, 20 and 50 denominations, were, upon my arrival, in the hundreds of thousands, and upon my departure, millions. A few months later, billions, and by the end of 2008, trillions.

---

60   According to Steven Hanke of the Cato Institute, the Zimbabwean inflation reached 89.7 sextillion percent by November of 2008. A sextillion represents a number with 21 zeroes.

Zimbabweans would clean out their bank accounts on paydays and buy what they could by the end of that day. Most of what they would buy was groceries. With the heavily devalued currency and the increasing prices, locals would carry multiple duffle bags of bank notes and patiently wait for the cashiers to count it all. With many exhausting their bank accounts on payday, a barter economy was unofficially established throughout the nation.

"Everything was constantly jumping up, and the jumps were sometimes small or sometimes more than double. You really couldn't keep track at what speed the money was losing value. A beer is still a beer, if you've got a beer. If you've got 1,000 dollars it might buy a beer today, and you might not be able to buy the bottle top tomorrow," remembered Tom of the self-proclaimed "mbira punk" band, Chikwata 263. His bandmate, Hector, joked, "Just get in and buy what you can buy, and keep it! When the bucks come, buy everything and stock it at home. And when you need bread, and you got your sugar, take that bit of sugar and go and barter trade. Or soon after selling it, you buy what you need to buy," he laughed, recalling those years. "Dude, it was black market shit," said Chris, rather emphatically. "People would be selling meat, selling petrol. You just had to know the right people. You didn't go to supermarkets, you went to houses."

The entirety of my 2007 trip was black market currency exchange. The American dollar had become so valuable to locals that every price point was a negotiation – at an unofficial rate, of course. One particular evening, I had negotiated a proper dinner for my new friends at a tourist resort (one of the few places that had a constant stream of food supply) that included appetizers, full course meal, desserts and mixed drinks for four of us at the price of 16 American dollars! I quickly learned of all the shops and restaurants where I could exchange bank notes on the black market so the owners could cross into the nearby nations of Zambia or Botswana for goods and supplies with hard currency. This was the reality of life for people in the country for years. Business acumen and economic savvy became so ingrained in everyday life that around 2009, the country unofficially adopted the South African rand and the American dollar as their currency, much to the chagrin of the government. By 2010, the American dollar was accepted as the official currency until the economy could regulate itself.

"We just tend to deal with whatever is going on," laughed the otherwise timid Gary Stoutmeister of the one-man melodic death metal project, Nuclear Winter. "We can't let it affect daily life. Everything is kind of a struggle here. We just tend to deal with whatever is going on," he repeated, adding that the two years of economic turmoil only toughened the spirit of Zimbabweans.

"Those days were really rough," recounted George, guitarist of the band Acid Tears. "You couldn't buy anything. It was a struggle. We did anything possible. Whatever you could to get through the day. You had to go to people that you didn't even know just to buy a loaf of bread," he chuckled, shaking his head back and forth. It was almost unreal to hear it from another's perspective. The bartering system was a necessity during that period.

Education was also a forgotten aspect of life in the country during that time. "We went to school three times the whole year. They even brought in kids to come teach, people that didn't know anything." His bandmate and best friend, Boyroc, chimed in, laughing at his recollection. "Did you go to school?" asked Boyroc, grabbing George's arm in hysteria. "That was my time to go to school. I didn't even go to school. They messed it up," he laughed.

The members of Acid Tears grew up in Mabvuku, a township outside of Harare, and a different world than the spacious suburbs. Mocking the collapse of their wonderful education system, once noted as one of the best in the world and still-surprisingly-not terrible, the three members of Acid Tears seated around me confessed that none of them even had a high school education. Music was their only escape from Zimbabwe. All of them were also currently unemployed. Unsurprisingly, the country's unemployment was still at a staggering 90%. "This is it. This is all we got," stated a frustrated Boyroc. He was right. In the land of nothing, their anything is heavy metal.

GUIDED BY FEAR IN THE ABSENCE OF HOPE

My sole reason for believing that this country, of all the ones I have visited, is the most difficult country to pursue a healthy musical culture in Africa is because of the very present ears throughout the network of their society. Though I have yet to research North African nations' metal culture, I am aware of metal fans being arrested in Morocco and Egypt and of the accusations of Satanism levied against metal fans in those countries as a result of the government controlled censorship. However, those countries harbor healthy rock and metal communities with acts that perform in Europe constantly, as well as host international touring bands in Morocco and Tunisia. Algerian, Egyptian and Tunisian rockers have performed all over the world, have released albums on international labels and have even hosted their own metal festivals. Zimbabweans, however, do not enjoy these privileges. Out of fear, they are silenced.

The government of Zimbabwe under Robert Mugabe is notorious and nefarious. Ranked as the second worst leader in the world behind North Korea's leadership, it is appropriate that both nations have been linked in the past to an atrocious act. In the mid- 1980s, Mugabe began to feel the weight of opposition in the country's central Ndebele speaking region, Matabeleland. Most of the people in this area favored the leadership of Joshua Nkomo. To quell what he viewed as an act of dissent, Operation Gukurahundi was carried out by Mugabe's North Korean-trained Fifth Brigade in hopes of destroying the opposition party's support base. It is estimated that over 20,000 people were killed. As the leader of this political party, the ZAPU (Zimbabwe African People's Union), Nkomo was said to have escaped into Botswana dressed as a woman before finding exile in London. Eventually, Mugabe got his wish. His ZANU party merged with ZAPU, forming ZANU-PF (Zimbabwe African National Union-Patriotic Front) in

1987. He was now in sole control of the only political party in the nation.

Mugabe's one party rule has been challenged, yet uncompromised. Musicians know this all too well. All musicians face the peculiar challenge of success within their borders. When sitting with the musicians I met, one of the matters discussed was whether or not rock or heavy metal bands could one day enjoy radio successes in Zimbabwe. The answers were those of trepidation. Radio is a wonderful medium to reach a large amount of listeners in a few minutes. But for musicians in Zimbabwe, their fear was that *everyone* would hear their music. "I don't want to see Robert Mugabe's henchmen. Rather play it for the people and let it get to the people that get it," expounded Chris.

Dividing The Element cited the successes of local traditional musicians, notably Thomas Mapfumo, as a validation of their fears. Known as the "Lion of Zimbabwe," Mapfumo is well known in the country for his style of *Chimurenga*[61] music. Playing a traditional style of music centered on the rhythms of the mbira, his success is largely attributed to the adaptation of modern instruments with the rhythms and hymns of the styling. Mapfumo was adored for his ability to stand up to the previous regime of Ian Smith and spent time as a political prisoner. However, it is his notoriety as a vocal critic of the Mugabe government that has many praising him now. Though, many argued it was his music that enabled the government of Mugabe to get into power. With the 1989 release of his album,

---

61   Shona word meaning "struggle."

Corruption, Mapfumo's fortunes turned against him. As Dividing The Element's guitarist Archie stated, "They wanted to kill him." The pressure got to be so intense that Mapfumo was imprisoned and eventually fled to Oregon in exile.

Another musician that also received heavy ire from the government is Oliver Mtukudzi, or as he is known locally, Tuku. A performer of traditional music, he came under fire after the release of his song "Wasakara," which translates roughly to "You Are Worn Out." Many interpreted this song as a stern attack on the aging Mugabe, and it was adopted by the opposition party Movement for Democratic Change (MDC) as a theme song. "Tuku is arguably the biggest music legend ever from Zimbabwe," shared Derek. "They [ZANU-PF] have been unable to persuade him otherwise, and he is too much of a superstar for them to attack him or intimidate him. I know that post-2006, he has become cautious of being too critical by avoiding pointing fingers at specifics, but I still feel that his music and lyrics continue to address social and political issues," he added. The lessons of Tuku[62] and Mapfumo reverberated with this generation of musicians who understand their reality well. The fact that those who were vital in the movement to overthrow Ian Smith could also be subject to arrests from Mugabe's henchmen terrifies them.

---

62   It is widely rumored that Mtukudzi was paid off by Mugabe to refrain from political messages in his music. Though the sourced article is merely speculation, rumors and assertions quickly circulated throughout the music community. "How Mugabe silenced Oliver Mtukudzi" by Dakari Mashava. http://nehandaradio.com/2015/04/04/how-mugabe-silenced-oliver-mtukudzi/

Perhaps the Zimbabwean musician with the strongest legacy is Andy Brown. Born to a German father and Zimbabwean mother, his music is still shared and loved passionately by everyone, even the metal community. Albert Chimedza explained to me just how important Andy Brown was to local music. In a way, he felt Brown had the same impact Bob Dylan had in the United States.

"The kids now all play his music," Albert laughed calmly, with his cigarette- clenching hand pointing at Chris and the members of Chikwata 263, who accompanied me to Albert's house. "The genesis *is* Andy Brown. He is rock and roll. There is no other musician that is this crazy," exclaimed Tom of Chikwata 263, who also felt Brown's impact to Zimbabwe changed the musical culture.

"Andy Brown was the best guitarist and songwriter ever from Zimbabwe," elated Derek, whose band performs a few of Brown's songs. "However, around 2006 or so, he was very critical of the government, which resulted in a backlash from authorities. He was apparently intimidated and 'politically cleansed' and then paid a fat bribe to turn sides. His next album [most likely *Chiedza*] was very pro-ZANU-PF, which resulted in a fan backlash at his concert at the national sports stadium. Fans were burning CDs and turned violent on the band. Several band members, including his mbira player, Noble, who is a friend of mine, were beaten up. Noble ended up leaving the band and moving to Australia. His career was never the same after that, right up to his death." Andy Brown died in

March 2012, just days after his 50th birthday, from an unknown cause.

Rock and metal musicians have been rather indirect with their lyrical themes. A few told me that they go into specific themes through obscurity. Tom warned that addressing matters directly would be dangerous. "That would be foolish," he said without any hesitation. "Most people would say, 'Hey there is a white guy screaming in Shona', then they would question what I was trying to say with the lyrics. So it doesn't get too deep. We are not seen as a political band, we are seen as a punk rock band." A genre traditionally rooted in protest silenced? It was pure fear.

Hector paused and questioned my motives for asking what their songs were about. I never faulted him for his trepidation. His concern was real. "There is Oliver Mtukudzi. He has messages that are really strong, and Thomas Mapfumo is more direct; 'the country that we fought for is now in rags'." "You can be more blatant about what you are saying, or more indirect," interjected Tom, expressing that in the West, "people are excited [about the hook] and won't get too focused about what they are singing about." Hector continued, this time with a smile and a look of relaxation after it was explained what I was really doing in Zimbabwe. "Once in a while, people will question what they [other musicians] are singing about. The best things about songs that are not direct is that situations repeat themselves. So if they are singing about unity, they can sing, 'let's unite'!" he shared.

"There are a lot of instances of people just disappearing. You can't just speak out," lamented Boyroc. His bandmates George and Billy sat quietly, shaking their heads, too. "You can't," uttered George under his breath, loud enough for all of us to hear. His tone carried disdain; Boyroc's carried disgust as he continued. "I think if someone notices, if someone just brings it out, it would be bad for you. I think someone would pay attention. You can't just be straight up open. It's not really much of a free country."

Aware of the arrests made in North Africa, a few came to me to address the fear that exists in Zimbabwe. My description of the country as the most dangerous nation in Africa to be a rock or metal musician was met with hesitations and thoughts. "It is possibly one of the most difficult countries to be a rock musician now. It wasn't say 25 years ago on the basis that rock is founded on freedom of expression and rebellion. Both of which the Zimbabwean government has gone out of its way to try and stamp out," shared Wes Niemandt. Gareth Reed, a Zimbabwean metal musician based in South Africa, agreed. "Yes, it's extremely difficult to be in a rock/metal band [in Zimbabwe]. Political reasons play a big role, but there are other reasons as well – education, upbringing, exposure to 'outside' music. I think the interest is there, but the education of metal isn't. No one is exposed to it, so they don't understand yet."

"It's all connected. I think Zimbabweans, more than any other nation in the world, have seen what happens when a system collapses," concurred Derek. "I'm talking about politics, banking, everything. So we're more distressful."

"Zimbabwe is one the most difficult places to be a metalhead," posited Chris. After seeing his frustrations throughout his everyday routines, I understood his statement. Frustrations piled high. Musicians here experience a different life than exists for musicians around the world. "There's a never-ending fear that all Zimbabweans seem to have. If we speak out in any way, a heavy closed hand of reprimand could fall upon us at any time. People here have to respect the fear or we risk leaving ourselves open to some shit."

We were both reminded of how heavy this hand of reprimand can be during a September day. Chris and I were in a conversation about an activist who had been missing since August 2015 named Itai Dzamara as we drove through downtown Harare. "Yeah, he's still missing. I don't know him, though." Dzamara disappeared after a protest in a central Harare park where he, and other activists, had taped their mouths shut, holding protest signs in front of government offices. A friend of Chris' was also involved in the same cause that led to the disappearance of Dzamara. I asked about his friend. "[He's] all right despite been beaten once, detained and thrown in the cells a couple of times. He also had an ongoing court case with bogus charges put on him for refusing to obey a position of authority. The charges were dropped a couple of months ago, though. Think he's just keeping his head down for now."

His friend did not want to speak, respectfully. Chris and I imagined that the words on those placards read something to the effect of, "Time To Go" or "Mugabe Must Step Down," the sort of material copy-and-paste slogans that are chanted in political protests all over the world without so much as a blink from government leaders. But in this country, like a few others, protests such as this were met with concern. Chris' reasoning behind his comment about Zimbabwe being a difficult place to perform metal was justified by this fear of being sought out.

Another instance that showed the kind of trepidation musicians here live with was shared by Albert. He invited me to his house with Chikwata 263 so that I could see the mbira business he ran from his property. A small box with metal tines played with the thumbs, the mbira is also called the "thumb piano" and is seen and heard in various southern African countries. Albert's instruments were crafted by hand, made to absolute perfection and sold all over the world. Showing me around his workshop and meeting his employees – one of whom was deaf and remarkably able to craft this instrument to perfection – I noted a photograph on the wall of Albert and Mugabe.

Albert explained that he noticed a few men who snooped around his property every so often. Once they approached, he was asked why he was making instruments. They wanted to know if he was running an illegal business. He joked – sort of – that he was "hoping to make the perfect instrument for the President," because, as Albert noted, he knew exactly who they were. So all he could do was give them a response that deflected their inquiry, as they wanted to catch him and probably arrest him for running his business outside the perimeters of tax offices. He offered them an instrument to give to Mugabe. One of them looked him in the eye and said, "give him one yourself." So he did.

Putting on his finest suit, he was escorted to the President's office where he presented Mugabe an mbira and, in return, received an official photograph to mark the occasion. Albert chuckled while pointing at the photograph. "Mugabe told me, 'I thought I was going to see some ugly thing'," he laughed hysterically. "They leave me alone now!"

"WE HAVE TO DO IT NOW."

Visiting Zimbabwe again was an eye opener. It was not just my love of the music, it was a better way of understanding how people lived and how they can keep a level of motivation with the circumstances that surrounded them. Music was more than just a vessel of escape. It was an identity in a land of compromised outcomes and filthy politics. Zimbabwe still has semblances of normalcy. Movie theaters still showed current films, shopping malls carried goods, grocery stores once again had steady stock, gas stations had gasoline and communications continued uninterrupted, schools were also still educating children and Internet usage was still constant and uncensored. Amenities served as distractions to the real problems.

Heavy Metal Africa had come full circle for me. I was getting ready to leave Zimbabwe wondering if I had met enough people or even had a full understanding of the history of the music in the country. Many of the musicians of the previous era were just not around anymore. After a while, none of that mattered. I came back to a country that had mesmerized me several years before and had now become a part of me for good. In 2007, I was certain that only hopelessness would continue to guide Zimbabwe. I was wrong. Zimbabwe is special because the people refused to have their souls crushed by tyranny.

"Despite what people might think, Zimbabwe is a beautiful country populated by amazing people from all backgrounds and races. I urge everyone to come see for themselves. My family is now scattered across the world, but I chose to return. I don't know why, but it feels right," shared Newbz, who reiterated that despite the political turmoil that could have led to his death and the heavy hand of the government today, Zimbabwe is and will always be his home. "It may sound unbelievable to a Westerner, but this is Africa, and things work differently here."

The Zimbabwean soul is a special one: loving, caring, kind and wonderful. I also saw just how powerful this music became to those seeking to move beyond the barriers of constraint. I saw that heavy metal matters.

Heavy metal and rock music are providing the escape and optimism that many need. "Most people look at us like there is something wrong with us, like we need help. Especially when you come from Mabvuku. People just don't understand it at all," reminded Boyroc. But as he shared, there is so much more to his life now that metal has a local inspiration: Dividing The Element. "Our goal is to try and push as hard as we can. We are inspired by Chris' band. We never thought it would be possible. We were blown away. These guys are actually doing it. We have to do it now. With Dividing The Element, now we have to push!" he boasted. Boyroc was not alone. Many in Harare admired Chris' aplomb and have supported his efforts and those of his bandmates.

Many musicians I met outside of the rock periphery were more than happy to support the band when it came time to orchestrate his concert. Chris and I frequented the venue of his concert often, an old theater in downtown Harare that also serves as a bar for a few dedicated regulars. This specific venue defied segregation during the era of division and stands as a reminder of what once was. But for Chris and the young generation, the Reps Theater is a symbol of what can be.

Introducing myself to a gentleman at the end of the bar casually sipping away his vodka tonics, I was surprised to hear he was British. "Paul," he said, as he introduced himself. Asking why I was visiting his adopted country, I explained my reasons. Chris was hoping I would meet him. Once running a metal band of his own in the 1980s, he was delighted to have the opportunity to see that things are turning around in the country.

"Metal is going to be a small and appreciative audience. It has got its following, maybe not nationwide, but we'll get pockets of good supporters. It has got its place in Zimbabwe society. Local music is not, I hate to say, very inspiring, so it's nice to have something different," he shared, pointing right at Chris. As another gentleman, Mario, a former blues musician who was overhearing our conversation, put it, "Chris is putting his ass on the line. We have to support him."

Having seen how Dividing The Element impacted Harare in a multitude of ways, as well as how Chris planned on moving ahead with his love of the music, I, too, was elated that many had taken to his cause. The community that assisted in organizing the event for his band was not even made up of heavy metal fans. They were just a group of "when we's" singing the praises of a generation making an effort to move beyond the difficulties that surrounded them – a group of people excited to see a Zimbabwe they assumed was lost, but is now in the hands of the ambitious.

GOODBYE FOR NOW

My last morning in Harare was slow and frustrating. Nothing seemed to be going the way I wanted. Things kept falling out of my hands, and I kept struggling for words. Chris' family had asked me if I would have lunch with them before I left. I was more than happy to sit one last time. As I packed up a few more things, I had a very odd feeling. This was not the feeling of uncertainty or discomfort, but the sense that there was more to be done.

Before I knew it, I found myself in the same car that Chris picked me up in, bouncing over and navigating around potholes. Desperation reveals itself around every corner in this part of the world. Men hurried to fill the potholes right in front of you with bricks, sand and mud so they could ask for money. As comical as it was, there was always tragedy behind their smiles. Or perhaps it was my smile hiding the sadness that I was leaving this spectacular country. Once again, Zimbabwe captured my heart. I sat silently thinking of how the people of this troubled country were continually able to carry themselves with dignity and grace.

The soul that permeates through this country's people is by far the most sincere, honest and kindest I have encountered in Africa. Zimbabwe is a complicated but special place. Through misery and famine, kindness and respect still radiated from their hearts and their smiles as authentic as the morning sun. I now knew why Zimbabwe was my favorite African country, because it is the most difficult place for me to say goodbye to.

I was also leaving Africa. Chris had done what so many others did throughout this adventure – he welcomed me into his home and life, without shame. They knew I could understand them, their lives, and their passions – without judgment.

Chris and his girlfriend were silent as the airport came into focus. They asked me what was next. I told them I was not sure. He opened the trunk of his third-generation Mercedes-Benz wagon to get my suitcase and shook my hand. This time, none of us was smiling. I could see he really enjoyed having me around as well, but I had no idea how to properly say goodbye. I was not just saying goodbye to him, I was saying it to all of those I had visited in the five countries prior. All of those who had opened their doors and lives to me – the American metal fan who wanted to ask a few questions. It began to sink in as the terminal got closer.

There were no questions asked as I approached the immigration counter, just a simple nod of two heads speaking the tacit language of understanding. I sat on a plain-colored bench, waiting for the flight announcement that would lead to Johannesburg and, eventually, onward to the United States. I had no idea what to think. I stared aimlessly. Entirely too many things came rushing through my head, as I did my best to gather my thoughts.

As the plane took off, I could see the twinkle of the deceiving city skyline in the distance amid the vastness below. This was not just Zimbabwe staring back; this was the collective of every place I had visited, every hand I shook, every eye gazed upon, and every single story told. These countries were no longer forgotten nations in the forgotten continent; they were etched in my heart forever.

*Sitting with Albert (L) and Tom and Hector of the
"mbira-punk" band Chikwata 263 at Albert's mbira shop.*

Derek of Evicted doing what he loves most.

Chris (R) and the rest of Dividing The Element.
Left to Right: Matt, Archie, and Newbz.

Zimbabwe's Evicted.

Photo credit: *Michelle Fortmann*

A true rocker, Ike Mhalanga, at his quiet suburban home.

A relaxing evening with the members of Dividing The Element and Evicted's Derek.

The future of Zimbabwean metal, Acid Tears.

POSTSCRIPT & ACKNOWLEDGEMENTS

I came back to the United States from Zimbabwe and sat quietly. I stared for a while at the pile of T-shirts, CDs, posters and instruments that I was given throughout my trips, reflecting on the memories staring back at me. The emotions that poured through my body were feelings I had never felt before. I did this. Somehow, I was able to muster the courage to pursue a passion and somehow I made it happen. Every single face, every handshake, every note I heard came back to me. The sights, the smells, the feeling of my feet on the concrete, the way the air felt and the way Africa was absorbed into me – all of it came back with each of those memories. They were unbelievable snapshots; glimpses of my past, locked into my future.

What you are holding is a snapshot of four years of dedication and countless hours of late nights and early mornings of working at home, in coffee shops, pubs, airports, bookstores and libraries to make this happen. *Heavy Metal Africa* is a burning curiosity that led to me to unexpected places, with some of the most endearing people I have ever met. I, too, was surprised by how deep rock's history fell in Africa's story and I hope that I have made a solid start of at least exposing a moment of that history. I feel there is more to come. Other countries in Africa have started to kick up their own rock and metal festivals, and more Africans than ever before are pursuing ambitions to form their own rock and heavy metal bands. Since I have started this book, a few nations have even enjoyed visits from international acts, notably South Africa, Kenya and Botswana. South Africa, in fact, is becoming the "go to" spot for touring international bands, and a blossoming metal festival scene, highlighted by the awesome Witchfest.

Africa is well on the way to gaining the validation it rightfully deserves.

I hope this book was able put Africa into a different spotlight for you. To say the continent is grossly misunderstood and greatly stereotyped is an understatement. Africa is a remarkable, diverse continent and I am glad to share it with everyone. Perhaps you now understand why I love this place so much.

I still maintain contacts with so many people interviewed in the book, and always will. Part of what made this experience wonderful were the new friendships that came to life. And another aspect of this has been watching many of the bands blossom into wonderful acts who are even getting fantastic international exposure. For rock and metal fans who want to hear the bands mentioned in this book and others I was not able to include, most of the acts mentioned have social media accounts with links to their music and videos.

Throughout this experience, I almost quit three times and I went flat broke twice – literally, flat broke! But I kept going. I knew I had to keep going. I wanted to finish what I set out to accomplish. Sometime between the moment I began to write and research this book and now, I received so many notes and messages of encouragement from complete strangers all over the world. People I had never met reached out through emails and social media to thank me for my work, and to say they believed in what I was doing. Somehow, things could never be that bad. I just had to completely put myself in the mindset where I also had to believe in what I was doing. Once again, thank you to all of you who believed in this from the first word and throughout this lengthy process. Your words, your encouragement and your energy exceeded anything I could have ever asked for. Thank you, again.

I am eternally indebted to those who helped along the way. From the bottom of my heart once again, I thank you. To each and every single musician, critic, fan, journalist and DJ who sat with me to share your stories, and your country: THANK YOU! How I ever could have imagined this was because of your willingness to take the time to meet with me, show me your homes and welcome me into your lives. Some of you made the effort to take days off of work, travel long distances, and even rearrange concerts and rehearsals just for this curious – wanderlust stricken – American. Again, THANK YOU! To those I was not able to meet in person and interview for the book, I am forever grateful for your understanding. I know that perhaps there is still more I could write in this book, and many more stories and historical insights I could include, but know that you are not without my gratitude.

To the rockers of Namibia, my sincerest apologies for not being able to include my visit to your stunning (and rather hot) country. Stefan Steyn, Penilane, Stephan Slabber and Safe 19, the Wenk family, Jaucques, Sue, Juan, Marco, Famaz Attack, SubMission, Arcana XXII (Robert), Sue and my Vilho: my sincerest gratitude and I promise to include your stories as soon as possible.

In South Africa: Herman and Suretha, and the Le Roux family of Pretoria and Cape Town. R.I.P., Mr. Le Roux, it was a sincere pleasure meeting you. Herman, if you only knew how much your time and wisdom meant to me. You are a proud African, and an extremely proud South African. You were the best guide I could have ever of had and you made sure I was taken care of from the second I landed. I am happy to call you a friend now and forever. Lucas Smith and family in Durban, thank you for putting me up for a long weekend. Lucinda and Brian Viljoen in Cape Town for taking in Herman and me at 3 in the morning, letting us wake up at 11 and having coffee ready. My apologies again for not being able to fit in the interview with Junkyard Lipstick. Patrick Davidson, you were a crucial part of this. And you know it! The Allemann family of Johannesburg. Alec Surridge for the sofa on such short notice. Thanks again, brother. If Craig Waring never set up our meeting at Eye Of Horus in 2009, this may never have happened! And Frank Marshall, your photographs introduced African metal to the rest of the world. I am glad we got to finally meet...actually, I am not just happy we met, I am proud to call you a friend.

In Botswana, I must once again thank the Sbrana family for taking me in and showing me their world. Sadly, Renato Sbrana passed away about a year after I visited Botswana. He was ever gracious with his time and wisdom, and I cannot thank his family enough for their generosity. To Ivo, Delia, Juice, and especially Cassandra, my sincerest sympathies for your loss. Gabriel for the short-notice accommodation. To all of my "brothers" in metal: SALUTE! And Stux, it goes without saying that a good reason why I knew this book was for real, and the fire of metal is special, is because of you. You will never be a stranger – ever again. Thank you a million more times for your push, drive, words, wisdom, encouragement and energy. Heavy metal is special, and it is special because of rockers like you.

Emmanuel Dominic in Nairobi (sorry again). Switch for driving three hours from your parents house just to come and fetch me. *Asante sana!* To the Kenyan metal community who checked up on me day in and day out to make sure I was OK, and for bringing me water and my medication. *Nakupenda sana! Nimefurahi kukoanana.* Until next time!

Romeo in Antananarivo – please thank your mother again for the nice vegetarian meals. Markus Verne, if you only how much your time and wisdom means to me and to the rockers of Madagascar! Thank you again for your help. The Rakotovao family of Fianarantsoa, for taking in Stephan and me and feeding us for a few nights. I do not know how I can thank you enough, *misaotra betsaka!* And Stephan, you are a brother now and always. I miss you and I miss Madagascar. I'm going to come "home" soon enough. Thank you always.

Thibault in Mauritius, for not only letting me stay at your place, but for allowing so many people to come and chat with me. I am very happy you allowed me to listen to Opeth at full volume and for introducing me to Oceansize! The Juret family and "Fly" in Reunion island: *Merci beaucoup!*

And lastly, to Chris and his family in Harare for welcoming me into your home. Keep your head up. We all know just how wonderful Zimbabwe can be. Better days lie ahead.

To those who meticulously read, re-read and re-read again these words and gave me the feedback I needed (and sometimes disliked!) to ensure I kept my focus: Thank you. Beth Winegarner for the "mid-season" push I needed. David Mollica for bouncing around ideas with me and for not telling me I was crazy. Terry Hooker, Chad Bower, Ben Jones and the beautiful Stacey Marie for making sure this book read like one! To Tom and Francine Costello, Jason Price and everyone at Word Association Publishers. Mark Loftus for the camera. Don DelVecchio. Sara Sutler-Cohen for the index. Ashley Reynolds for the photograph. Patrick Rigney, John Weeks, Kirshna Egor, Wayne Boucher, Paul

Blom, John Weeks, Sven Oberg, Natalia Kouneli and Raffaele Mosca, Jimmy Crabb, Craig Halliday, Tony Ernst, Christer Jassons, Johnny Olsson and "newtrendinslavery" for your generosity. To Dr. Aimee Kanner-Arias, and Dr. Stephen Chan, thank you both for guiding me through my intellectual pursuits. Dr. James Caraway, I am forever grateful for your guidance and mentorship. You challenged me to find a passion in my interests, and you kept believing in everything I followed. Also, those who received postcards from me on my travels: cheers! Nelson Varaz-Diaz, Jeremy Wallach, Keith Kahn-Harris, Bryan Bardine, Mark Levine and Nathan Snaza for your words of encouragement. To my family, a never-ending *gracias* for not thinking I was crazy in doing this. *Mami, tu creiste en esto el primer dia, y siempre me estaba empujando. Gracias por todo.*

ON AFRICA!

ABOUT THE AUTHOR

EDWARD BANCHS holds an MA in African Studies from the University of London's School of Oriental and African Studies. His research on rock and metal in Africa has been featured in several publications, including *The Guardian, O Globo, This Is Africa,* and *FactsMag.* A lifelong metalhead, he lives in Pittsburgh, PA, where he is planning his next African adventure.

INDEX

melodic death metal, 39, 231, 339; melodic hard rock, 51; power metal, 217; progressive metal, 25, 41, 256; symphonic metal, 188, 215; thrash metal, 7, 32, 48, 94, 193, 209–210, 223–224, 270, 291–292, 294
Hellchild, 95
Helloween, 230
Hendrix, Jimi, 199, 324
Henn, Louis, 41
Heretics (Mauritius), 266
hip-hop: in Kenya, 146; in South Africa, 56; and Western influence, 49, 113
Hippo Camp (Mauritius), 260
"Holy Diver" (Dio), 295
Hope Era (Madagascar), 188, 216, 239
Housewife's Choice, 29
Humanoid (Mauritius), 263–264

"I Just Called To Say I Love You" (Wonder), 38
Iklwa (Skinfint), 114
Ile Bourbon, 288
Impish (Kenya), 138
In Oath (Kenya), 166–167, 171, 177
Inay (Madagascar), 189
INOX (Madagascar), 194
INOX Studios (Madagascar), 194
Inside Africa (CNN), 96
Intellectual Metamorphosis (Wrust), 108, 113
International Criminal Court (ICC), 165
Internet: and access to heavy metal, 136, 170, 327; era in Zimbabwe, 327, 349; and file sharing sites, 170; and rise of bands in era, 210
Iraimbilanja (Madagascar), 189

Iron Maiden, 23, 34–35, 83, 114, 122, 197, 256, 321–322, 326

Janis Joplin, 324
Japanese, use of language in music, 218
Jax (Paranoid), 255–256, 259
Jean-Paul (Skeptical), 273, 279, 283
Johannesburg, 23, 25–27, 39, 43, 50–52, 54–55, 62, 65, 68, 93, 96, 103, 106, 116, 309, 354, 362
John Iyate and The Sparks (Zimbabwe), 318
Jojo (Murfy's Flaw), 151
Jomo Kenyatta International Airport, 132
Jonah (Inay), 189
JonJoRomBona (Madagascar), 209, 213, 222–223, 231
Joss (Allkiniah), 217, 221
Jozie (Murfy's Flaw), 144, 162
Judas Priest, 43, 75, 125
Juggernaught (South Africa), 24, 43, 50, 65, 70, 101
Juice (Skinflint), 88–91, 95, 111, 114, 363

Kadradraka 2000 (Madagascar), 190
Kalahari, 73, 77, 87–88, 93, 101, 121
Kaltz (Sasamaso), 211–212
Kamikaze Test Pilots (UK), 326
Kamp 13, 107
Karim, Sadiq (Moment of Silence), 165
Kawangware, 161
Kazar (Madagascar), 190, 192–193, 238
Kebonyi (Skinflint), 90, 95, 100, 114
Keireini, Saidimu (Dove Slimme), 144–145, 163, 168
Kelly Brown (Kenya), 135

WA